Strange Sects and Cults

Egon Larsen

STRANGE SECTS AND CULTS

A Study of Their Origins and Influence

HART PUBLISHING COMPANY, INC., NEW YORK CITY

Contents

Introduction

There has been such an astonishing flowering of sects, such an increase in their number, diversity and oddness in the middle decades of our century that there must be some explanation for the phenomenon. Its most puzzling aspect is the fascination which these new and old cults and creeds seem to have in the western world in this age of scientific and technological achievements, of mass communication, of a general rise in the level of education: not the kind of soil in which one would expect irrational or superstitious notions to grow.

The variety of answers that we are being offered is just as puzzling. The psychologists explain the popularity of sects as man's reaction to the nuclear Sword of Damocles that hangs over us all, to the threat of universal destruction – as a retreat into an esoteric world where salvation can be obtained by some magic formula. The theologians, on the other hand, admit that the failure of the established religions to solve the supreme problems of our time has emptied the churches and is driving people into the arms of eccentric and often phoney prophets. Some sociologists argue that Messianic sects, with their promise of a millenium just round the corner, are almost a necessity in a society where many find it increasingly difficult to cope with our complex reality; others see the popularity of mystical cults as an escape from the materialistic rat-race of modern life. An African writer, observing the attraction that the Day-of-Judgment prophets hold for his compatriots, speaks of their obvious 'gloating over the approaching doom of mankind' – yet he could find plenty of sects with the same message and attitude in the 'advanced' hemisphere between London and Los Angeles.

So it seems that there is no general or even regional explanation for the flowering of sects today. But there are at least a few pointers, and they lie in our nature. The wise Christian apologist Tertullian wrote 1,800 years ago: *'Credo quia impossibile'*, usually translated as 'I believe because it is absurd'. This, indeed, is one of the most human traits in man, the reasoning animal – probably a subconscious protest against the faculty of thinking which nature has bestowed on him, and which has landed him in so much trouble throughout history. One might almost say that a sect's chances of success are the greater the more uncritical the belief which it demands. In order to believe you don't have to think, know or comprehend; it saves a lot of mental energy if you are ready to accept, unquestioningly, what some prophet or dogma tells you. And if the sceptics try to shake your faith you can floor them with Hamlet's over-quoted hint that 'there are more things in heaven and earth than are dreamt of in your philosophy'.

Is it, then, the simpler kind of soul that is most liable to join a sect? Another pointer seems to confirm this. We all know from our schooldays that boys and girls love to form esoteric groups with secret rites, coded languages and terrible oaths of loyalty. As a rule, it is a harmless phase of development which fades away with puberty, when sexual and intellectual interest take over (or when, under unfavourable social conditions, the groups transform themselves into violent adolescent gangs). However, that youthful tendency to form secret circles may remain latent in people whose personalities never fully mature, to break through again when boredom, frustration or a feeling of life's emptiness sets in and a new esoteric group, a sect, happens to be available. Since truly mature personalities are rare, there is always a vast reservoir of such potential candidates for sect membership.

Judging by the enormous number of sects of whose existence we know – and we may safely assume that there are at least as many that have so far escaped being talked or written about – we might think that only a small minority of people have never joined one. But this would be a miscalculation. Those who tend towards sectarianism for one reason or another are usually not very choosy; many are members of several sects, and even more join first one, then another, and eventually perhaps a third. There is a substantial 'floating population' in the world of sects, and particularly among the more eccentric ones; for if you believe in one absurdity, you believe in all.

Sects are good business and often big business. In a world which many enter because they want to give their critical faculties a rest, prophets who are merely after profits abound. They perform their transcendental confidence tricks according to the great showman Barnum's motto that there is a sucker born every minute – though they will never rise to his admirable frankness in revealing the basis of his business. It is arguable whether they do much damage to their followers apart from relieving them of their money: but there is certainly something more despicable in trying to manipulate people's souls for gain, in 'taking them for a spiritual ride' (in our African writer's words), than in emptying their pockets for some fraudulent commercial venture. Real damage, of course, may be done where alleged faith-healing is part of a sect's activities, as it so often is, when sick people are prompted to refuse conventional medical treatment in favour of some pseudo-religious magic. To be sure, those who claim to have been cured by faith-healing may be speaking the subjective truth; but their deceptive euphoria is either only of a short duration or their illness is psychosomatic, caused by their mental state. All that has happened is that they have responded to an autosuggestive belief in a supernatural healing power. In either case, the real causes of the trouble remain.

The sad thing is that although innumerable false prophets and sham cults have been exposed, their business often goes on as usual, or soon flourishes anew under another flag after an interval caused by the leaders' temporary absence in jail. Frequently, exposure makes the faithful rally even more enthusiastically around their master 'maligned' by the press and 'persecuted' by the authorities, and the stream of new members continues to flow. Sects rarely die all of a sudden; some fade away but as a rule they have a very long life. Among those that had their heyday in the past, there are still some that just refuse to give up their ghosts, decades or even centuries later. Thus the old sects that linger on today add their numbers to those that have begun their existence in our time. It is a cumulative effect and explains to some extent why there are such a lot of them.

In this book I am dealing only with the strangest sects, the bizarre tip of the iceberg, so to speak: Western European and Far-Eastern, American and African, with a sprinkling of historical ones. Selecting them was not an easy task, for the choice is large; even the definition of a sect is open to discussion. Strictly, the term means a group of people believing in doctrines and practising rites different from those of an established church from which they have separated; but in colloquial language one tends to include all groups of believers in transcendental tenets or philosophies different from conventional religion, whether they have separated from the main body of a church or gathered their followers on the basis of some completely independent set of notions. I have taken the colloquial meaning of the word as my guideline because this book is not supposed to be a history of religious schisms but a layman's dip into the ocean of human folly and ferocity, extravagance and gullibility. A few of the samples I have come up with may revolt the reader; however, even such an incomplete survey as this cannot ignore the more unsavoury aspects of the subject. At least I have refrained – difficult as it sometimes was to check my temper – from pointing a moral. The reader, I hope, will do it himself.

E.L.

Strange Sects and Cults

1

Prophets of Doom and Bliss

Joanna Southcott

The English love their eccentrics as much as their lords, and to become one or the other, or both, is probably a secret dream as widespread among Englishmen as that of becoming a matador is among Spaniards. Every now and then, the newspapers and other media of mass communication drag some eccentric into the limelight – as a rule, with his eager cooperation – just to show with pride that the traditional spirit of whimsy and fantasy is still alive in the island race. Whenever some new space spectacular hits the headlines, for instance, some paper is certain to send its man down to Dover to interview the secretary of the International Flat Earth Research Society to let him explain how the flat-earthers reconcile the latest exploit with their creed. On other occasions we read or listen to interviews with the distinguished old gentleman, a retired director of the UK Atomic Energy Authority, who has been waiting every afternoon since 1917 for the second coming of Our Lord according to the prediction of his 'Prophetic Witness Movement', which numbers quite a few ministers of religion among its members. The first indication that the millenium is about to begin, we are told, will be the disappearance of several prominent industrialists from their offices; they will have ascended to meet Christ on His way to us. Or the spotlight turns to Wales where a country welfare officer by the name of Morgan runs Britain's smallest sect, the Morganites, founded in 1742. It consists of twelve men who meet once a month late at night in an old farmhouse above Aberystwyth to reaffirm their belief that industrial civilization will soon collapse and men return to the land under a system of oligarchies, a belief based on the Morgan-

15

ites' ancient scripts on theology, astrology, world history and sexology.

But there is one eccentric English sect which never waits to be discovered for yet another generation of newspaper readers; it brings itself to their attention, at irregular intervals, by advertisements in the national press. These have had more or less the same wording for decades:

CRIME AND BANDITRY,
DISTRESS AND PERPLEXITY
will increase
until the Bishops
OPEN
Joanna Southcott's Box

This prediction is usually followed by a few Bible quotations from Revelation, and always by the invitation to write to the Panacea Society, Bedford. 'There is nothing to pay,' the ads end reassuringly.

Those who respond to the invitation receive a whole bunch of pamphlets and leaflets, obviously printed a very long time ago, which lends them a certain period flavour. One of the brochures is a biography entitled *The Truth about Joanna Southcott,* first published in 1917 and reprinted a few times. It begins with the simple statement that 'there is not, and never has been, a man or woman in the world who is Joanna Southcott's equal in brains, courage, perseverance, unselfishness, honesty, purity, loyalty to her country and devotion to her God', and that this is 'the truth that will prevail over the contemptible articles in Encyclopaedias, from which newspaper writers continue to get their information'. Fortunately, there are some near-contemporary sources of information on the lady in question, which enable us to piece together her life story without having recourse to those contemptible works of reference. It is quite an extraordinary story.

Joanna Southcott (or Southcote) was a farmer's daughter from a village near Exeter in Devon, born in 1750; her father was said to have come from a wealthy family which, however, disowned him because he had married beneath his inherited station in life. So he was reduced to having to earn his own living and his daughter, after minding the cows as a child, had to go into domestic service in Exeter when she was still quite young. Subsequently, she worked as a shop assistant, and eventually took up wallpaper hanging. There is no indication that during the first four decades of her life she ever aspired to higher things except, perhaps, to marriage, which seems to have been rather difficult, because she was as fat as she was plain.

She had joined the Methodists and met a man called Saunderson, who claimed to have prophetic notions; and gradually it dawned on Joanna that she too was suited for the career of a prophetess. At the age of forty-two, though still semi-illiterate, she began to write about her visions, partly in prose and partly in rhymed doggerel verse. A circle of followers gathered round her, quickly increasing when she declared what a still small voice had told her: that she and no one else was the woman referred to in Chapter 12 of the Book of Revelation: 'A woman arrayed with the sun, and the moon under her feet, and upon her head a crown of twelve stars.' For the time being, she did not go any further with Revelation in the matter of 'being with child', which she saved for a later occasion.

She had left her domestic job and made her living by selling seals which were to secure the salvation of the buyers. Her confidence, not to say audacity, increased with her reputation and she challenged the bishop and clergy of Exeter to a public investigation of her miraculous powers. The churchmen ignored Joanna, who told her converts that this was due to their fear and jealousy.

For a prophetess of her calibre Exeter had become too narrow, and she went to London on the invitation (and at the expense) of a well-known engraver by the name of Sharp. Business was so good that she was able to build a chapel for her sect at Newington Butts, next to the Elephant and Castle Inn. Her writings, with nearly unintelligible prophecies, foretold a speedy approach of the millennium; they sold like hot cakes, and to increase her supply of visionary raw material she employed a boy who pretended to have revelations, which he dictated to her. Mr Sharp, still the most devout of her followers, sealed up her manuscripts, 'with great caution', in a box which he secured in his house in Paddington, to be opened at a later day.

There was a schism among the sect; a rival prophet revealed himself and threw Joanna out of her own chapel in Newington Butts. But she was by now so well established (contemporary sources put the number of her followers at a hundred thousand), that she had nothing to fear from any competitor.

In January 1803, she and Mr Sharp staged a grand performance for the benefit of the sect. The sealed box with her writings from 1792 to 1794 was opened and examined for a week by 'twenty-three persons appointed by divine command'; the result, pronounced before an assembly of selected believers, was 'that her calling was of God'. They came to this conclusion, declared Mr Sharp, from the fulfilment of the prophecies in her writings – largely illegible scribblings, however. Joanna's own comment was: 'This must be so, to fulfil the Bible. Every vision that John saw in Heaven must take place on earth; and here is the sealed book that no one can read!'

The trade in seals was highly commercialized. Applicants had to 'volunteer' for the destruction of Satan's kingdom on earth. At a price varying from twelve shillings to one guinea, each of them received a folded paper endorsed with his name and closed with Joanna's seal in red wax, showing a circle around the initials JC (for Jesus Christ), with a star above and one below, and with the words 'The Sealed of the Lord, the Elect Precious, Man's Redemption to inherit the Tree of Life, to be made heirs of God and joint-heirs with Christ'. The paper was also 'authenticated' by the illegible signature of the prophetess. By the purchase of the document, the believer was then said to be 'sealed'; but to maintain a certain degree of exclusivity Joanna declared that there would be no more than twelve times twelve thousand 'sealed' people, conforming to Chapter 12 of the Book of Revelation.

It was the last year of her life which brought the most dramatic episode in Joanna Southcott's career as a prophetess; if there was ever any doubt that she herself believed in her 'mission', as she called it, this episode with its anguish and hysterical exaltation proved that she did, poor soul. It was a phantom pregnancy.

The 'dropsical old woman', as a contemporary Londoner called her, had fallen victim to some unidentified illness which made her belly swell up, and she was convinced that she was – in her sixty-fifth year! – 'with child'. And not just with anybody's, as she had never been intimate with men, but with the Holy Ghost's. The still small voice had made itself heard again, telling her that she was to give birth to Shiloh, the second appearance of the Messiah, mentioned in Genesis 49.

The good news was proclaimed to the world. The great event was to take place, she said, at midnight on 19 October 1814, before the end of the harvest. She allowed herself to be examined by eight doctors; three said she was not pregnant, but five said she was. The Archbishop of Canterbury was informed by her enthusiastic followers; he did not, however, share their happy excitement. Considerable sums of money were contributed to receive Shiloh in style; the most expensive item was a satinwood cradle for £200. A hymn was printed, to be sung to the tune of *Rule Britannia*; it ended with the lines: 'Praise God for giving us a King / To make this earth resemble Heaven. / Rule King Shiloh! King Shiloh rule alone / With glory crowned on David's throne.' Joanna spent most of her waiting time in bed, ate much and often, and had 'longings' characteristic of pregnant women. On one occasion, it is said, she longed for asparagus, and ate 160 heads 'at no small cost'.

But the harvest ended; 19 October came and went, and still there was no sign of an imminent birth, though she was in pain. So she consulted London's most famous physician, Dr Richard Reece, who has recorded the scene he witnessed when he visited her at her house in Manchester Street:

Five or six of her friends, who were waiting in an adjoining room, being admitted into her bed-chamber, she desired them to be seated round her bed; when, spending a few minutes in adjusting the bed-clothes with seeming attention, and placing before her a white handkerchief, she addressed them in the following words : 'My friends, some of you have known me nearly twenty-five years, and all of you not less than twenty; when you have heard me speak of my prophecies, you have sometimes heard me say that I doubted my inspiration; but at the same time, you would never let me despair. When I have been alone, it has often appeared delusion; but when the communication was made to me, I did not in the least doubt. Feeling, as I now do feel, that my dissolution is drawing near, and that a day or two may terminate my life, it all appears delusion.' She was by this exertion quite exhausted, and wept bitterly.

On reviving in a little time she observed that it was very extraordinary that after spending all her life in investigating the Bible, it would please the Lord to inflict that heavy burden on her. She concluded this discourse by requesting that everything on this occasion might be conducted with decency. She then wept; and all her followers present seemed deeply affected, and some of them shed tears. 'Mother,' said one, 'we will commit your instructions to paper, and rest assured they shall be conscientiously followed.' They were accordingly written down with much solemnity, and signed by herself, with her hand placed on the Bible in her bed. This being finished, Mr Howe (the above-mentioned follower) again observed to her, 'Mother, your feelings are human; we know that you are a favourite woman of God, and that you will produce the promised child; and whatever you may say to the contrary will not diminish our faith.' This assurance revived her, and the scene of crying was changed with her to laughter.

Surprisingly, Dr Reece, though anything but a believer in Joanna's role as a prophetess, pronounced her condition as pregnancy; her symptoms must have deceived him. Eventually, of course, he had to admit the 'folly and absurdity' of his diagnosis.

Another doctor examined her and told her in as many words that she was a very sick woman and had better prepare for the end. Joanna, her confidence restored, insisted that her sufferings were merely forebodings of the birth of Shiloh, which had been postponed until Christmas by divine command. Eventually she admitted the possibility of a 'temporary dissolution', and ordered that her body should be kept warm for four days after that event, whereupon she would 'revive and be delivered'. Christmas Day came, but no Shiloh; Joanna, very much in pain, was again beset by doubts. 'If I was deceived,' she whispered, 'it must have been by some spirit, either good or evil,' – words which show that she was no deliberate fraud.

On 27 December 1814, she died, and her *entourage* did as she had wished and kept her body warm for four days. When it showed no signs of revival the doctors were admitted; there seems to have been quite a scramble among medical men to assist at the post-mortem of the famous prophetess, for no fewer than fifteen of them took part. She was, of course, not pregnant; by common medical consent her condition had been due to 'bile and flatulence, indulgence and want of exercise'. While the post-mortem was going on an enormous crowd was gathering outside in Manchester Street, waiting for news of some miracle. Mr Sharp, still Joanna's most faithful disciple, feared that a riot might start if the doctors made their verdict public, and he told the crowd that she was not dead but merely in a trance. He really believed it; later he predicted that Joanna would return to earth in July 1822, 'but if she would not, nothing would shake my faith in her divine mission'. That faith continued to be shared by a great number of her followers; in 1817 a whole procession of them marched through Temple Bar, a trumpet was sounded, and the leader of the demonstration declared the coming of Shiloh, the Prince of Peace, while his wife shouted: 'Woe, woe to the inhabitants of the earth!' The Londoners who were watching pelted the fanatics with mud, there was a brawl and some people were arrested.

Joanna Southcott's funeral was carried out in secrecy for fear of disturbances. A plain hearse, followed by a coach with only three mourners, made its way from an undertaker's in Oxford Street to the new cemetery at St John's Wood Chapel; the grave had been taken under the name of Goddard, and not even the minister who read the service knew whom he was burying. Only in 1828 did the faithful provide the grave with a black marble tablet, with biblical quotations in gilt letters, now illegible through decay. For a long time Joanna's followers used to visit the cemetery, in the firm belief that there would be a resurrection of her body, and that she was still to be the mother of the promised Shiloh.

The extraordinary thing about Joanna Southcott's sect is that it did not die a natural death after she herself had ended her days on earth. She had lived and prophesied at the time when the French Revolution was shaking the western world and her influence had grown particularly strong during the anxious years of the Napoleonic Wars. One would have expected that, with peace and prosperity prevailing in Victorian England, the sect would disappear without trace.

But it did not, and Joanna herself had seen to it unwittingly. She had published no fewer than sixty-five works, mostly tracts and pamphlets; many of them emerged from the box which she and Mr Sharp opened in 1803. But this near-illiterate woman wrote so much that another mountain of paper with scribblings, yet unpublished, was found after her death. It seems that her votaries stacked it away in a box, sealed it and left it in the custody of a clergyman among her followers, the Rev Thomas Foley,

Vicar of Old Swinford, Worcestershire. His son, also a vicar –
they were relatives of Lord Foley and ancestors of a Bishop of
London – kept the box in his parish at North Cadbury, Stafford-
shire, for the next twenty-two years. So it was passed on from
clergyman to clergyman, making the rounds through the English
provinces until, early in this century, a group of Southcottians
founded an organization with the explicit aim of guarding the box
until the conditions for its opening, supposed to have been laid
down by Joanna herself, would be fulfilled. One of these is that
twenty-four bishops of the Church of England (or their official
representatives) must be present as witnesses. If it was really the
prophetess who thought up this request (according to the Book
of Revelation, which speaks of twenty-four 'Elders'), then it may
have been as a kind of revenge for the haughty neglect with which
the Anglican hierarchy, with the exception of a few vicars, treated
her during her lifetime.

The box-guarding organization is the Panacea Society in Bedford, whose name we know from its advertisements warning us
that things in England will get worse until the box is opened. The
'Box of Sealed Prophecies' by Joanna, weighing 156 pounds and
secured with copper nails, is now 'in safe custody' at a secret
place, presumably with a clergyman in or near Bedford. The attitude of the Church of England, however, still seems to be the same
as in Joanna's days : its bishops ignore all requests, warnings and
promises by the Society. The promises are that if they obey 'the
divine commands to open the Box, England will be proved to be
the New Jerusalem', grave national danger will be averted, and
'the glory will burst from the Church', to mention only a few of
the benefits to be expected.

The Society is rather secretive about its own history and the
personal data of its founders, but it seems that it came into being
as a result of the great expectation of revelations on the centenary
of Joanna's death in 1914. Instead, the Great War occupied
people's minds with other worries; the sect explained it as 'Satan's
final attempt to secure the kingdoms of this world' after he had
failed in Joanna's lifetime, when he 'entered' Napoleon, the 'first
Beast' of the Apocalypse. He tried again, they say, in two more
final attempts, via the Kaiser and Hitler, so it is now high time
the box was opened and the ultimate danger overcome. Among
the innumerable other tenets of the Society's faith are: that every-

body with an immortal soul will go to heaven, but that Socialists have not got a soul; that some lucky people will undergo physical resurrection; and that man has a second brain in his solar plexus, which is hidden away there so that Satan cannot get at it – this is the brain used for understanding prophecy, particularly Joanna's. The sect is furthermore convinced that she did after all give birth to Shiloh two days before her death, but he was 'caught up' immediately to the Throne of God; no wonder that no one saw him. ('Damn me if the child isn't gone,' Dr Reece had exclaimed.)

To the uninitiated it may seem that the Panacea Society, which claims a hundred thousand followers, has no other activity but to spend thousands of pounds on its advertisements and pamphlets. However, the pamphlets explain that while waiting for the bishops' appearance for the opening, it is 'healing, helping, and protecting thousands' :

No one was more surprised than ourselves when, in May 1923, we discovered that Divine Healing was within our reach by a simple process, which proved to be the key which unlocked the prophecies. After most crucial tests, the Healing proved to be sure, though slow; and when every individual of the Society had been benefited, it became our obvious duty to give the Public an opportunity to participate ... Results have proved that nothing but obedience to and patient perseverence in the treatment is necessary.

In other words: no sudden miracle cures are promised, a wise policy on the part of the Southcottians. The range of complaints from which 'slow but sure deliverance by treatment through Water and the Spirit, without money and without price' can be obtained is rather impressive, as a special leaflet states:

Cancer, Nerves, Consumption, Epilepsy, Paralysis,
Rheumatism, Eye, Ear and Throat Troubles,
Mental Anxiety, Business Worries,
Faults of Disposition.
PROTECTION can be secured in the Tribulations and
Perplexities that are preceding the Coming of the Lord.
Do not write for particulars, but send
your list of complaints in as few words
as possible ...

The leaflet ends with the Society's maxim: that there is no cure for the complaints of England as a whole until the bishops open Joanna's box.

As a matter of fact, four boxes supposed to contain Joanna's prophecies have already been opened since her death; none of these openings, however, was attended by the required number of bishops and the contents proved disappointing in each case. The last of these occasions was in 1927. A petition, signed by ten thousand people, had been sent to the Archbishop of Canterbury, who again refused to take action. A kindly suffragan bishop offered to put the Southcottians out of their misery and attend the opening; although the rest of the required number of church dignitaries were missing, the box was opened. It contained no divine message to humanity but merely a horse-pistol, a lottery ticket, one earring, a dice-box, a child's nightcap and a copy of an early nineteenth-century book entitled *The Surprises of Love, or an Adventure in Greenwich Park*. Clearly it had been the wrong box.

Undaunted, the Panacea Society organized a new petition to the Primate, and got nearly thirty thousand signatures by 1935. But to this day the 'real box', according to its guardians, still remains unopened. However, Joanna was such a prolific writer that pamphlets and manuscripts from her pen keep turning up. Some of them are in the British Museum; another bunch found its way, via a vicar in the Isle of Wight, to the Greater London Council's records department as recently as 1970. This includes prophecies and very bad verse, with an unintentional touch of humour added by her eccentric spelling – she foresaw 'earthquacks' and told the story of a 'Great Snake Serpant' which 'attact' a ship's crew at night but was eventually disposed of by 'choping of his head'.

It is all a harmless and splendidly eccentric enterprise, as British as the Union Jack, in its combination of the fantastic and the realistic. The Panacea Society succeeded in getting registered as a charity; this means important tax concessions, but the accounts have to be disclosed to the Charity Commissioners. Thus it became known in 1966 that the Society's investments alone totalled almost £290,000, most of them in the form of property; the Society bought up some houses in Bedford many years ago, and their value, together with the income from the property, has of course gone up considerably. So the Society can afford its expensive advertisements. Perhaps the sect is quite happy to have its headquarters in provincial Bedford – whose main tourist attraction is the jail where John Bunyan spent twelve years, mainly occupied with writing *The Pilgrim's Progress* – instead of London, which is bound to suffer 'dire distress', according to the Southcottians. The Lord 'will sweep London as a man sweepeth the yard with a besom, for one half of it will become a lake, and men-of-war will be able to enter it'. Still, let us be of good cheer, for we are assured that 'the 6,000 years of misery caused by the Fall are drawing quickly to a close, and the promise of Prosperity, Health, and Happiness on earth is slowly but surely coming into operation through Water and the Spirit, as prophesied by Joanna Southcott', definitely before the year 2000.

The British Israelites

Few among the many puzzles in the Bible have stirred people's imagination in the last two or three centuries more than that of the ten 'lost tribes' of Israel. The Old Testament, otherwise fairly detailed as a tribal history of the Jews, offers hardly a clue to their fate after their disappearance from Palestine. What happened was that Solomon's son Rehoboam, who ascended the throne of Israel in 922 BC, was faced with a great deal of discontent among the northern tribes due to his father's policies of high taxation and forced labour. They eventually broke away under a king of their own, Jeroboam, thus dissolving the unity of the nation, and only the tribes of Judah and Benjamin remained loyal to the dynasty of David which continued to rule the southern part of the country from Jerusalem. The Bible calls Jeroboam a 'mighty man of valour' who, however, 'made Israel to sin'.

Under his rule and that of his successors, paganism and immorality increased; eventually the country's internal struggles, its economic and military weakness tempted the aggressive Assyrians to invade it. After a three-year siege, the fortified capital Samaria fell in 721 BC. The northern kingdom had come to an end and large sections of its people were deported to Assyria and Media as slaves. One must assume that, as nothing more has been heard of them since that time, 2,700 years ago, these ten tribes lost their identity and became submerged in the gentile population of the Middle East, while their former kingdom was re-settled with Assyrian colonists.

The southern tribes of Judah and Benjamin, with part of the tribe of Levi, survived. Tough and austere, and despite some temporary deviations loyal to their traditions and their God, they survived the Babylonian exile, the destruction of their Temple and capital, Jerusalem, by the Romans, and their dispersion all over the ancient world; they went on to survive two thousand years of religious and racial oppression, of enforced migration and, in our own century, of mass murder. They are the Jews of today.

It is a historical miracle of the first order, but it is taken for granted; mysteries appeal to the playful human mind more than facts, and the supposed survival of the lost tribes is just such a mystery. Over the centuries they have been 'discovered' in innumerable guises and countries – as Tartars and Red Indians, in Afghanistan and the Sahara, in China and Japan. 'No race has escaped the honour, or suspicion, of being descendants from the subjects of Jeroboam,' wrote a British historian, A. M. Hyamson, at the turn of our century. They were even said to have been involved in the destruction of Atlantis!

Movements or groups claiming to be the lost tribes exist all over the world. There is, for instance, the Ahmadiya sect in Pakistan, founded by Mirza Ghulam Ahmad, who was born at Qadian in the Punjab in 1839. He was a devout Moslem who had dreams and visions in which he saw himself as a regenerator of Islam, and at the age of fifty he announced that he had received a revelation that he was the Mahdi, the expected Messiah of the Mohammedans, as well as the great teacher of the whole world prophesied in Hindu, Buddhist and Zoroastrian writings, representing the incarnation of Krishna and the second coming of Christ, though not in the flesh but in the spirit.

Ahmad developed his role in detail. He was crucified as Jesus Christ, he claimed, but was taken down from the Cross in a swoon, still alive. He recovered and went to Afghanistan and Kashmir, where he found the lost ten tribes, to whom he preached. Ahmad had been told, in a revelation, that the tomb of a Moslem prophet called Yus Asaf at Srinagar was in fact that of Jesus, 'Yus' being a corruption of Jesus and 'Asaf' the Hebrew verb 'to gather', for it was here that Christ had gathered the lost tribes.

The sect did not organize itself properly until after Ahmad's death in 1908, but split up five years later on questions of dogma. Both branches are still carrying out active missionary work; they have a number of religious centres in Pakistan, publish journals in Urdu and English, and Ahmad's successor Mohammed Ali, a learned and educated man, made a new English translation of the Koran; it presents Islam as a 'rational faith' which appeals to the modern scientific age. According to the Ahmadiyans, the lost tribes of Israel are still alive among the people of Pakistan, though their founder's more extravagant claims have been forgotten.

On the opposite side of the globe, in the West Indies, the Ras Tafari movement teaches its fundamental tenet that the Negroes are the descendants, or at least reincarnations, of the lost tribes of Israel. The sect began its early life in 1918 with the United Negro Improvement Association, founded by the American evangelist Marcus Garvey who, perhaps inspired by the Balfour Declaration which promised the Jews a national home in Palestine, advocated a mass return of the Negroes from the western hemisphere to Africa, their 'homeland'. This Black Zionism, as Garvey's movement was often called, tried to give the American and West Indian Negro an identity and a philosophy as well as a political-religious purpose, expressed in the slogans 'Africa for Africans' and 'One God, One Goal, One Destiny'.

Garvey's ideas did not catch on very well in the United States, but were all the more popular in Jamaica, where they underwent a significant change in 1930 after the coronation of Ras Tafari Makonnen (later to be known as Haile Selassie) as Emperor of Ethiopia. Somehow the event, of great importance to the Abyssinians, made a deep impression on Garvey's followers in Jamaica; they took the new ruler's subsidiary official titles, 'King of Kings, Conquering Lion of Judah, Elect of God', very seriously. Ignorant of African geography, the poor, uneducated masses of the island, particularly in the slum districts of West Kingston, began to look upon the Emperor as their Messiah who would lead them, the exiled tribes of Israel, home to an African paradise. Thus the Ras Tafari movement, as it now began to call itself (*Ras* means Prince in Amharic, and *Tafari* is the family name of the Emperor), promised its followers freedom and salvation, embroidering its beliefs with all kinds of notions based on biblical quotations: that the ten lost tribes were exiled into slavery because they had transgressed the law of God; that the white man is inferior to the black man; that the black man's revenge will be to make the white man his servant; that Jamaica is the black man's Hell, Africa-

Ethiopia his Heaven; that Haile Selassie, descendant of King David, is the living God. Some statements of the Rastafarians must have embarrassed the Emperor: that he swore 'Death to the white man' or that he 'started the Mau Mau rebellion'. In their street processions they carry the green, gold and red flag of Ethiopia with giant photographs of him.

In a way, therefore, the Ras Tafari sect has been a forerunner of the Civil Rights Movement, preceding it by some thirty years; but it has never been activist or militant. Instead it has developed its own curious brand of religious doctrine, a Judeo-Christian mixture with elements from African tribal cults, for 'the white man's interpretation of religion is a fraud to keep the black man back'. The most acceptable Christian faith, they feel, is that of the Coptic Church, because it developed on African soil and half of the Abyssinian people belongs to it.

One has to see how and where most of the Rastafarians live to understand that it is essentially an escapist movement. Their homes in West Kingston are what the French call *'bidonvilles'*, clusters of rusty tin shacks or cardboard huts without water supply or drainage, let alone electricity. Illiteracy and unemployment are very high among the 150,000 people or more who vegetate in an area of less than four square miles. Fewer than a quarter of them are married, yet many of the women have eight or nine children, usually by different fathers.

This is the soil on which the Rastafarian sect has grown. The belief that they and their brethren are the lost tribes of Israel has given them a certain pride, and their trust in the Ethiopian Messiah a definite hope of better days to come. But although Haile Selassie did in fact make a land grant of some five hundred acres in the Arushi area of Ethiopia for receiving West Indian re-migrants as settlers, very few Jamaicans have come so far: money for transport and settlement has not been forthcoming, for one thing, and there may also be an instinctive fear of the disappointment which the return to the African 'paradise' may bring.

Escapism among the Rastafarians also takes the form of smoking *ganja*, a drug similar in its effects to marijuana. They believe that is is a 'holy herb' (and quote the Bible on this point) and say a short blessing before lighting the match. Some members of the sect make a living by growing or selling *ganja* and the Jamaican police carry out regular raids to discover its illegal cultivation. The Rastafarians wear long hair and beards, in accordance with Israelite custom, and express their protest against having to live in exile by not conforming to the rules of the Jamaican 'establishment: they avoid marriage, do not vote at elections and gather at their chapels to celebrate Ethiopian and Coptic holidays instead of Jamaican ones. When Haile Selassie visited Jamaica in 1966 thousands of Rastafarians gave him a truly Messianic welcome at the airport, very much to his surprise.

Perhaps the most curious among the various sects claiming descent from the lost tribes are the British Israelites, curious because of the extensiveness of their claim and because here we have no escapist movement of a poor and ignorant people, but an association of citizens from the educated middle classes, with more than a sprinkling of upper-class people, in the midst of modern, prosperous Britain. One only has to visit its impressive headquarters in London, literally a mere stone's throw from Buckingham Palace, to realize that the British Israel World Federation, with branches in the United States, Australia, Canada, South Africa, Rhodesia, and New Zealand, is an organization of considerable magnitude.

It has been called a 'prophetic persuasion' because its basic creed serves as a starting point for claims, warnings and promises of things to come according to its special interpretation of the Scriptures. That basic creed, of course, is that the Anglo-Saxon peoples in general and the British (including their Celtic elements) in particular are the direct descendants of the lost tribes of Israel. Those who accept this tenet will also believe that the British are the Chosen People to whom God has promised national and spiritual supremacy, protection and prosperity if they abide by His laws. World events and political developments, say the British Israelites, can be understood and their future course mapped out only if the present identity of the Chosen People is accepted.

History has no shred of evidence about the survival, as tribes, of the captives whom the Assyrians deported, but the total absence of factual knowledge on the subject has cleared the way for all those strange theories and beliefs. The origins of most of these myths are impossible to trace, but we know very well how the notions of the British Israelites have developed.

One of the earliest sources of British Israelitism was a book published in 1649, entitled *Rights of the Kingdom, or Customs of our Ancestors*. Its author was a favourite of Oliver Cromwell by the name of John Sadler, born in Shropshire in 1615, who was for some time town clerk of London and sat as a Member of Parliament for Cambridge. He was a political writer and student of Oriental literature, and it occurred to him that England's constitution was similar to that of ancient Israel; although he did not formulate a precise theory in his *Rights of the Kingdom*, he implied that parts of England's population might be descendants of the lost tribes. They might have come with emigrants from Phoenicia; Sadler believed that the name Britain originated from the Phoenician *berat anac,* 'the land of tin and lead'. At any rate, he seems to have advised Cromwell on the question of re-admitting Jews to England, a plan which the Protector discussed with the French biblical writer Manasseh ben Israel in1655.

Contrasting strongly with the scholarly Sadler, Newfoundland-born Richard Brothers, who came next in the line of British Israel pioneers, was a religious fanatic. Dismissed from the British Navy, where he served until the age of thirty, in 1787, he began writing pamphlets in which he claimed to be 'a nephew of the Almighty and Prince of the Hebrews, appointed to lead them to the land of Canaan' from Europe, among whose nations they were dispersed. In 1795 he demanded of the King that the latter should hand him his crown as God had committed to him 'the Government of the Jewish Nation', which he vaguely identified with the peoples of the western world. He was promptly arrested for treason, found guilty but insane, and sent to the London madhouse for a number of years. Yet he found sympathizers in educated circles, among them the Orientalist and MP Nathaniel Brassey Halhed, who tabled a motion that Brothers's case should be reheard before the House; he did not find a seconder, and Mr Hansard, in one of his outspoken comments, wrote of Halhed's initiative as 'a memorable and melancholy instance of the eccentricity of the human mind'. A leading Quaker, William Bryan, also sided with Brothers, adding a revelation of his own: 'That very many of those called Christians are the true descendants of Jacob, who is called Israel; that by various dispersions and captivities, conversion to Christianity in the early ages of that Church, etc, the distinguishing mark of the Jew was lost'; and he came to the conclusion 'that the greater number of the inhabitants of this land (called Great

Britain) are Israelites' (*A Testimony concerning the Spirit of the Truth*, London, 1795).

Then there was a Scottish lawyer, John Finleyson, who elaborated on Brothers's theories in various pamphlets; claiming divine inspiration and adding some astrological data, he announced that 'nearly all' the English, Germans, Dutch, Irish and two-thirds of the French were 'descendants of the Hebrews'. For good measure, he also included the Persians and the North Africans, half the Russians, Poles, Swiss, Italians, Spanish, Greeks, Mexicans and Peruvians. Descendants of the lost tribes, he said, 'abound in the Turkish Empire and even in China, Japan and Ethiopia', while the great majority of North Americans were also among that not very select company of descendants. Finleyson published the last of his pamphlets as an old man in 1849, but already thirty years earlier he had managed to secure the release of Brothers from the asylum. He seems to have been an efficient lawyer, at any rate.

Today's British Israelites, however, prefer to look upon Ralph Wedgwood as their predecessor. In his *Book of Remembrance*, which was published in 1814 when Napoleon was approaching the end of his rule, Wedgwood pronounced the definite claim that the British Empire was the Messiah's 'promised possession and naval dominion' in fulfilment of the prophecies in the Books of Daniel and Revelation. He, like Joanna Southcott, was among quite a number of British prophets who identified Napoleon as the anti-Christ, and Britain as the principal nation on the side of the angels.

Then came the actual begetter of the British Israel philosophy, John Wilson, the son of a poor weaver from Kilmarnock, who used to recall how the idea that the English (he did not say the British) were the lost tribes first occurred to him 'as a bright flash of light' when he saw his children pasting pictures of English bowmen at Agincourt and other notable battles in their scrapbooks: England was the bow of Ephraim, the lost Israel. He expounded his claim in lectures first in Ireland, which he toured in 1840, and then in England and Scotland. He was an impressive speaker, who appealed most of all to the middle classes, and the book he wrote on the subject, *Our Israelitish Origin*, was a great success. He also started the first journals of what was later to grow into a vigorous movement but remained only a loose group of sympathizers and believers during Wilson's lifetime. He died in 1871.

He argued that although England was a modern, spiritual Israel there was also a strong possibility that the English were literally the lost tribes. While Judah was the 'first-fruits', Israel was the 'harvest', and God's warning that He would 'cause them to be lost among the gentiles till Seven Times should pass over them' referred to Israel only, and the Jews could not be the beneficiaries of the divine promises.

Wilson, who was of course not a scholar, collected his arguments in favour of the Anglo-Saxons' identity with the lost tribes from any source that came his way. There was, for instance, the philological proof: the word 'Britain', far from deriving from the Phoenician *berat anac,* meant the Land of the Covenant, *brith* in Hebrew. He took great pains to explain the migration of the ten tribes with similar arguments; the Danes and the Danai (Greeks), the rivers Danube, Don and Dnieper, were these names not obviously derived from that of the tribe of Dan? The Saxons were, in fact, Isaac's sons; and so on. In short, the tribes of Israel, far from getting absorbed by the heathens, migrated north and west as though compelled by an inner impetus, to meet again in the British Isles, in England, the Land of the Angels, to establish the true kingdom of God and to be 'recovenanted in Christ'.

Subsequent British Israel writers and speakers have enlarged upon these claims, and it is not always clear which of them were Wilson's contributions to the saga and which were later put forward by his disciples. There is, for instance, the matter of the British monarchy. It all began with Pharez and Zarah, the twin sons of Judah, Joseph's elder brother, and a younger son of Judah called Shelah. While some of the Zarah clan settled in Spain, as evident from the name of Zaragossa, Shelah's descendants became 'the families of the house of them that wrought fine linen', as the Bible says. To the British Israelites, 'the combination of fine linen weaving and the name of Shelah points irresistibly to Ireland', as a latter-day writer of the movement declares. In this style, interpreting Bible passages imaginatively while slightly twisting the arm of history, the argument continues 'irresistibly'. The royal family of David were descendants of Zarah's twin brother Pharez, and according to British Israelite lore these two seem to have sired all the major royal families of Europe, starting with the Trojans and the Greeks and going on via the Vikings and the Saxons to Ireland, Scotland and England, where the families of Zarah, Pharez and

Shelah all met again and intermarried, 'so that our present beloved Queen is descended from them all and unites the various ruling branches of Judah in her own person. . . . It is the family divinely chosen to hold the sceptre. It is significant that while the nations of mixed race have thrown off the yoke of royal rule, the Israel nations remain faithful to their monarchy.'

Wherever the British Israelites look they find evidence of their nation's identity with the lost tribes: the famous Redcoats of Britain's army (see Nahum's description of Israel's soldiers); the Stone of Scone, which was already David's coronation stone, still serving the same purpose in Westminster Abbey; England's weights, measures and currency, retained until recent times, all based on ancient Palestinian standards; the Union Jack(*sic*) with Jacob's emblem, the letter X, which is also the Greek *kh* and the symbol for Christ; circumcision being practised among the Anglo-Saxons more than in other Christian nations, and particularly in the British royal family. Even good old John Bull provides an interesting scrap of evidence: was not the bull Ephraim's heraldic beast?

But this is not all. The mere name of Great Britain is a pointer: Genesis 12:2 speaks of a 'great' nation; elsewhere it is called a maritime nation, having command of the sea, occupying islands and coastlands; an undefeated nation; a company (or Commonwealth) of nations. Slightly out of date, however, is the claim that the new Israel, Britain, 'possesses the wealth of the earth' (Genesis, Deuteronomy). But that it excels in keeping the Sabbath is still true; after all, the longest Sabbath in history, the Friday-to-Monday weekend, is without doubt an English invention. In short: the British 'have all the Marks of Israel . . . if only they realized it'.

To return to John Wilson: he did not endeavour to organize a movement based on his ideas, which he regarded as a system of prophecy on the strength of the revelation that had come to him: that 'wonderful evidence of Almighty Providence'. It was only after his death that his followers stepped up their proselytizing efforts within the framework of a missionary association. A new advocate of the British Israelite creed, Edward Hine, aroused much public interest with his books and pamphlets, but also much internal dissension within the movement when he attacked its

'Teutonism', the 'excessively foolish' writings of a number of its protagonists and the 'nonsense taught by some who have espoused the Identity cause'. It took many years to sort things out and establish some kind of doctrinal unity: and the British Israel World Federation came into being, linking groups which had sprung up in all countries with Anglo-Saxon populations, open to membership candidates from all denominations, though the Federation emphasized the Protestant element in its evangel. It would be interesting to know whether any practising Jews ever applied for membership and what the British Israelites' attitude to these candidates was; after all, the pamphlets from Buckingham Gate say: 'Jesus, well knowing that the Jews' Devil-inspired rejection of Him, through their evil leaders, would be final, pronounced sentence of disinheritance upon the Jews as God's nation: "The Kingdom of God shall be taken from you, and given to a nation bringing forth the fruits thereof" ', and that nation, of course, is the British.

Like the Southcottians, the British Israelites complain about the lack of cooperation on the part of the Church: there is 'little response from those acknowledged as the leading shepherds of the Christian flock . . . Would it be too much to suggest that our Church leaders might dwell for a while on these deep issues in the light of the Scriptures?' Neither the Anglican nor other Protestant leaders want the scriptures explained to them by the British Israelites, and their attack on the 'fallacy that Christianity was brought to us from Rome' does not sound very conciliatory in Roman-Catholic ears. Individual churchmen, however, have always been found in the ranks of the sect, and there is the odd archbishop or two among the honorary members of the past, on a list headed by Queen Victoria, who held 'drawing-rooms' with British Israelite guest speakers, and King Edward vii, and including enough admirals and generals to staff a navy and army at wartime strength. Some leading members even whisper that Queen Elizabeth ii is among their supporters.

A major source of annoyance to the movement is that 'modern historians are far from helpful' in the matter of the lost tribes' alleged migrations – understandably, for although British Israelite literature is brimful of biblical quotations, each of them with chapter and verse, there is a great dearth of authentic historical references; one rarely finds anything more objective and reliable than Herodotus's hearsay tales; many archaeological discoveries and interpretations are mentioned without reference to sources and dates, so that it is rather difficult to check what is fact and what is wishful thinking. The latter seems to have played a particularly large part in the British Israelite saga of the Celts who reached the British Isles as the 'advance guard' of the ten tribes; they started out, we are told, as the 'sons of Omri', King of Samaria, changing into the Khumri, the Gimira, the Cimmerians, the Cimbri of Jutland and eventually the inhabitants of Cymru on their way from Palestine to Wales, populating the other Celtic countries *en route*.

Nor do modern historians accept the British Israelite belief that the Scythians were in fact Israelites who migrated from Media to southern Russia and from there later to central Europe, where the Romans called them Germans. Some of them, the saga continues, 'came to Britain as Anglo-Saxons, AD 450–600; others, after moving north through Jutland, became known as Danes and Vikings', who of course invaded England; and others again 'settled for a short time in France and were called Normans'. Under William the Conqueror they were the last Israelites to arrive in 1066 for the great rendezvous of the lost tribes. Orthodox history, however, has traced the movements of the Scythians in a different direction : probably coming from North-west India, they extended their kingdom to the west, invading Assyria and penetrating as far as Palestine; in Europe, they seem to have got no farther than what is now Rumania and Bulgaria.

After the Church and the historians, the Establishment: while expressing its gratitude for 'the incomparable blessings conferred by the Davidic Throne as now represented by our Gracious Queen', the sect often criticizes her government, and that of the United States, in no uncertain terms. A wealthy Canadian member paid for enormous press advertisements in the 1960s, setting out the British Israelite creed in detail, with the usual abundance of biblical quotations. One paragraph reads:

As Samson of old, when blind, saw that he could destroy the enemies of his people by bringing their house down upon them, so the people of the British and American empires when they realized that they have been betrayed by their leaders—financial, political, and ecclesiastical—into surrendering their sovereignty, will, while still blind to their identity, lay hold of the two main pillars of the

hidden government—international finance and organized religion—
and bring the whole structure down like a millstone cast into
the sea [Revelation, chapters 17 and 18], completely destroying the
present world order. As these two chapter of Revelation declare, God
will put it into the hearts of the ten horns—'my people'—to give unto
the 'beast' [Europe], their power [sovereignty] for one hour. This we
now see taking form. He then instructed His people to throw off the
old woman that has been and is riding, manipulating and controlling
the rulers, and to 'eat her flesh, and burn her with fire'—confiscate
her assets and utterly destroy her Babylonian system of international finance and organized religion. Soon thereafter the visible
phase of God's Kingdom in power and great glory will be established
on earth, by which and through which He will bring about the
blessing of all the families of the earth. The people of the British and
American empires, and other nations of the ten tribes, awakening
to their identity, will rise again, not as they are at present constitu-
ted but as Israel. . . .

And so we come to the prophecies as revealed to the believers.
The 'End of the Age of the Gentiles' is at hand; the signs are wars,
famine and pestilence, 'phenomenal tides' and earthquakes, and
the 'distress and perplexity' of nations. But not because the bishops
refuse to open some old box; rather because the world is rehearsing
for Armageddon. In the Second World War, the British Israelites
saw Stalin, although he was Britain-Israel's ally, as a latter-day
Antioch Epiphanes, the evil King of the North, and the Soviet
Union as the new Babylon. Stalin's agents were the Zionists, whom
he sent to Palestine to prepare, as a fifth column, for Russia's
takeover of the Holy Land; for he wanted to conquer Jerusalem
and destroy, with one blow, the seat of three religions.

Now, say the British Israelites, the final conflict between the
kingdoms of God and Satan 'looms close'. The menace is 'not
merely Slav, but also Mongol and worse' (sic). The slumbering
East has woken up and prepares 'an assault upon the nations which
stand for decency, law and justice'. But when the 'Sign of the Son
of Man' appears in heaven, the 'righteous ones among the holy
ones will have entered the Marriage Supper and will be beyond
the power of Communism'.

The 'Message of the Great Pyramid', which used to be quoted
by the British Israelites before the Second World War, has let
them down and is no longer among their campaigning arguments.

According to it, Hitler's most critical day was to be 27 November 1939 but nothing remarkable happened on that date. It is, of course, safer to refer to past and existing situations, such as the conflict in the Middle East. 'The greatest of all timemarks was, of course, the deliverance of Jerusalem from gentile oppression by British and Anzac forces in the First World War,' we are told. 'It marked the Beginning of the End.' Now, however, the fronts have shifted, and Bible interpretation has had to be revised accordingly : the Zionists are no longer Satan's agents, for it is the other side, the Arabs, who are 'headed and sustained by the northern power', i.e. Russia. It follows that the British Israelites are, for a change, on the side of the Jews, although it is rather unfair that the latter, just to confuse the issue, call their country Israel.

Armageddon is near and another sign of its approach is space travel, particularly the moon landings, the Tower of Babel all over again. An American British Israelite has had his lectures on the subject published. 'The launching of the Apollo flights,' he says, 'and earth and moon orbiting devices, as well as sending instrument-laden rockets to probe the planets in our solar system, all signal the imminence of divine intervention. . . . Because he is still in his sinful state, man's efforts to explore, and perhaps exploit, outer space, are endangering God's universe,' and these activities will accordingly be stopped by divine intervention: 'The Lord will now be compelled to move to protect His universe from contamination by sinful human beings . . . The unrighteous will not be allowed to consummate their plans for the conquest of outer space . . . God is about to restrain the wicked and prevent the realization of their intentions. Then He will cleanse the earth of all evil in order that men of peace and goodwill may bring about the ultimate establishment of righteousness upon earth, from whence its blessings will spread throughout His universe.'

A strange sect indeed. In the midst of an advanced, well-to-do society they seek a new status symbol for all the English-speaking peoples, 'along with their kinsmen in the countries of the North Sea fringe' (including, presumably, the Germans), by tortuously identifying them with a long-lost group of tribes, assuming the parts of modern prophets in continuation of their biblical prede- cessors. They take pride in being the advance guard when the twentieth-century 'Israelites' will one day march through the golden gates into the millenium, and they want to be able to say: 'We told you so,' when that day comes. They foretell general doom if their voices go unheeded, and bliss if the message is accepted. Other messianic sects may hope for material benefits; the British Israelites are content with transmitting the 'instruction of Almighty God to the English-speaking and kindred peoples for the Crisis of the Ages, now upon us'. These are the message and instructions as pronounced by the prophet Isaiah 2,500 years ago : 'Come, my people, enter thou into thy chambers and shut thy doors about thee; hide thyself as it were for a little moment until the indignation be overpast. For behold, the Lord cometh out of His place to punish the inhabitants of the earth for their iniquity.'

2

Quiet Fanatics

The Amish People

To define the main characteristic of the Amish sect by saying that they have opted out of the twentieth century would be wide of the mark. They never lived in it, though technically they are our contemporaries. For them, time has stood still for the last quarter of a millennium; to be precise, since 1727. Within a range of little more than three hundred miles from New York, there is the early eighteenth century : not its architectural relics but its everyday life, its way of thinking, its people.

One might even say that the origins of the Amish go back to the heyday of the Reformation. In 1523, only two years after Martin Luther had made his great confession of faith before the Diet at Worms, a Swiss lay preacher, Konrad Grebler, founded the Protestant sect of the *Schweizer Brüder*, the Swiss Brethren, at Zürich. The new faith spread to Germany and Holland. Assailed by the Catholic Church, disowned even by the Lutherans, they suffered a terrible bloodbath in 1529. Fifteen years later the survivors rallied round the Dutch Anabaptist, Menno Simons, calling themselves Mennonites. They refused to baptize young children, to serve as soldiers, to take oaths. It was another Swiss, Jakob Amann from the Canton of Berne, who provoked a split among the Mennonites towards the end of the seventeenth century; the rules and practices of the sect were not strict enough for his liking, particularly those concerning the outlawry of recalcitrant members. His followers, the *Amisch* (later called Amish) were soon to be found in Bavaria and Alsace, in the Netherlands, and even as far as Galacia in southern Poland. What they were seeking was peace and quiet to live in their faith and enough land to farm in large communities.

The New World seemed to offer them both. In 1727, the first contingent of two hundred brethren from Pirmasens in the Palatinate arrived in Pennsylvania to join the 'Plain People' : the English Quakers, the Swedish and ''Dutch' (in fact German) Anabaptists who had already settled there, secure from religious and political persecution. Many more members of the 'Old Order Amish', as they began to call themselves, followed them during the course of the eighteenth century. Large communities were established in Ohio, smaller ones in Iowa and Indiana as well as in Canada. There are altogether some fifty thousand Amish people in North America today and their numbers are growing; none are left in Europe.

They are peaceful, quiet fanatics, and they are said to be among the richest farmers in the world, although they cultivate their land just like their peasant forefathers in early eighteenth-century Europe. They are a living anachronism. If you told them so, and if they understood what you meant, they would smile and reply that it was you who were out of step; with nature, with life, with God. But most likely you would not be able to understand them, nor they you; for the majority of them still speak an archaic Alemannic, the south-west German idiom which the first Amish immigrants brought to America. It isolates them from their fellow-citizens, and this is what they want: to be left alone.

Lancaster County, Pennsylvania, is still the heartland of the Old Order. Twentieth-century American life may be hustling by on the highways with their fast-rushing stream of powerful automobiles; but behind that wood, on the far side of that hill, the modern world has ceased to exist. A team of well-groomed horses pull a wooden plough through the earth, perhaps the most fertile in the whole of the United States. A bearded man walks behind the horses, gripping the plough handles. The country road skirts acres of tall, thickly leafed tobacco plants and rolling fields with fat dairy cattle; ducks are chasing each other in little ponds, hens cackling in their spacious runs; the trees in the orchard seem to be waiting quietly while the sun ripens their abundance of fruit. A large, low house built of stone is the centre of the farm. Smoke curls up from the chimney; the farmwife is baking bread. She wears a long white apron and a little white prayer cap at her housework. The children, the smaller ones usually barefoot, also wear headgear: the girls caps and the boys wide-brimmed, dark hats like men. When the women go out or go to town, for instance, shopping in Lancaster City, they wear ankle-length grey gowns with girdles and dark bonnets like the Puritan women a dozen generations ago.

The men let their hair grow down to the backs of their necks, with straight-cut fringes over their foreheads; the married ones have 'Uncle Sam' beards, which leave the upper lip free. They rarely take off their enormous black hats. Their clothes, too, are black and simple; in the strictest communities all cloth is woven by hand, and the men's suits have no buttons but hooks and eyes: buttons, and also moustaches, are banned because they have military associations.

No machine noises disturb the pastoral peace. There are no tractors, no cars, no power-driven implements, in fact no power apart from that of human or animal muscles: no electricity or gas, no petrol or oil except in the oil lamps. Cooking and baking is done with wood fires. There are, of course, no refrigerators or washing-machines, no radio or television sets, no telephones or air-conditioning. Transport is by horse-drawn buggies with high, slender wheels and by farmcarts pulled by oxen or mules. The horse and buggy play quite an important part in the Amish community; when a boy has reached the age of puberty, at about sixteen, his family present him with his own horse and buggy so that he can *rumspringa,* Alemannic for 'jumping about', and take his girl for a ride after the day's work. For a strict religious sect this seems quite a broadminded attitude; in fact, courtship is encouraged because it leads to marriage and to the propagation of the community.

The Amish scorn every kind of labour-saving device; when they buy a farm with electricity they rip the cables out. Instead, they build windmills for grinding and irrigation. If a member of the community is discovered riding in a motor-car without special permission, let alone driving one, he may be expelled as a sinner without hope of redemption. Pride and ostentation are deadly sins; so are sloth and frivolity; but the deadliest is marrying outside the faith.

It is a plain faith. There is no other guide in daily life but *'s dicke Buch,* 'the fat book', the Bible; the command that man must earn his bread by the sweat of his brow is supreme in this pastoral existence. Therefore, the world outside and all its ways are sinful temptations of the devil. From these stern convictions spring the sect's attitudes to the various manifestations of state power. 'He who does not take anything from the state does not owe it anything,' is the Amish tenet. As their faith forbids violence, they refuse military service; their young men may, however, serve in, state labour camps. They refuse to pay social security taxes, for they hold that such 'insurance' implies a lack of faith in God. This has led to lengthy conflicts with the US Internal Revenue, and at one point Amish livestock was seized and auctioned by the authorities. In the end Congress granted them exemption from the social security tax as well as from social security benefits. 'We can look after our old people and the sick ourselves,' the Amish declared. However, they do not refuse to pay normal taxes; but they do not vote in any elections.

Education causes the most severe friction between the Amish and the authorities. The brethren say that, according to the Bible, children belong to the parents and not to the state; they should not be confused and tempted by irreligious teachings, and they need not learn more than the three R's – everything else is in the Bible. The Amish fear that in those larger, modern state schools the children would be drawn into the world of the devil; even gym classes and sports, where 'immodest' clothes are worn, present a danger. There would necessarily be much contact with all kinds of machinery, with radio and television and motor-cars. The children would also have to adopt English as their first language. '*Du bleibst deutsch*,' 'You remain German', Amish fathers demand of their offspring.

So they receive their elementary schooling in the community for eight years; but the state demands twelve. When it came to the crunch in Ohio in 1960, for instance, the Amish communities set up their own high schools to keep their children there for the additional four years. The state inspectors decided that these Amish schools were anything but 'high', but the parents refused to let their children go to town. There have been compromises here and there, but the school problem as a whole has remained unsolved. The state will not make special laws for the Amish, and the Amish know that once they allow their children to mix and learn with those of the rest of the population, the end of their faith would be near: 'The wisdom of this world is foolishness with God', says Corinthians 1:3.

The schools set up by the Amish communities are part of a simple, all-embracing and efficient mutual-aid system based on biblical concepts. They provide their own homes for the aged, help for the sick, assistance in cases of emergency. Just as they scorn the social security scheme operated by the state, they abstain from taking up fire insurance policies. They even refuse to have lightning-conductors; it would mean a lack of faith in divine providence. When a barn burns down, which happens once or twice each summer in almost every community, all the men rally round to build a new one; they are so efficiently organized that the 'barn-raising' is done more or less in a day, and in the evening there is a great feast for which the women prepare a mighty meal. New farmsteads are built in the same cooperative way.

The Amish are efficient farmers. It is something of a miracle that despite their archaic methods – even chemical fertilizers and pesticides are banned – they have become most prosperous by raising cattle, growing vegetables, producing tobacco (although they themselves do not smoke). Basically they only want to meet their own requirements; but their large surpluses, and particularly their whole tobacco crop, are sold in the towns and the money is used for buying up more land. A certain amount of shopping is also done by Amish housewives on their horse-and-buggy trips to the market centres. And strangely enough the Amish like to visit relatives in other, distant centres of their faith, but only the older members of the community are permitted to travel. Then, of course, they have to use such infernal contraptions as airliners, railways and motor-coaches. On returning, however, they never seem to be influenced by the ways of the outside world, never tempted to become part of it.

Religious services are held only every second Sunday, and there is no church, for 'the Lord dwelleth not in temples made with hands'. Worship takes place in rotation in the various homesteads of the community (which, as a rule, comprises about forty families and whose area does not extend beyond the horse-and-buggy radius). Outside the house the older men assemble before leading the way into the large, plain room, now filled with the communally-owned, backless wooden prayer benches. The women follow behind and take their seats opposite the men, and the boys and girls bring up the rear. If the room is too small to hold them all, 'overflow' meetings are held in the other rooms of the house.

These 'preaching services', as they are called, last for four hours; at half-time there is a short interval during which the children get 'half-moon pies' to keep them from getting fidgety and disturbing the severe solemnity of the sect's worship. Everybody, of course, wears their Sunday best, which means, for the men, black, lapel-less, hook-and-eye fastened suits and white, collar-less shirts, and long, plain-coloured dresses, white batiste aprons and prayer caps for the women. The children, even the smallest ones, are dressed like little replicas of their elders. Oddly, the men with their dark reddish or grey beards and their large black hats, which they keep on during service, look very much like a congregation of Orthodox Jews.

Their hymn books are verbatim reprints of a sixteenth-century edition of 'true Christian songs, composed by the Swiss Brethren in the prison of Passau'. Many of the 140 hymns recall the dreadful persecution of the sect in Germany, Holland and Switzerland; one of them goes even further back in history, telling of all the terrible sufferings of believers and including the 'cutting-up of the Prophet Isaiah with a wooden saw by King Mannas', in thirty-five stanzas of thirteen lines each. A typical note introducing one song says: 'The following hymn of martyrdom was written by Hans of Amsterdam who, with many other brethren, was betrayed, imprisoned and executed . . . Very comforting.' The tunes of the hymns are merely indicated by reference to old German folksongs; the precentor of the congregation intones the first words alone, very slowly, and then the worshippers join in.

A number of communities share the service of a 'bishop', who has come down for the day. Before the hymn-singing begins he retires with two or three 'servants', meaning local lay preachers, to decide which of them will have to carry out *'s schwere Deel,* 'the hard task', i.e. preaching the long sermon. When joining the congregation they shake hands with the men, and the chosen 'servant' begins his sermon, which lasts for some three-quarters of an hour or more. He has not been given any time to prepare it; he relies on the 'inspiration of the Holy Ghost' and the innumerable Bible stories and quotations which every Amish knows by heart. As a rule, the moral is one of the basic tenets, such as: pride is the root of all evil.

There follows a silent prayer, with the congregation kneeling; then a reading from the Bible and a last hymn. The service is over. The host family have laid out a buffet lunch for all. Late in the afternoon the black buggies roll off. But in the evening the young people of the community return to the host farm for another bout of hymn-singing; now, however, they use a book with 'quick songs', as they are called, and eventually no book at all; in fact, the later the evening, the less religious become the young people's songs; but no musical instruments are permitted.

They have come in their 'courting buggies', the light, fast, open vehicles which the boys are given when reaching maturity. These buggies are an essential prop of teenage love-play. After a sing-song evening, young couples are expected to drive off into the countryside. As the courting grows more serious, they arrange to meet at night when both their parents have gone to bed or just pretend not to notice. The boy drives towards the girl's home, ties the horse up at some distance, and throws pebbles at her window. This is the signal for her to open the kitchen door and let him in, very much in the tradition of the village custom called *Fensterln* in Bavaria and Austria.

There are many stories about courting customs among the Amish; the strangest seems to be the so-called 'bundling' of engaged couples, but as the sect keeps silent about it one cannot say whether it is still being practised. According to rumour they go to bed together, fully clothed; the girl lies under her blanket and the boy, at her side, on top of it, with some barrier like a bolster between them. Tradition says that this is supposed to test the couple's powers of resistance to temptation. However. 'bundling' could have had a more realistic origin: in a severe winter the whole family may have taken to sleeping together to keep warm.

An elaborate show of tongue-in-cheek pretence is put on by all concerned in an impending Amish marriage. The whole thing has to be kept secret from everybody except a go-between, usually a minister of the faith, to whom the boy confides that he and his girl have decided to get married. The go-between breaks the news to the parents, who pretend to be greatly surprised although they have probably known all along. There follow talks between the heads of the families, about roughly the same topics as farmers would discuss anywhere when their offspring intend to marry. The girl's trousseau is already complete; starting with her first birthday she has been given everything an Amish bride needs, from bed linen to saucepans, while her mother and elder sisters have made sure that she has learnt how to run a home. No Amish girl has learnt more than that, or even thought of training for a career of her own; if she has the bad luck to remain single, she will always find enough housework to do either at home or with relatives. Secrecy prevails until the banns are up two weeks before the wedding; then, for the first time, the young man can visit his girl openly. Weddings take place only after the harvest, usually on Tuesdays or Thursdays – not on Mondays because no preparations may be made on the Sabbath, not on Fridays because it would bring bad luck.

An Amish wedding, always at the bride's home farm, is a long and strange ceremony. The bride wears a homespun, plain-coloured dress, perhaps blue or pink but not white, with a round, collarless neckline and long, wide sleeves, and over it her every-day white batiste apron reaching down to her ankles. Her bonnet, tied under the chin, is black; all the unmarried girls taking part in the ceremony have already exchanged their usual white prayer caps for black ones. The bride carries no flowers, ribbons, jewels or veil, but a triangular *Halsduch*, or neckerchief, instead: only once more in her life will she wear it, when she lies in her coffin. Her two best friends, dressed like herself, are her 'waiters', or bridesmaids.

There is no best man, no giving away, no wedding ring, and of course no photographer. The bridegroom wears his lapel-less black Sunday suit, but on that day his white shirt has a large black bow-tie. He may already have started to grow a married man's beard, but his upper lip must remain clean-shaven; his hair is half-long, cut straight at the nape and the customary fringe at the front peeps out from under his big black hat. While the congregation starts the ceremony with a warming-up spell of hymn-singing, bride and groom are instructed in the duties and responsibilities of married life by the bishop in an adjoining room, with the bridesmaids and the groom's attendants waiting outside the door. When they all join the congregation the actual service begins with prayers, continuing with more hymn-singing and an endless series of sermons by the bishop and the lay preachers as well as by some of the elders of the community. At long last, the bishop pronounces the couple husband and wife.

After the ceremony there begins a feast as lavish and gay as at any village wedding in a well-to-do European peasant community. Huge masses of food and drink are served and consumed, singing and folk-dancing and games go on until late at night, and there is a good deal of horse-play and practical joking. Strangely enough, the Amish sect has no objection to alcohol; their home brews, especially their wines, are quite strong. After all, Christ himself drank wine, and the Good Book does not disapprove of drinking. As to the practical jokes, these too take customary forms: the groom, for instance, is seized by a group of his bachelor friends and tossed over a fence into the arms of another group of married men, symbolizing his transition from one state to another, while the bride is made to jump over a broomstick.

But this is not yet the wedding night, in our traditional sense, for the young couple. The groom returns home with his parents after the feast; he will visit his bride during the following days at her own home, but it is only after the next Sunday, when they have attended service, that they remain together. As a rule they then start out on a honeymoon trip by buggy, travelling from one community of the region to another; at each of them, they are again lavishly fêted and given wedding presents on departing. The gifts – only useful things for household or farm are permitted – are stacked in their buggy, which is not the courting one but a larger closed-box vehicle, indicating their married state. The tour may last for two or three weeks, and when the couple arrive back they stay at the groom's family home while he is building his own house with the help of his friends, or equipping a purchased or leased farmstead with plain hand-made furniture.

In the midst of modern America, with its record rate of divorces, the Amish know of no unhappy marriages or broken homes (and, by the way, there are no serious crimes in their communities); once a man and a woman are joined in matrimony, they will stay together until death parts them. They take their marriage vows seriously.

To produce as many children as possible is the overriding function of an Amish marriage. Seven or nine children are the rule rather than the exception; birth control is, of course, unthinkable. But nature exacts penalties for continuous inbreeding. From the Amish records it becomes clear that marriages inside the communities, i.e. within a circle of three or four dozen families, have been customary since the sect settled in America; inter-community marriages are often between second cousins, and occasionally between first cousins. The Amish may not believe in science, and least of all in genetics, but it hits back at them with a vengeance. Pernicious anaemia kills off some of their babies, haemophilia afflicts other children, muscular dystrophy turns teenagers into prematurely senile men and women, who become completely helpless within a few years.

Perhaps the most bizarre havoc caused by the recessive genes takes the form of six-fingered dwarfism. Medical researchers who have been able to study hereditary defects among the Amish have traced almost sixty such cases which occurred during the last hundred years, while only fifty cases are recorded in the entire international medical literature. The geneticists came eventually upon the original carrier of this disorder, which produces stunted bodies and shortened arms and legs but gives the victim one additional finger and toe on each hand and foot; one of the founders of the Amish settlements suffered from it, and whenever two of his descendants marry, thus bringing the recessive genes together, the chances of such an abnormal child being born are great. For the geneticists, the Amish, with their closed communities and their reliable family records, are most valuable for the study of inherited defects; but the Amish sect, including the victims, takes these afflictions as God's inscrutable will. Still, some inkling of the true cause is slowly filtering through to them, and it seems that some communities have begun to encourage young people to seek their mates outside the range of their horse-and-buggies, though not yet outside their faith.

What breaches the isolation of the Amish much more than the first dawnings of scientific understanding is tourism. The mass media have got hold of the curious anachronism of the sect in the midst of modern America, and idle snoopers love to drive their cars through the settlements in the hope of finding some 'quaint' scenes for their cameras. There have been many collisions between motor-cars and buggies, with the latter and their occupants getting the worst of it. Contact with the tourists – about two million of them per holiday season in Lancaster County alone – also means an infiltration of the outside world into the Amish way of life, and it is of course the youngsters who can resist these temptations least of all. Transistor radios can be heard playing pop music inside some of the courting buggies as they carry young couples across the countryside; fortunately, the lads' big hats provide good hiding places for the devilish contraptions if some older Amish happen to come along. Cameras, too, have been discovered in the hands of the younger generation, although photography is anathema to the sect. The films are brought surreptitiously to the drug stores in the nearest towns for processing.

Worse still, the high wages paid by factories and builders tempt some of the young men to defect and move away from the settlements, while housing developments encroach on the land which would otherwise be acquired for new farms by the Amish. A few groups of the sect on the fringes of its territories have split from the rest and made their peace with the modern age, adapting themselves to it in their dress and habits while keeping their basic religious beliefs and rites. There is a new word for these semi-renegades: 'Automobile Amish'.

Will the sect, then, disappear within the foreseeable future? Certainly not. Their extremely high birthrate more than makes up for any losses in numbers they might suffer from reduction by temptation. Since the beginning of this century, they have increased enormously: there were twenty-nine Amish districts in 1905 in the United States and Canada; there are over 270 today, including, however, splinter groups and sub-sects. No doubt the overwhelming majority of the fifty thousand Amish will stick to a way of life which they have found good, and which many of those who have opted out or are dropping out of our western society may be unconsciously seeking.

3

Noisy God

Father Divine

'I don't have to say I'm God, and I don't have to say I'm not God,' said the man who called himself 'Father Divine', answering a question in court. 'But millions of people think I am God.' He was a bald and ugly old Negro, fat and little more than five feet high : not exactly cut out by nature for the part he played so successfully and over such a long time; that he did it against the heavy odds of his physical appearance and limited intelligence was the only miracle Father Divine ever performed.

According to the mythology he created around his origins, he first appeared on earth in Harlem in a puff of smoke; according to temporal records, however, he was born George Baker some time between 1874 and 1880 on a rice plantation in Savannah, Georgia, earned his living as an itinerant hedge-cutter, but turned up in Baltimore in 1899 as an assistant preacher to a black Baptist minister. They toured the Negro districts, and soon Baker began to call himself 'The Messenger' and 'God in the Sonship Degree', but assumed the alias of 'Major J. Divine' when he bought a house in Sayville, Long Island, with his first wife Peninah in1915.

The time of the First World War was a period when many Negroes migrated from the rural, segregationalist south to the industrial north where factory workers were wanted. Uprooted, hungry for spiritual guidance, the black proletariat welcomed 'The Messenger' with his pseudo-religious patter as a visible link with another, better world. Besides, Mrs Divine ran a free soup kitchen for those in need. Within a few years, Sayville had become the centre of a new black cult. There was a lot of rather noisy worshipping, and 'Major Divine' was prosecuted for disturbing the peace. Sentenced to a year in jail and a $500 fine, he accepted martyrdom and went to prison without a word of protest. Four days after pronouncing the sentence, the judge, until then an apparently healthy man, dropped dead. Divine broke his silence and commented from his cell, 'I hated to do it.'

So the reputation of a miracle-worker went ahead of him as he moved to Harlem after his release. It was the time of the great depression; workless Negroes and quite a number of dispossessed whites flocked to the saviour, now calling himself Father Divine, who promised eternal life to his followers and death to his detractors; security and dignity for men and women of all races, subjects to which he kept returning in his sermons and speeches, must have seemed like impossible dreams to the sceptics, but in fact he proceeded to make them come true within the movement he built up.

Aided by some of the better educated among his sect – there were, in fact, a few university graduates – Father Divine founded cooperatives, starting with Harlem boarding-houses and two dozen restaurants where good meals were served for a few cents. Somehow he had managed to get the capital for these first cooperative enterprises; the profits, however, had to be handed over to the cause. Jobs were found for more and more followers, and as the economic crisis lost its momentum later in the 1930s, Father Divine found it increasingly easy to attract money for new projects. By now, his sect, called the Worldwide Kingdom of Peace, had been joined by numbers of middle and upper class whites who saw in Father Divine the only man who could lead the black underdog out of his degrading predicament. Conditions in Harlem, however, were still terrible. Up to fifty per cent of the population were on the dole; twice as many Negro mothers as white ones died in childbirth; the tuberculosis rate was four times higher than for the whole of New York, the figures for venereal diseases seven times higher.

Against this background, Father Divine's achievements look splendid indeed. From his Harlem 'heaven', as he called this and the provincial community centres, each a combination of chapel, soup kitchen, and propaganda office, he built up a formidable system of cooperatives where members lived communally; branching out into the countryside and other towns, he added farms, workshops, hotels and food stores to his empire as time went on. With that economic network the number of his followers grew steadily. Although his own estimate of twenty million followers was no doubt vastly exaggerated, there were eventually several millions who believed in him, handed part of their earnings over to him, and revered him as the greatest man on earth, if not God himself re-incarnated.

'Peace, it's wonderful' was the movement's greeting, devised by Father Divine and echoed by the mass of his followers in their daily lives. One of them, however, did not leave him in peace; disappointed, she sued him in 1941 for the return of her contributions, nearly four thousand dollars all told. A New York court found in her favour. Enraged, he threatened to 'evaporate for another 1,900 years', but then decided to move his headquarters to Pennsylvania instead, cursing New York: 'I will dry up your rivers and your streams!' As the curse was uttered in the midst of a drought, it did not cut much ice outside the sect.

At the zenith of his power, a few years after the end of the Second World War, he built his central 'heaven' in wealthy Montgomery County near Philadelphia. It was indeed magnificent. Presented to him by a disciple who called himself John De Voute, it comprised a seventy-three-acre estate with a thirty-two-room château in mock-Gothic style. Father Divine turned the inauguration of the 'country seat of the world', as he called it, into a great interdenominational event by inviting another Negro sect leader, 'Prophet Jones' of Detroit, for a ceremonial visit in 1953. Jones accepted with 'cosmic and best wishes'.

The occasion, fully covered by the American press, is worth recalling, as it shows the pomp and flamboyance of sects which had originated among the underprivileged of the slums. At the Philadelphia railway station, the Detroit Prophet, 'Dominion Ruler of the Church of the Universal Triumph', arrived with twenty-six pieces of luggage, containing some of his four hundred suits and his $12,000 white mink coat, and with his *entourage*: two valets, two secretaries, two bodyguards, one hairdresser and one cook. 'Peace, it's wonderful!,' cried the assembled crowd of 1,500 believers, barely held in check by the police, as Father Divine welcomed his visitor: 'I'm happy to meet you, Your Holiness.' 'God bless you, Your Goodliness,' replied Prophet James F. Jones, playing his part to perfection and with suitable ecstasy. A fleet of fifteen chauffeur-driven Chryslers and Cadillacs took the party first to a press conference, where the Prophet's bracelet with 812 diamonds attracted attention, and then to Father Divine's 'heaven'. After a grand tour of the grounds and the château, the two leaders and their retinue sat down to a twenty-seven-course dinner including seven varieties of ice cream (but only soft drinks). The magnificence of Father Divine's headquarters impressed the Prophet, but this was of course principally a spiritual meeting of kindred souls. 'I know,' said the guest at the farewell handshake, 'that the chassis of your mind has been lubricated with divine lubrimentality.' Making up words of this kind, which one looks for in vain in dictionaries, was just another knack common to both dignitaries; Father Divine, for instance, defined the deity like this: 'God is repersonified and rematerialized. He rematerialates and he is rematerializatable. He repersonificates and he repersonifi-tizes. . . .'

There was another press conference which the Prophet had arranged for himself alone. 'God is going to stop death before the end of the twentieth century,' he declared. 'Yes, I want to put undertakers, gravediggers and casket factories out of business.' Was his meeting with Father Divine of any significance with regard to future collaboration between the two leaders? a reporter asked. 'There is a significance,' replied the Prophet. 'But I don't know whether God will let me disclose it.' However, God seems to have changed His mind, for the two never met again, going their separate ways of salvation for the masses.

Hostess at the château had been 'Mother Divine', Father's second wife, who was twenty-one years old, and he well in his seventies, when they married in 1946: a pretty white Canadian ex-typist by the name of Edna Rose Ritchings. They were an odd couple when they stood side by side at the altar and his nose reached only to her shoulders. But neither the discrepancy in height nor in age was what caused an uproar among the sect; it was the fact of marriage itself. For one of its rules was strict celibacy; Father Divine permitted no sexual relations to his followers, marital or otherwise, and in his many Peace Mission hotels married couples were not allowed to share the same room; there were men's wings and women's wings and double rooms were given only to guests of the same sex. Father Divine, naive as he basically was, probably never realized that he was furthering homosexuality.

Why did he ask his followers to forgo normal sexual relations? Probably for the same reasons as those underlying his ban on drinking, smoking, using make-up and visiting places of entertainment, prohibitions which have always held a paradoxical attraction for salvation seekers. Man's masochistic streak wants to be satisfied, self-denial makes him feel virtuous, and he expects to be rewarded with heavenly bliss and spiritual immortality for his sacrifices on earth. To be sure, these are considerations which the primitive mind of George Baker could not grasp intellectually, but his empirical understanding of human nature certainly told him that sex would always raise its ugly head amongst his flock, and that the guilt he instilled in them by his ban would only serve to bind them more securely to the movement. Other sects, other religions have prospered on guilt ever since Man ate from the Tree of Knowledge – in other words, since he developed into a thinking, feeling human being.

Father Divine weathered the uproar caused by his wedding very cleverly. Miss Ritchings, he declared, was the reincarnation of his late first wife; the new marriage was a purely spiritual one. 'Father Divine has kept me pure from my infancy to this present day,' said the bride. Both vowed to live together like brother and sister, black brother and white sister: the union of the two spirits, housed in skins of different colour, was to be understood as a symbol for the interracial basis of the Kingdom of Peace; or, as Father Divine explained, it might be likened to 'Christ's marriage with His creation'.

Mother Divine had been one of the twenty-six secretaries and helpers, black and white 'angels' with angelic names like Miss Smile All the While, Miss Buncha Love, Miss Rapid Integration, Miss Gladness Darling; Edna Rose was called Miss Sweet Angel. She proved to be an efficient administrator and a good hot-gospeller who could rouse her followers, mostly women, to hysterics nearly as well as Father himself. She certainly added a great deal of glamour to his personal appearances and looked much more at home than he in their Rolls-Royce and Duesenberg limousines, both cream-coloured. But what did it matter that the unbelievers laughed at the undersized Messiah, so long as the sect accepted him as 'Dean of the Universe', 'Dynamo of Salvation', 'Master of Omnipotence', and as 'the author and the finisher of atomic energy', who was busy 'bringing all atomic energy into submission', according to his claims? In 1945, of course, it was Father Divine who had the atom bomb dropped on the wicked Japanese.

Each year the wedding anniversary was celebrated on an increasingly lavish scale. On the fifteenth, in 1961, there was a mammoth banquet at the château; thousands of sect members were fed in the grounds with the invited guests' leftovers. Gluttony was not listed in Father Divine's register of sins.

Father Divine's Kingdom of Peace was the most powerful movement America's black population had ever seen, and the only one also attracting a substantial number of white followers, estimated at twenty-five per cent of its membership. The sect was made the subject of a book, published in 1953 under the title of *Father Divine: Holy Husband* (in Britain: *The Incredible Father Divine*); it was a serious 320-page study of the man who had then been 'dominating the Negro religious scene' for a quarter of a century, written by a white sociologist, Mrs Sara Harris, with the help of a Negro assistant, Harriet Crittenden, after two years of investigation and observation. To get the inside information they needed the two women spent ten weeks at Father Divine's 'country seat of the world', with his permission; he also granted them a series of lengthy interviews. Yet when the book appeared his wrath was truly divine.

He had expected a reverential eulogy, but Mrs Harris had compiled a critical analysis, revealing facts he would have liked to be forgotten, and recording impressions that made him and his movement look ridiculous, such as the hysterical adoration of his female devotees:

A trembling woman in a skintight, black-satin dress keeps whispering: 'I love you, Father, I love you, my sweetheart, I love you, I love you ...' Her body jerks in spasms. A middle-aged woman in a red coat starts to snake her way up and down the aisle of standees. She is half dancing, half stumbling. She cries: 'God, God, God' ... Nobody pays any particular attention. Father, being accustomed to the peculiar form his followers' adulation often takes, pays less attention than anyone. 'They love, love, love me so much,' he says.

Mrs Harris tells the tale of how he had picked up his trade from a Baltimore hot-gospeller, Samuel Morris, before striking out on his own at the time of the First World War; how he was once certi-

fied insane, but harmless, in New York; what happened to his
'true followers' when they died although Father had promised
them that they never would: they were hustled away to a pauper
burial. And there was the embarrassing story of how Father Divine
wangled his accounts so skilfully that he never paid a cent of
income tax, although living in the utmost luxury. Except during
the annual 'open house' parties for ordinary followers each
September, only the 'angels', the 'rosebuds' (girl novices) and
privileged guests were admitted to the château with its forty-
three-foot buttressed ceiling over the foyer, its valuable oriental
rugs and rosewood furniture, and the gold and silver plate in
the chapel-like banqueting room lined with alabaster carving.

The book also ventured an evaluation of Father Divine's empire.
It appeared that ten million dollars was a conservative estimate;
twenty million may have been nearer the truth, as the movement's
property holdings in Pennsylvania, New York and Newark alone
were worth more than six million dollars. And that was only a
minor part of the movement's, or rather Father Divine's possessions. 'Today,' wrote Mrs Harris, 'he is a property tycoon with
properties in England, Australia, Austria, Germany and Switzerland.' To which, of course, must be added the enormous number
of churches, hotels, stores and so on throughout the length
and breadth of the United States. 'Our blessings,' said Mr De
Voute, Father's patron and public-relations officer, 'are so
numerous that we don't count them. We just share in the
blessedness.'

Mrs Harris listed the good points of Father Divine's rule objec-
tively: his unflinching opposition to racial segregation, which
won him the hearts of the American Negroes; the countless
'heavens' he organized where generous and wholesome meals were
served at fifteen cents, or even free for the poorest, during the
depression; the immaculate rooms at the Peace Mission hotels for
two dollars a week; the chain of employment agencies providing
jobs for the needy. Crimes among the sect members were
extremely rare. A white social worker in Harlem said in those
years: 'Father Divine rendered an inestimable service, and he did
it with genuine goodness.' What did it matter if his flock's noisy
hymn-singing disturbed the neighbours? The sect, Mrs Harris
concluded, served a real need in the lives of its members; but that
such a need should exist at all was 'the shame of America'.

Yet Father Divine refused to take the rough with the smooth of the book; accepting Mrs Harris's praise as his due, her factual revelations made him see red. Through the medium of the movement's newspaper, *New Day*, edited by Mr De Voute, he pronounced a formidable malediction against the book's 'writers, publishers, republishers, readers, sympathizers, harmonizers, believers, critics, followers, preachers and priests, as well as nations and others that coincide with those lies published in that book . . . They are cursed with consumption, with fever, with inflammation, with the sword . . . They shall be smitten with botch of Egypt, with fire, with burning, with emerods, with madness and blindness and heart trouble. . . .' He concluded his Bible-style fulminations with the plain statement: 'I am a dynamo of salvation and yet destruction to those who contact me inharmoniously. I have cursed them down to the bottomless pit on earth. I curse them without mercy. I curse them without pity. I curse them without compassion or any sympatheticness. Aren't you glad?' he asked the faithful at the end of his malediction; and one could almost hear them shouting the answer in unison: 'Yes, Father, we're glad!'

On the eve of the 1965 annual open house party, with thousands of followers streaming into the grounds of the 'country seat of the world', George Baker lay dying, with his 'spotless virgin bride' and a dozen and a half of his angels around his fourposter. There were no tears, only hymns and prayers, for Father Divine was merely 'dematerialating', as he himself called it, to be 'repersonifitized' in some other body, though the event would perhaps be delayed for yet another 1,900 years. Reckoned in earthly terms, he must have reached the age of at least eighty-five. During his temporary absence from the movement, Mother Divine assured those present, she would guide it according to 'his instructions received through his spirit'. And she ordered that the open house party should go on as he himself had said it should.

We do not know what happened to that poor angel, Miss Love Dove, quoted in Mrs Harris's book as saying: 'If Father dies, I sure 'nuff would never be callin' on myself to be goin' on livin' in this empty ol' world. I'd be findin' some way of gettin' rid of the life I never been wantin' before I found him.'

For the mass of his followers the news of his death was a deep shock. Many began to drift away, some to other prophets, but probably a considerable number to the Civil Rights Movement which was then gathering momentum among American Negroes, and which had already attracted some of the better educated, politically interested members of Father Divine's inner circle. A year or so before his death, his PRO John De Voute had organized a platform discussion on the subject between two whites and three Negroes, all faithful disciples, at the Divine Fairmount Hotel in Jersey City, obviously in an attempt at calming down a dissident group which threatened to split the sect, or lead it into left-wing political waters. 'For us,' said Mr De Voute, opening the discussion, 'there is only one family, one race. We don't even call people N's [Negroes] or C's [Caucasians]; we consider that a sin.' 'Father has freed us from within,' declared Miss Blessed Mary Love. 'We move unhampered in the world because God in the fathership degree [Father Divine] has harmonized us with one another. The spirit will protect us.' 'We can see now what Father has done for us,' said Miss Magnetic Love. 'We have sympathy for those who are working for integration, but we know they will never achieve true success except through the Christ-life of Father Divine.' As expected, the discussion team came to the conclusion that there was no need to fight for integration outside the Worldwide Kingdom of Peace.

But others thought there was, and while the faithful, singing hymns, were filing past the bier on which their dead leader was laid out, his empire was already crumbling away.

Some of it still exists, and may do so for many more years, yet it is only a shadow of its former grandeur. There is no new leader who could be called the successor of that wily, extravagant, outrageous man; he was symptomatic of a past phase in the development of the American Negro. Perhaps Father Divine's real successor is Black Power.

4

The Cream-Cheese Apostle

Germany's Age of Unreason

To all intents and purposes, the National Socialist Party began as a sect. The lost war, hunger, an accelerating inflation, unemployment and a floundering government had created a general sense of frustration and hopelessness in Germany; any group offering spiritual uplift and promising radical changes found adherents in all social classes. The party in which an uneducated but mesmeric ranter, Adolf Hitler, had become the most prominent personality attracted, by its extremist programme, many dropouts who neither wished nor expected to come to terms with the new democratic state. One only has to look at the leaders of the so-called Hitler putsch of 1923 in Munich to understand to what kind of people the party appealed: there was Hitler himself, the artist *manqué*; Goering, the drug addict and airman whom the Versailles Treaty had deprived of his joystick; Röhm, the ex-officer, at loggerheads with society because of his homosexuality; and General Ludendorff, who had been Hindenburg's right-hand man in the Great War, but had fled in disguise to Sweden when the German army was on the run in 1918. He was now devoting himself to attacks on the sinister, supranational powers that ruled the world: the Jews, the Catholics and the Freemasons. He dreamt of restoring his somewhat stained reputation by becoming the new hero-figure of the fatherland, bringing back the Hohenzollern rulers and liberating Germany from the clutches of its international oppressors. The beer-cellar sectarians of Hitler's group were kindred souls; he headed their column and braved the bullets of the government forces on the rebels' march through Munich in November 1923.

The putsch broke down, and Hitler was sentenced to confinement in a fortress, where he wrote *Mein Kampf*. With the publication of that book the party ceased to be a bothersome sect of misfits and crackpots. Some German industrialists, worried about their power and profits in the face of growing pressure from the trade unions and the Communists, helped Hitler with their backing to build it up as an alternative mass movement for the discontented. Yet it retained a certain element of sectarianism, with a Messianic leader who promised to bring the nation, after its time of 'shame and slavery', into the millenium (*das tausendjährige Reich*); with elaborate, pseudo-religious ceremonies of initiation and dedication; with a variation of the cross as its emblem; with the ritual greeting '*Heil*' (an intentional association with *Heiland*, the Saviour). Moreover, the Nazi Party assemblies, with their skilfully produced mass hysteria, had more in common with the gatherings of some primitive sect than with political meetings in a civilized country.

Indeed, Germany's 'golden 1920s', as they were often called in retrospect one world war and one 'millenium' later, were a time of unparalleled prosperity for Messiahs and mountebanks, quacks and prophets, impostors and tricksters: a golden age of gullibility. Miracle men gathered flocks of paying believers round them with the greatest of ease, con-men swindled with a minimum of effort the multitude who longed to be deceived. There was, for instance, the incredible episode of the false Hohenzollern prince, a young loafer who, a decade after Germany had become a republic, was mistaken for a grandson of the Kaiser all over central Germany and, without having to pretend very hard, was adulated and obeyed, wined and dined by aristocrats, provincial bigwigs, and even *Reichswehr* commanders; in short by all those who longed nostalgically for the old imperial establishment. The *Reichswehr* was also fooled by at least one 'death-ray' inventor who tricked its experts into believing that he could detonate explosives over considerable distances.

Ludendorff, who had withdrawn from Hitler after the failure of the 1923 putsch, came more and more under the influence of his lady-friend, later his wife, Mathilda, a muddle-headed upper-class virago, steeped in mystic notions about the supremacy of Nordic man. They ran a weekly journal dedicated to that philosophy, but got into debt with the printers to the tune of some hundreds of thousands of marks. However, a rescuing angel appeared just in time to save them from the bankruptcy court. His name was Franz Tausend, an unemployed chemist who claimed to have found a process for making gold from lead, potassium, mercury, sodium and so on by melting and cooling the mixtures in turn. Ludendorff fell for the swindle and agreed to lend his name, which still carried some weight in nationalist circles, to a sect-like secret society for the exploitation of Tausend's 'discovery'. Incredibly, dozens of Germany's leading industrialists, who, or whose experts, ought to have known better, were taken in by Tausend's trick demonstrations and contributed large sums to the society. Ludendorff had secured for himself the lion's share of the expected profits, to be used for what the agreement described, rather vaguely, as patriotic purposes.

Tausend established himself in the midst of the Bavarian forests in a secluded mansion, where he developed his process. Here, too, the atmosphere of a religious sect prevailed: young men and their girl-friends drifted in, doting on the 'miracle-worker', talking about his 'Christ-like' eyes, calling him 'master'. There was a steady stream of businessmen and industrialists whom Tausend admitted to some of his experiments; they would stare with fascination at the great man's tweezers as he carefully fished out little golden globules from the crucible. Analysts found them to be genuine, and factories were secretly bought in Bremen and Frankfurt to take up mass production of gold as soon as the process was perfected; 'gold vouchers', later to be exchanged for the real thing, were sold to investors.

Tausend's luck ran out only after nearly five years of amazing success. A major backer became suspicious and asked the authorities to investigate the miracle man's affairs. The preparations for the trial took the best part of two years, because out of nearly five dozen victims of Herr Tausend's scheme, only a single man was ready to testify against him; the rest, among them some of the best-known names in German industry, finance and politics, were so thoroughly ashamed of their own gullibility, so embarrassed by the prospect of being ridiculed by the press as suckers and simpletons, that they refused to complain of his having duped them. Ludendorff, after having paid his debts out of the invested money, had already withdrawn from the society; perhaps he had smelt a rat. At the trial Tausend's secret was revealed by a police officer who had watched a gold-making experiment: the deceiver, pretending to check his formulae, was holding a fountain pen, and out of that pen the officer saw a small gold pellet drop into the crucible. Tausend went to prison, and when he was released the Nazis were in power; he tried his old scheme again, but the nationalist circles he approached had no need for a goldmaker now that their champion Hitler was master of the Reich and of all the gold in the country.

In Austria, too, a miracle man was busy in the 1920s trying to restore Germany to her position as a world power; not by making gold but by means of the 'space energy' he claimed to have discovered and tamed. Karl Schappeller, born in a poor-house, had been a carpenter's apprentice and then a village postmaster until he was certified as a lunatic and pensioned off. Six years later, in 1925, he owned a beautiful old castle and a splendid new luxury car, the prophet of a home-made creed in which religion and science, politics and philosophy, ethics and economics were inseparably mixed. His sect, for this is what his large following of believers really was, extended to the same aristocratic, political and industrial circles, mainly in Germany, from which Tausend recruited his victims, and which were still hankering after the good old days of the Kaiser; Schappeller's 'space-energy machine' was to bring them back.

All the disciples and visitors were shown was a laboratory model, a little globe of some rough metallic material; inside, Schappeller would assure them, an eternal fire was raging, as in the larger model, the earth. He had succeeded in concentrating the whole energy of space in that globe. Properly exploited, it would revolutionize everything – life, science, technology, economy. It would drive ships, trains and cars, aircraft and factory machines; substations distributing the new power without cables would be built at distances of 10 kilometres. Their radiation would also influence the weather, heat the homes, provide a new kind of light, power the communication networks (including personal radio telephones), heal the sick. No more digging for coal or drilling for oil would be necessary. The consumed energy would be automatically restored by earth magnetism. Only Germany and Austria would be permitted to benefit from Schappeller's space energy, which would have to be operated as a state monopoly, bringing untold wealth and prosperity to these countries, including free homes, food and clothes for every citizen.

Not a bad idea for a science-fiction novel or film, but Schappeller, though a certified lunatic, was no fool. He knew how to coin money from sheer fantasy. His cleverly controlled and directed publicity, a combination of news stories for the sensation-hungry popular press and mysterious rumours spread in exclusive circles, brought the money rolling in. The more underhand and selfish the motives of those who wanted to benefit from his 'invention', the larger the sums they invested in his scheme. First it was the feudal landowners near Schappeller's Upper Austrian village who fell for his patter; then the circle of the initiated widened, and the fable of his world-shaking scheme quickly spread in the German Republic. The years 1927–8 marked the climax of his success; yet even crazy Schappeller never dreamt that he would one day see among the space-energy supporters no less a personality than the ex-Kaiser himself.

One of the most enthusiastic novices of the Schappeller sect was a titled lady who happened to be intimate with the wife of Kaiser Wilhelm's court physician in his exile at Doorn Castle in Holland. The two ladies talked with considerable excitement about the prospects of turning the tide of vulgar democracy back with the help of Schappeller's space-energy machine, and of restoring the Hohenzollern monarchy. The foolish women found an eager listener in Princess Hermine, Wilhelm's second wife, who would have liked to be Empress not only in name. There was already in existence a secret organization set up by the Kaiser's private treasurer, von Nitz, for the purpose of conducting monarchist propaganda in the German Republic and abroad. It appears that Hermine convinced the ex-Kaiser that this Austrian fellow Schappeller could help the deposed dynasty to stage a comeback. At any rate, von Nitz was empowered to back the space-energy development with considerable sums; it was said that altogether one million marks was paid to Schappeller from the imperial coffers. His boasts that he had intimate personal connections with Doorn were never denied, and of course, his prestige rose immensely.

It came down with a bang in 1929 when the leading physicist of Vienna University, Professor Thirring, published his report of an interview he had had with Schappeller. He summarized his verdict on the space-energy machine in one word, the German equivalent of 'codswallop'. The golden showers from Doorn stopped abruptly; so did many other regular contributions from shocked believers. Schappeller's creditors began to clamour for their money. He disappeared, and the bailiffs moved into the old castle. The press revealed the ex-Kaiser's financial interest in the ex-postmaster's absurd project. Schappeller's son gave an interview to reporters; the Kaiser, he said, had never thought of regaining his throne and empire by promoting space energy; he had backed the scheme, according to a letter he had written to Schappeller Sen., 'because he wanted to free himself from the heavy blame for Germany's collapse (i.e. in 1918), with which he was now being burdened, by taking part in measures towards a social renewal of his former empire'.

Gullibility and unreason had their heyday in the hectic atmosphere of Berlin in the late 1920s. There were said to be, among its four million inhabitants, three thousand occultist practitioners and a thousand sects. Professional astrologers abounded. The rich and the influential flocked to the famous clairvoyant, Hanussen, who enjoyed the reputation of being able to foretell everything accurately; but he obviously failed in his own case, or he would not have ventured into the Grunewald forest that day in 1933 when the SS were waiting there to murder him. The Buddhist creed got its first foothold in central Europe among the Berliners, with a temple and a community settlement in a suburb. The more eccentric and exotic the tenets of a cult, the greater its snob value; one called Mazdaznan, an offspring of Zoroastrianism, was quite fashionable among women but endangered many marriages because it required a lavish consumption of garlic. Another cult, Carezza, had to be joined by husband and wife together because it demanded *coitus sublimatus* as the basis of married life (with a rather erroneous reference to Dr Marie Stopes): the sex act begins as usual, but 'freezes' at once – there must be no movement and no orgasm, but 'sublime, pure, poetical, divine happiness'.

Perhaps this and many other cults were (and still are) the expression of a genuine yearning for a better, more fulfilled life, attainable by some magic formula. But seekers are rarely critical and often unable to discern the shrewd businessman behind the mask of the prophet. This eagerness to believe may become dangerous when the sick turn away from the medical practitioner to look for a supernatural cure through faith-healing. On a less spiritual and religious level, there was also in Berlin in the 1920s the bizarre episode of Hartwig's Mineral Water which, within a decade, 'cured' thousands of sufferers of diabetes, stomach ulcers, kidney and liver complaints, catarrhal diseases, hardened arteries, gout, uric acid and gallstones, at least according to the patients' own testimonies. From the billboards, the newspaper advertisments, the posters in the buses and under-ground trains, the Berliners were exhorted to drink Hartwig's Mineral Water in case of any complaint, and they were proud that such a potent panacea was being produced by nature under their very feet. And so it was indeed: in 1929 the Supreme Court of the Republic pronounced its finding that it was nothing but ordinary Berlin tap water, with a slight addition of artificial carbon dioxide to make it fizzy.

Joseph Weissenberg

No other sect that bloomed in Berlin in the 1920s was as perni-cious, and at the same time as symptomatic of the hysterical gulli-bility among the German lower middle classes, as Josef Weissen-berg's 'New Jerusalem'. From the facts of the case arises an almost inconceivable story.

Josef Weissenberg was already past seventy, with a chequered life behind him, at the time when he appeared in the limelight. He had come from Silesia, where he served in one of the Kaiser's grenadier regiments before the turn of the century. After many years in the army he had worked as a shepherd, bricklayer, waiter, cabby and innkeeper; the latter two occupations, he would say, he had to give up 'because Jesus Christ told me so'. From then on he described himself as 'mesmerizer'.

It was little more than a police report which mentioned his name for the first time in an official matter: a Potsdam shopkeeper had died and his family had failed to notify the authorities; when the police came to make enquiries, they found the family gathered around the dead man, fervently praying for his resurrection under the guidance of a 'disciple of the Divine Master Josef Weissen-berg'. From then on, the Divine Master and his sect never failed to provide the newspapers with sensational stories, and the police and judicial authorities with tricky problems. The next case was that of a Berlin housewife, Martha S, who had become increasingly violent towards her bewildered husband. All he could make out from her incoherent rantings was that she had come under the influence of Weissenberg. In the end she had to be taken to a lunatic asylum and the husband sued Weissenberg for damages unsuccessfully, as it turned out, despite this evidence submitted to the court by two psychiatrists who had observed her at the asylum:

During the observation period Frau S. said that she was now reconciled to her fate as she had found the right way. Weissenberg had taught her the true faith. At his meetings, some people had seen Jesus in the flesh, and she still kept seeing the image of Christ. This gift of vision could not be bestowed upon others by an ordinary man, only by a 'deity' like Weissenberg. During a meeting, the Saviour and the Holy Spirit, in the shape of the Dove, had appeared beside Weissenberg, the Divine Master.

The psychiatrists came to the conclusion that the patient had become mentally ill through her association with the 'prophet' Weissenberg, but the court found that the poor woman was already unbalanced when she joined the sect. Four similar cases kept the courts busy for years.

Clearly, this man Weissenberg wielded extraordinary power over the members of his sect, particularly the female ones. However, a male disciple, a dead one, and a nineteen-month-old blind baby were the victims in the most sensational of all the numerous court cases with Weissenberg as defendant. The hearing took place on a bleak November day in 1930. A Berlin paper wrote:

The scenes inside and outside the Criminal Court must have opened many eyes—including, presumably, those of the justiciaries —to the evil influence which this former cabby and waiter, together with his helpmates, exerts on a great mass of people. It is incredible that this semi-illiterate man is allowed to damage the physical and mental health of thousands of people. The crowd of excited and hysterical women that filled the corridors and stairs, spilling out into the street, seemed to have got out of a madhouse.... As soon as Weissenberg appeared in the corridor during an interval in the proceedings, they screamed, 'God bless you, Divine Master!' and jostled with each other for a glance from their lord and hero. It is well known that Weissenberg has ruined a great number of marriages and that, as a result of his 'spiritual cures', many women have ended up in the lunatic asylum, as the public prosecutor stated in his opening speech. And there sat the dead man's wife—a typical case of extreme hysteria. We know that members of some sects have had themselves crucified in their religious mania; this woman has merely tried to saw off her own arm.

The case of her dead husband, a dispensing chemist by the name of Wernicke, and that of the blind baby, Hildegard Hensicke, were linked by the fact that in both instances Weissenberg had done irreparable damage by treatment with his panacea – cream cheese, slightly salted. He never explained intelligibly why cream cheese, plus faith in himself and prayers, should be able to cure virtually all ills, but it was assumed that he chose it because of the similarity of the German word – *Weisskäse* – and his own name.

Wernicke, like his wife a member of the sect, had suffered from diabetes and developed a carbuncle, perhaps as a result of neglect of the disease. As a chemist who dispensed prescribed medicaments every day he ought to have known better than to put himself into the hands of an uneducated quack; yet he accepted Weissenberg's treatment of the carbuncle with cream cheese. Within a short time, Wernicke was dead.

The case of the baby was even more tragic, for the poor thing was of course too young to decide for herself who should treat her eye infection. Her parents, both passionately devoted to the Divine Master, took her to him; he applied his panacea and exhorted the parents to recite the Lord's Prayer a few times daily. When Hildegard was eventually taken to a hospital it was too late: she was blind in both eyes.

In the dock, charged with criminal negligence, stood a tubby old man of less than medium height, round-faced, with receding grey hair and a thick, drooping white moustache that gave him a somewhat military air, with ruddy cheeks and staring blue eyes under heavy lids and bushy brows. He held himself straight, his movements were brisk, his voice was sharp: there was still much of the former sergeant-major about him.

When describing himself as a mesmeriser, he was asked by the judge where he had received his training. 'I do only what the Holy Writ prescribes,' replied Weissenberg. 'So you have no medical knowledge?' asked the judge. 'I have a supernatural vision, hearing and feeling about diseases,' Weissenberg replied.

At a later stage of the proceedings, Weissenberg agreed to put these faculties to the test. An usher volunteered for the part of the patient, and the self-styled miracle healer was asked what was wrong with the man. Weissenberg stared at him, and then pronounced his diagnosis: 'You have a cold in the kidneys and the bladder. Fifteen – no, sixteen years ago you showed clear symptoms of mental and spiritual depression. You've had much grief and a lot of troubles. Your nerves are in a very bad way.' 'Can you give a short description of the man's condition?' asked the judge. Weissenberg: 'Nervous debility.' 'And what do you prescribe for the patient?' asked the judge.

Weissenberg did not fall into the trap of prescribing his favourite cream-cheese cure. Instead, he suggested 'water soup, buttermilk, two recitals of the Lord's Prayer and of the first Psalm before going to bed. Then a man will be able to sleep well; he knows he has done his duty to God.' The usher was asked whether there really was, or had been, something wrong with his physical or mental health. Yes, he had been suffering from renal stones, gastric ulcers and pleurisy a long time ago, but he was now completely healthy. He had never had any nervous disease.

When the cream-cheese treatment of Wernicke and the baby was discussed in court, the judge asked, 'But there isn't a word about that in the Bible, is there?' Weissenberg, very solemnly: 'So a man has no faith, even I cannot help him.'

Nearly all the witnesses testified for the Divine Master. The blind baby's parents, very primitive, almost illiterate people, would not say a word of accusation against the man whose 'cure' had robbed their child of its eyesight. The thirteen-year-old son of the dead chemist, who had spoken up against Weissenberg during the preliminary investigation, now retracted everything; reporters had seen him in the corridor before the hearing, a bewildered lad amidst a group of excited women; his mother admitted to the court that she had influenced him in favour of the accused.

Among the witnesses for the defence was a former police officer who testified, with considerable emphasis, that Weissenberg had healed him merely by making the sign of the cross. Questioned by the prosecutor, he admitted that he was now employed by the Master as assistant and preacher, and that it was he who, under Weissenberg's direction, had applied the cream cheese to Hildegard's eyes. 'Is there no legal way of smashing this organized gang of crooks?' asked a Berlin paper. The press was rather angry when the verdict was pronounced: Weissenberg was found not guilty in the case of Wernicke – it was not proven that salted cream cheese had caused the death of the diabetic, and he might have died anyway; guilty, with six months in prison, in the case of little Hildegard.

Both prosecution and defence appealed against the sentence, with the result that it was quashed. Weissenberg went scot-free.

The house where the miracle healer practised his art for the benefit of the members of his sect stood in one of the dirty and depressing streets of Berlin's working-class district, an old, dilapidated tenement building with dark, narrow stairs, flaking paint and a permanent smell of boiled cabbage. On a second-floor door appeared the name of Josef Weissenberg, with the warning that there were no consultations on Sundays and Wednesdays, and that it was no use ringing on those days. A wizened old woman, acting as receptionist, opened the door, asked the caller whether he had come for the first time, and gave him a battered disc with a number on it. He was shown into a large waiting-room, poorly furnished, where those already present would greet him with the salutation of the sect, 'God bless you'.

But when the door to the consulting-room opened, there appeared a personable young blonde, ushering the patient in. Those who expected to come into the presence of the Divine Master were disappointed, at least for the moment; there was only another young girl in the room, occupied with office work, and the two would chat about everyday trifles while the first one, after a brief enquiry as to the patient's ailment, passed her hands down his arms and legs, swiftly and mechanically. Many patients came for this routine 'treatment' alone, answered the leading question as to whether they already felt better with 'yes', paid one mark and went away. First-timers, and those who looked as though they could afford considerably more, would be admitted to a third room, with the Master himself in it.

A dreadfully depressing room, even more so than the whole slum house – gloomy, dirty, smelly, with an unmade camp bed as the main piece of furniture and many fly-blown, vulgar pictures of saints pinned to the walls. The Master, too, would enquire what was wrong with the patient, whether he had seen a doctor and what the doctor had said. Without paying much attention to the answers, Weissenberg – after a piercing look at the patient's face – would immediately prescribe one of his herbal teas, plus a couple of Lord's Prayers every night, and perhaps some extra refinement such as putting arnica leaves on the abdomen in case of a kidney complaint. If improvement was too slow, he would say, then a course of cream-cheese treatment would be indicated, perhaps in three weeks.

Consultation plus a packet of Weissenberg's tea cost two marks. The packet showed a picture of the Master wearing a naval cap – *de rigueur* for members of the sect at formal occasions – opposite a list of the ailments which the tea would cure 'with success guaranteed': tuberculosis and piles, heart diseases and rheumatism, coughs and menstrual irregularities, liver trouble and gout.

Had Weissenberg been merely a quack making a quick profit out of psuedo-medical advice and the sale of herbal tea, no one would have bothered much about him; there were too many of them in Berlin as everywhere else. But the flat in that north Berlin tenement was merely the tip of an iceberg; the bulk of it lay in the sandy hills south of the capital, about an hour's drive away. Its name: Peace Town New Jerusalem; its ruler: Joseph Weissenberg; its inhabitants: the brothers and sisters of the 'Community of St John, Researchers into This Life and the Beyond'; its motto: 'Through Struggle to Victory'.

The village, with homes and facilities for several thousand people, consisted of a few streets of bungalows, a large old people's home, a big assembly hall, administration buildings, workshops, a steam laundry, a large coffee-house with a beer garden; it had its own waterworks and a dairy farm – cream-cheese a speciality – amidst acres of meadows and cultivated fields. There was also an enormous 'museum' – but more about that later.

The uncommitted visitor could not help wondering where the money to build all this had come from and with what means it was being maintained. Few of the villagers could have earned money by outside work; there were no factories or large farms in the area, and the nearest town was Berlin. A high proportion of the New Jerusalemers were old-age pensioners, with ridiculously small allowances in those years of a world-wide economic depression. So what Weissenberg and his *entourage* told inquisitive outsiders must have been true: sect members everywhere paid one mark per month towards the upkeep of the community; perhaps it was also true that their number was one hundred thousand, most of them in and around Berlin and in the rest of northern Germany. But there were also other explanations for the financial miracle. At one of the large parades of the sect held near Berlin, the right-wing German National Party was officially represented – a party backed by heavy industry and the big landowners, the *Junker* clique. It was also said that Weissenberg was on good terms with the National Socialists.

To be sure, Peace Town, like its ruler, had a distinct militarist aura about it. Two First World War field-guns were stationed outside the administration building. At roll calls the Master loved to appear in his old uniform with decorations, flanked by other members in similar attire. Several groups of New Jerusalem inhabitants called themselves 'veteran associations'. And the flag of the community showed the former imperial colours of Germany, black, white and red.

Old-time militarism was also a recurring theme in that most curious assembly of odds and ends called the museum – 'worthy of the pen of a Zola,' wrote a newspaperman. It was housed in a vast, brightly lit hall. On entering, the visitor passed a series of coloured life-size photographs of Weissenberg as a grenadier, followed by twenty-six paintings of the 'trance artist' Grete Müller, the Master's principal assistant; the pictures, crude and extremely childish, purported to show scenes from the Gospel of St John. A whole room, roped off because it was so highly valued, was furnished only with pieces made from antlers, and enlivened by the figure of a stuffed pig. Then again photographs of the German Emperors, the air ace von Richthofen and other war heroes. Pictures made of silk and of fur. A bust of the Great Elector of Prussia. An altar of wrought iron, made by an 'inspired' blacksmith at New Jerusalem. German and foreign military medals in showcases. . . .

The centrepiece of the 'museum' was an enormous group of larger-than-life wooden models, painted white. On the left Jesus Christ, on the right Weissenberg (in a white suit), in front of them two angels and a lectern with an outsize Bible. The whole thing was illuminated by electric bulbs shining through stained-glass panes. Brothers at Wittenberg, said a notice, had been working at it for eighteen months under the guidance of an 'inspired' turner.

Sunday morning at New Jerusalem: about a thousand brothers and sisters, prayer books in their clean-scrubbed hands, the men wearing naval caps, were moving in orderly double file towards a large, low hall with a double-vaulted roof, the assembly hall. At one end the altar, with a white cross between two candelabras and vases with flowers; behind it, a large picture of Weissenberg, flanked by paintings of scenes from the Scriptures; around it, a backdrop of blue cloth. On one side, under a picture of the Saviour, a statue of Weissenberg in a little artificial mountain landscape. There were no pews; the faithful sat down on white garden chairs. Prayers were said, hymns from the books sung under the direction of a man with a moustache like the Kaiser's, wearing a long black preacher's gown. Then Weissenberg appeared, breaths were bated, some shouted, 'God bless you, Divine Master!' But he did not preach yet; two new members had to be accepted into the sect, a routine ceremony, with the Master laying one hand on each of the two heads. Then he retired to a seat at the side and left the stage to the first star turn of the programme: Grete Müller, the trance artist and now the trance preacher.

A humdrum name, a humdrum woman : middle-aged, podgy, round-faced, her dark hair parted in the middle, with piercing eyes and a long, pointed nose over a pinched mouth. She was dressed in a straight blue gown. Holding an outsize Bible in her hands, she began to preach, monotonously, solemnly, but with sudden eruptions of screamed words or half-sentences. Most of her sermon was nothing but a chain of platitudes, no more than what a fifth-rate country vicar could produce. Only the screamed words were different; they all referred to the Master: ' . . . Whosoever follows Josef Weissenberg will never be in need . . .', . . . any work by the sweat of the brow is hallowed by the Master . . .'

It did not seem to matter what words were screamed, it was the screaming itself that had an extraordinary effect on many listeners. Their eyes closed, their bodies stretched, their legs began to tremble; heads were jerked back, arms stiffened; deep groans came from open mouths, then yells, roaring, bellowing – animal sounds. The ecstatic faces betrayed the close connection between their rapture and the sexual act. The preacher, too, had screamed herself into a trance; with closed eyes, the Bible held stiffly above her head, she now spoke 'in tongues' – unintelligible words, then again sentences in a high-pitched voice : that of the dead Chancellor Bismarck who, the congregation knew, liked to take possession of Grete Müller.

Hands were being raised in all parts of the auditorium: the signal that someone nearby had thrown a fit and needed help. One of the Master's 'tools' – assistants in the New Jerusalem idiom – rushed to the brother or sister writhing in convulsions, and tried to wake them up. If this did not work the Master himself would come down the aisle, lay his hand on their foreheads, murmur something into their ears. Then the convulsions would cease, the screaming stop; one more ecstatic groan, and the eyes would open again. Grete Müller, too, emerged from her trance after one more shout towards heaven: 'Make us one! Make us free!' She fell on her knees, Weissenberg helped her up, she stumbled off the stage. Organ music. The Lord's Prayer. A short interval.

A mother brought her newborn baby up to the altar. Grete Müller reappeared, fell promptly into another trance and baptized the child with the voice of a deceased pastor.

And then, at last, the Master himself. He, of course, did not need either trance or spirit voice to produce his effects. As soon as he started to speak, shouting almost unintelligibly, like the commands of a sergeant-major, accompanied by denture-clicking, the hysterical scenes recurred, only more so. Now the groaning, roaring, convulsing spread like a chain reaction. Within minutes no one in the audience seemed to sit still any longer; everywhere rolling eyes, waving arms, bodies in obscene movements, people jumping and falling, screaming 'in tongues', a Breughel picture brought to ghastly life, a hellish concert.

Then, suddenly, the Master stopped as abruptly as he had started. The hysterical crowd woke up with a last, massive groan. Eyes opened again, limbs went limp, mouths closed. Organ music. The doors opened, letting in the bright midday sun. Chairs were scraping, a double row of people began to move through the aisles and out as though nothing had happened.

As the assembly hall emptied, the beer-garden filled. There they sat, middle-class couples in sober dark suits and dresses, workers in their Sunday best, pasty-faced widows and pimply youths, young girls in their dirndls, calling the waitresses, drinking beer from litre mugs, munching sausages, six tier gateaux or open sandwiches with – of course – the local speciality, cream cheese . . . as though nothing had happened.

In the end, the law got old Weissenberg for his last unsuccessful cream-cheese cure; but he died before he was called upon to serve his sentence. New Jerusalem disintegrated. Those who needed a hysterical outlet among masses of fellow-believers found it in the rallies and marches of that other sect that had taken over the State, and a new Master, an ex-corporal, directed them and excited them now that the former sergeant-major had gone.

5

California:
Sectual Breeding Ground

Occult Communities

California, of course, has more experience than any other country in dealing with, and tolerating, strange cults and sects, fringe religions and eccentric communities, which have often created a great deal of trouble. One might think that developments such as the gold rush of 1848 or the establishment of Hollywood as the centre of America's film industry early in our century, causing the influx of heterogeneous elements into the western coastlands, have been responsible for the birth and spread of weird beliefs. But this is only a partial explanation, for it was probably the whole phenomenon of migration to the west, and not just the arrival of a few thousand gold diggers and film people, which produced a spiritual climate favourable to unorthodox creeds. 'History is replete with instances of corruption of religion among migrating people,' wrote an American theologian, Dr William W. Sweet. In the process of moving westward, he explained, the customs, practices and religious habits of the migrants underwent important changes: old ties were loosened, old allegiances weakened. A church survey made in Los Angeles in the 1940s said that new beliefs proved to be such strong influences because traditional attitudes were not reaching people in the Californian community, and even conventional churches were 'adopting measures unsanctioned in other parts of the country for a more effective hold upon their people'.

Then there is southern California's geographical location. On the one hand, Los Angeles is the largest metropolitan centre west of Chicago, and cult movements find their last stop here on their usual westward trek through the States; on the other hand, in case of trouble with the authorities, the Mexican border is only 'a hop, skip and jump' away (as the first Hollywood film people, always looking over their shoulders for the bailiffs, used to say). Many a prophet and sect leader has taken the road down Mexico way when things grew too hot for him in the Golden State.

Southern California's fabulous economic growth towards the end of the last century attracted some extraordinary characters. There was a Mrs Katherine Tingley from New England who became the first major prophetess on the West Coast. Encouraged by Mme Blavatsky's success with her Theosophical Society, she teamed up with a leading New York theosophist, William Quan Judge, over whom she acquired such a strong influence that he proclaimed her Purple Mother. After collecting a lot of money on the East Coast for building 'a White City in a Land of Gold beside a Sunset Sea', she established the Point Loma Theosophical Community near San Diego, fifteen miles from the Mexican border, in 1900. It consisted of about forty buildings in a hideous mixture of styles, some Moorish and some fake Egyptian with a central dome of opalescent green. Visitors were greeted by bugle calls from a bugler hidden in an Egyptian gateway.

It was a residential establishment. Three hundred believers, of two dozen different nationalities, lived here, paying handsomely for board, lodging and spiritual enlightenment; newcomers were expected to hand to Purple Mother a personal present. She ruled as an authoritarian, but her cult did not follow any strict lines: there was not only a theosophical university but also a Yoga College, a 'School of Antiquity' and a Greek theatre. Residents wore fancy costumes and raised chickens and silkworms. Stories about orgies at Point Loma were probably exaggerated, but in 1923, at the ripe age of seventy-six, Purple Mother became involved in an affair with the husband of one of the sect members. There was quite a scandal; she decided to get away from it all, left her faithful to their fate and went to Europe, where she died a few years later.

Mrs Tingley's early success prompted other prophets to try and emulate her formula. Some years before the First World War, when Hollywood was still in its infancy, a retired Virginia lawyer by the name of Albert P. Warrington bought a fifteen-acre estate in the centre of the film town and called it Krotona, 'the place of promise'. Soon it had an Occult Temple, a vegetarian restaurant, a number of tabernacles, and a 'psychic lotus pond'. He also rented a meeting hall on Hollywood Boulevard, where he organized lectures in the 'esoteric interpretation of music and drama' and the 'human aura' as well as courses in Esperanto. In 1920, he took his colony of believers out of Ojai Valley, to the home of a fellow-prophet who claimed to have flown to Ojai from a place he called Lemuria on board a great flying fish. But there was also a more serious-minded sect leader in the valley, London-born Mrs Annie Besant, the socialist and theosophist, a pupil of Mme Blavatsky, who founded a centre of the Theosophical Society. It was there that she brought a young Indian called Krishnamurti, grooming him as a spiritual teacher. The valley is still a great attraction for sects as well as for people wanting spiritual guidance, the majority, however, elderly neurotic women.

Prophets have abounded in southern California particularly since the end of the First World War; the most famous of the female ones was without doubt Mrs Aimée Semple McPherson. A young, poor and poorly educated but extremely ambitious widow, she turned up after 1918 in San Diego, holding revivalist meetings in a boxing arena. Business was not too good, and in 1922 she moved to Los Angeles in her panting old motor-car, with no more than $100 in her handbag. Within a few years, she had made her first million and proceeded to build her Angelus Temple holding five thousand people, with a broadcasting station attached. Her sect, which she called the Four Square Gospel, boasted a brass band bigger and louder than Sousa's, a female choir bigger and more beautiful than the Metropolitan Opera chorus and a costume wardrobe comparable to Ziegfeld's.

Sister Aimée, as she was now calling herself, owed much of her success to religious histrionics. She would entertain her audiences with dramatized versions of the story of Sodom and Gomorrha or drive an actor made up as the devil around the platform with a pitchfork. At the height of her career as a hot-gospeller she was said to have more than forty thousand followers who would flock to her 240 'lighthouses', as she called her local chapels.

In 1926, she staged her most exciting show by disappearing from the Ocean Park beach; as she had last been seen wearing a bathing costume, it was assumed that she had drowned, and thousands of her followers gathered on the beach to pray for her soul. An aircraft was chartered to drop wreaths on her wet grave, and an overzealous disciple was drowned trying to recover what he thought was her body. At a memorial meeting in the Angelus Temple, $35,000 was collected for a monument to be set up for Sister Aimée. But lo and behold – within a few days she turned up, safe and sound, on the Mexican side of the border, telling the press and police that she had been kidnapped. Her story sounded too odd to satisfy the newspapers, and they sent out their reporters to check it. In due course, they found a love-nest where Sister Aimée had spent a couple of days with the radio operator of her Angelus Temple station before her re-appearance in Mexico.

The police arrested her for giving false information but her lawyers managed to get the charges dropped. The interlude did not reduce the number of her followers very much; they were too happy to have her back. However, gradually the old charisma waned, Sister Aimée got more and more depressed, and in 1944 she was found dead from an overdose of sleeping pills.

It was probably from California that the Yoga cult started to sweep through America and Europe in the 1920s, crystallizing into myriads of large and small sects. The Theosophists, with their Krishnamurti, had raised western man's hope of salvation from the mysterious east, and cults centred on, or founded by, genuine or fake Indians, Tibetans and other prophets from east of Suez are still extremely popular. Around 1970, small groups of smiling English youngsters of both sexes, in flowing robes and with Mohican hairstyles, could be seen slowly dance-marching in file through London's West End during the day, to the accompaniment of some tinkling Oriental instruments, chanting 'Hare Krishna' and offering passers-by literature on their 'Krishna Consciousness Movement'. Founded by Lord Chaitanya, a fifteenth-century guru, it has its headquarters, of course, in California, where its leader, His Divine Grace Swami Prabhupada, presides over what he claims to be 'the fastest growing religious movement in the world'. The Swami sometimes descends on the English followers who rush to kiss his feet as soon as they touch the airport tarmac. He leads the faithful in their chanting of mantras, incantatory prayers, which they say have a 'cleansing, blissful effect'; and he reminds them of their vows to refrain from smoking, drinking, drug-taking, gambling and illicit love. Most important of all, he strengthens their morale and helps them to keep a stiff upper lip when friends and neighbours make fun of their shaven heads, their outlandish garments, their assumed Indian names and their un-English ecstatic grimaces. But they are a gentle, harmless and inoffensive lot, these Krishna people; and if they feel happy braving ridicule, there is no reason why anyone should try to stop them.

In California itself there are several Krishna cults in rivalry; the largest one claims thousands of members. Over twelve acres of the Box Canyon region belong to them. Here is the colony of the WKFL Fountain of the World: W stands for Wisdom, K for Knowledge, F for Faith, L for Love. The community, originally consisting of about a hundred men, women, and children, was founded in 1949 by 'Krishna Venta', as he called himself. He claimed to be the twentieth-century Messiah, the Only Begotten Son of God. His followers walked around barefoot in pastel cotton robes, coloured according to their occupation and state: light blue for a healer, lavender for artists, pink for pregnant ladies. They were well liked in Box Canyon because they helped to fight fires and did emergency rescue work in earthquakes and floods. Krishna Venta's biography as told by himself does not sound so realistic. 'I came from the planet Neophrates approximately 240,000 years ago via a rocket ship,' he explained, 'and landed in the Euphrates Valley in Turkey, which was the Garden of Eden. All these years I have been in earthly physical form.' Inside information had it that the bearded Krishna had no navel, sure proof that he 'materialized himself'.

The authorities, however, were sceptical. Police files were said to show that he had been arrested from Florida to California for burglary, theft, vagrancy, passing a dud cheque and not supporting his wife and children before becoming the Messiah.

For rich neurotics who have nothing better to do, or whose analysts have given up in despair, the Esalen Institute offers the poshest and most exclusive way of spending their money. Here, in one of the most beautiful coastal landscapes of the world, 150 miles south of San Francisco, one Michael Murphy, inspired by Aldous Huxley's propaganda for eastern philosophy, established that cult colony in the 1930s, naming it after an Indian tribe; today, more than a hundred Esalen centres, modelled on the Californian original, exist in the US. According to the cult's publicity, it wants to 'explore those trends in the behavioural sciences, religion and philosophy which emphasize the potentialities and values of human existence' under the motto 'Awake, tune in, unfold'. What this looks like in practical terms is, to put it crudely, a good deal of mutual exploring of cult members by touching, stroking, sniffing, gazing, rubbing, wrestling, which produces much excitement, sexual and otherwise. William C. Schutz, a former psychiatry lecturer at Berkeley University, has 'programmed' present-day Esalen courses, which cost up to $5,000 a head, including massage.

When the cult opened a centre in London in 1970, leading British psychiatrists warned against the dangers which this kind of treatment might bring in cases of serious mental disturbances.

Prophets for Profit

'Religion, like most other things in the US, is a fertile field for the entrepreneur,' wrote the London *Sunday Times* in 1965. 'It is a fair bet that anyone, of suitable loquacity, whackiness or even sincerity, could go to California today, set himself up as a religious leader, and soon acquire an appreciable number of followers, mostly female, elderly, and prosperous.'

Californians will subscribe to this statement but object to the word 'today'; for in the early 1930s, the time of the economic depression, entrepreneurs were even more numerous and cults even weirder than lately. There was, for instance, a man by the name of Guy W. Ballard, who had been indicted in Illinois for a gold-mine promotion, and fled to Los Angeles with his wife Edna, a medium, in 1932. It took him little time to find out what the easiest and quickest way of making money was in California: he founded a new cult, and called it 'The Mighty I AM Presence'.

He began by publishing a book entitled *Unveiled Mysteries*, in which he told the following story: on a hiking trip near Mount Shasta, a deity named 'the Ascended Master Saint Germain' appeared to him 'out of the void', tapped him on the shoulder, and gave him 'a cup of pure electronic essence' plus 'a wafer of concentrated energy'. Ballard ate and drank, whereupon he found himself 'surrounded by a White Flame which formed a circle about 50 feet in diameter'. He and Master Saint Germain then took off for the stratosphere inside the flame circle; they continued with a grand sightseeing tour, visiting the Egyptian pyramids, the secret Inca and Amazon cities, and Yellowstone National Park, discovering treasures everywhere.

Whatever Ballard's imaginary riches were, the hard cash he earned with his *Unveiled Mysteries* proved more useful; he sold thousands of copies at $2.50, and with the proceeds he bought radio time to promote his 'Mighty I AM Presence' cult. Within a few weeks, he and his wife had assembled a sizeable sect whose members responded well to the request for 'love gifts' instead of membership fees. The former tabernacle of a defunct sect was taken over and decked out in would-be oriental and antique style, with a large neon sign outside proclaiming the name of Ballard's cult. A flourishing cash-sale and mail-order business, run by Edna, brought the dollars rolling in – for a monthly magazine, gramophone records with 'music of the spheres', a cold cream prepared specially for I AM believers, a Chart of the Magic Presence, and a toy for adults called Flame in Action, represented by coloured electric lights (it cost up to $200 according to size).

When the police eventually caught up with the Ballards and charged them with mail fraud, it turned out that they had amassed a fortune of more than three million dollars.

Then there was a sect called 'Mankind United', also launched in the early 1930s, the brainchild of one Arthur Bell. He, too, started his movement with a fantastic revelation: that a group of anonymous researchers had succeeded in making contact with a superhuman race of metal-headed little men in the earth's centre as far back as 1875; he, Bell, was still in touch with them, and they had offered him help in establishing a paradise of peace and wealth on the surface of the earth. Once two hundred million people had joined Mankind United, he declared, no one would have to work for more than four hours a day, four days a week and eight months a year up to the age of sixty, in order to enjoy princely comfort in a luxurious home equipped with all the wonders of technology and surrounded by orchards and hot houses, not to mention a swimming pool. All the potential beneficiaries had to do now was to surrender their wordly possessions to the sect, which would have to remain secret for the time being. Believe it or not, fourteen thousand Californians fell for this crude confidence swindle, most of them, according to the police, 'either elderly persons or individuals who had suffered severe economic losses'.

Of course the project did not remain as secret as Mr Bell would have wished, and he was questioned by an investigation committee of the Californian legislature. With an arrogance that was almost disarming he warned the committee that he was in possession of a 'ray machine' that could exterminate his enemies over a distance of thousands of miles, and that he could go into a trance and be whisked off to any corner of the earth at will. Investigations were still going on when America entered the war in 1941 and he was arrested and convicted, together with his associates, on charges of spreading seditious propaganda.

Like all church organizations, the Californian sects have so far been exempt from disclosing their income to the revenue men and paying tax on it. Since the beginning of 1971, however, a state law requires that they list their proceeds from 'non-religious activities', which include business activities such as running chains of hotels, canneries, wine distilleries, laundries and so on in competition with heavily-taxed commercial enterprises. Many sect leaders fear that this law is only the thin end of the wedge, and that their income from 'religious activities' may also be scrutinized and decimated by the tax man in the not too distant future.

Prediction of Disaster

However, there are some sects in the Golden State which ought not to worry, for they believe that God has decided to destroy southern California anyway; the original date set for the event was the end of 1970, and there were in fact some earth tremors in that winter, which caused some damage. Already in 1968, the Rev Donald Abernathy, of the Apostolic Gospel Church in Los Angeles, revealed that he had a series of visions which convinced him that the whole region would soon be 'torn apart by an earthquake, with buildings crumbling, freeways buckling, water gushing up from cracks in the ground, and volcanoes erupting'. In another vision, he saw an aeroplane ticket marked with the destination Atlanta. The Reverend was, no doubt, influenced by the seismologists' warnings that a major earthquake may be due because of the observed stresses along the San Andreas fault.

At any rate, Mr Abernathy persuaded 180 members of his congregation to emigrate to Atlanta, where they have resettled. Smaller religious groups and sects followed their example, such as the 90 members of the Friendly Bible Apostolic Church from Port Hueneme who made their-exodus to Tennessee under their leader, Pastor Robert Theobold. He told them not to be sorry about leaving the wickedness of southern California – 'Hollywood, big business, prosperity, homosexuality and topless places'.

Is the exodus of some of these sects a straw in the wind? Will the Golden State lose its status as the world's greatest show of 'vertiginous confusion of modern idolatry, sorcery and superstition', as an American sociologist put it? To be sure, its economic basis has undergone a marked change as the result of America's recession at the end of the 1960s; the paradise where everything used to be bigger and better than anywhere else had reached an unemployment level of seven per cent, higher than any other state in the USA, by the end of 1970, and three counties in southern California were classified as 'economic disaster areas'. That wicked prosperity which disgusted so many preachers and their flocks had begun to fade. The character of California's sects may therefore change in due course: from the cults of the rich neurotics to the messianic beliefs of the dispossessed. But sects there will be, and plenty of them; most Californians are sure of that.

6

Searching
for God and Gold

The Mystical Brotherhood of the Rosicrucians

There are good reasons for doubting that the fraternity of the Rosicrucians ever existed, at least as an association; so it is all the more surprising that it had such a profound influence on western minds in the seventeenth and eighteenth centuries, an influence which extends even into our own times.

Sorting out the different versions of Rosicrucian lore and tradition is a fascinating task because it shows the deep longing of men for mystical beliefs, which grows in strength and tenacity the more realistically science can explain the world around us: a longing to turn back the clock to the Middle Ages when knowledge was scarce and faith was all. It also shows that, given ingenious publicity, men will believe anything.

If we stick to tangible facts we must assume that the sect began its curious life only with the appearance of an anonymous manuscript which was passed from hand to hand among scholars and other educated people in Germany and Austria early in the seventeenth century, inviting all men of good will to join a secret brotherhood called the *Rosenkreuzer,* or Rosicrucians, forgetting about their differences of opinion and their jealousies, so that untold benefits might accrue to mankind through such a fraternal union. The name, it was explained, came from one Christian Rosenkreutz who had founded it two centuries earlier; he was a man who possessed occult powers and knew all kinds of mysteries, which he shared with the brother members of his circle. The manuscript was printed at Cassel, Hesse, in 1614 under the title of *Fama fraternitatis des löblichen Ordens des Rosenkreuzes*, later translated and published in England as *Universal and General Reformation of the Whole Wide World;*

together with the Fama Fraternitatis of the Laudable Order of the Rosy Cross. It told the story of the founder of the fraternity, of whom no one had ever heard anything before.

Christian Rosenkreutz, it was said, was born of a noble German family in 1378. At the age of five he began his education in a monastery, learning Greek and Latin. A brother from the monastery took Christian as a sixteen-year-old lad on a pilgrimage to the Holy Land; but when they had got as far as Cyprus the monk died, and the boy had to fend for himself. He was invited to stay and study in Damascus, where the local 'sages' took care of him, teaching him medicine, mathematics and Arabic. Then he went on to Fez to study magic and the Cabbala, and from there to Spain where, however, his occult knowledge met with scepticism.

The same happened to him in many other countries he visited, until he decided to settle in the Tyrol, in the Austrian Alps, where he put down his philosophy and experiences in writing. This took him five years and in the end he came to the conclusion that the reform of the world which he had in mind was too formidable a job for one man alone. He went to his old monastery and enlisted the assistance of eight disciples whom he bound to be 'faithful, diligent and secret'. Their main tasks were to heal the sick according to Rosenkreutz's methods, and to write down 'all that men can desire, wish or hope for' to be offered to humanity as a free gift. They were 'all bachelors and of vowed virginity', and after having lived as a community for some years, they split up and went as missionaries of the new sect into various countries. They entered into an agreement: none of them should claim any other power but to cure the sick; each should give his services without reward; they would meet at Rosenkreutz's house once a year; each should nominate 'a worthy person who after his decease might succeed him'; and the fraternity should remain secret for one hundred years.

Rosenkreutz himself, it was claimed, died at the age of 106 in 1484; some even said he grew to be 150 and passed away not, like the rest of us, because he had to, but because he wanted to. He had appointed another centenarian among the brethren as his successor; this man became the instructor of the 'third succession', who compiled the *Fama* from the founder's writings. At any rate, the one hundred years of silence had expired, and it was time to make the world acquainted with the way in which Rosenkreutz had planned to make it a better place.

According to the *Fama*, the founder's original writings had disappeared at the time of his death; but at the turn of the seventeenth century, when his house, the 'House of Fraternity' in the Tyrolean mountains, was undergoing repairs, Rosenkreutz's tomb was found in a secret vault, and in it a manuscript all written in golden letters. The brethren interpreted this as a sign that the fraternity of the *Rosenkreuzer,* or Rosicrucians, should now be opened to all men of learning and philanthropy who desired to work for the common good under the sign of the Rosy Cross.

In the turbulent and confusing state in which Central Europe was at the time, only a few years before the outbreak of the Thirty Years' War, the publication of the *Fama* caused great excitement among the intelligentsia. For many it meant a new approach to God and religion, in tune with their nostalgia for the calm, monastic atmosphere of the Middle Ages, undisturbed by doubts and scientific discoveries; the Rosicrucian spirit seemed to them pre-Reformation; pre-everything, in fact, for the brotherhood claimed that Rosenkreutz's notions came largely from the Egyptian Pharoah Akhnaton or Amenhotep IV, whom they regarded as their first 'Grand Master', thus going one better than the Freemasons, who traced their origins merely to either the Tower of Babel or the construction of Solomon's Temple. Akhnaton, in the fourteenth century BC was a mother-dominated religious fanatic who proclaimed monotheism and founded a new capital dedicated to the worship of his one and only god, the sun disc Aton; his 'heresy' was supported by his beautiful and influential sister-queen, Nefertete.

General interest in the mysterious brotherhood was much enhanced by the publication, only a year after that of the *Fama,* of a new document allegedly compiled by the Rosicrucians, entitled *Confessio* and written in Latin for the exclusive perusal of the *Eruditi Europae,* the learned men of Europe. It enlarged upon the general ideas and aims of the Rosicrucians, and scholars believed to discover in it a post-Reformation tendency, with the result that now the sect appealed to Protestants too, making escape into Roscrucian mysticism, as it were, interdenominational.

Yet there were genuine doubts whether the sect existed at all.

It had no address, the Tyrolean headquarters remained secret, and there was no centre where eager candidates could apply for membership. Letters by people who wanted to join the fraternity appeared in print, and so did others by scholars who claimed they were high-ranking members of the order. Presently pamphlets were published denouncing the whole thing as a fraud, or a hoax, perhaps even a parody of Freemasonry.

Whatever the truth was, it soon became clear that the alchemists, trying to prop up their reputation amidst the new tide of genuine scientific discovery, were beginning to muscle in; or perhaps they had been in it all along, despite the fact that the *Fama* denied the possibility of transmuting metals. At any rate, one cannot discard the theory that there never was a man called Rosenkreutz, and that the name of the fraternity derived from *ros crux,* Latin for 'dew cross'. Dew, according to alchemical tradition, is the most powerful solvent of gold, while cross is the symbol of light because the shape of the cross contains the three letters L, V and X, forming the word *lux,* light. Hence the Rosicrucians would be alchemists using dew for digesting the 'red dragon', or corporeal light, for making gold.

One edition after another of the *Fama* and the *Confessio,* sometimes combined in a single volume, came off the printing presses in Germany. The last one before the Thirty Years' War, published in Frankfurt, contained a kind of manifesto, perhaps written by some Rosicrucians who had become aware of the alchemists' designs on the sect. It denounced those who were seeking admission for unworthy motives: 'But men have either scorned our writings, or else have supposed we are going to teach them how to make gold by alchemical methods, or bestow upon them riches to satisfy their ambition and love of pomp, their wars and greed, their gluttony and drunkenness and lust.'

If the fraternity did not really exist, if it was merely a utopian dream, then it was a most extraordinary case of *quod volunt, credunt,* as Caesar put it – men are apt to believe what they wish to be true. The continent was suddenly full of self-styled Rosicrucians. During the Thirty Years' War, when secret societies were virtually banned all over Europe, regular meetings of Rosicrucian groups were held clandestinely in Hamburg and Nuremburg, Danzig and Erfurt; one at least, in Amsterdam, was broken up by the authorities. Each group seems to have worked out its own dogma and rituals as it went along, for neither the *Fama* nor the *Confessio* offered much detailed guidance in these matters.

Rumours as to the authorship of one or the other of these publications abounded; some believed that a famous Lutheran theologian from Württemberg, Johann Valentin Andreae, had written the *Confessio* in the early 1600s, when he was only in his twenties, for the purpose of disseminating Protestantism. In fact, he did claim to be a Rosicrucian, but later denounced the brotherhood as being undermined by Catholics who had infiltrated it and made it subservient to Rome; as a counter-move he founded another organization, the *Fraternitas Christi*.

Another widespread belief was that no less a man than Martin Luther himself had penned the *Fama*, for did not his coat of arms show a rose and a cross? However, there was little in Luther's life and letters that would have pointed to him as a likely founder, or founder member, of the secret sect of the Rosicrucians. The confusing and contradictory rumours around it go only to show that it was, at least in its early phase, all things to all men.

The man who gave Rosicrucianism a definite direction for a long period was an Englishman, Robert Fludd. England, backward, isolated and locked in its internal struggles until the last decade or two of the sixteenth century, had been left behind by the great experience of the Renaissance that excited and inspired the Continental countries. Then, with one mighty swoop, it surged forward, caught up with the rest of the western nations and surpassed them in many fields. Spiritual, intellectual, artistic experience crowded in upon the Englishman's mind, contacts with other peoples opened up, a two-way traffic of ideas flowed across the Channel. Rosicrucianism was one of the ideas that were imported into England, put into a more precise shape and exported back to the Continent.

Robert Fludd probably came from a Welsh family called Lloyd who had settled in Kent, where he was born in 1574. He entered St John's College, Oxford, at the age of seventeen, then went to Continental universities to study medicine for five years, and eventually returned to Oxford, where he took his medical degree in 1605. Like many doctors of the period he was a follower of Paracelsus, the Swiss physician, Renaissance philosopher and natural scientist, who had established a new medical school three-quarters of a century earlier. Fludd worked out a philosophic system founded on Paracelsus's ideas and teachings, but he was by nature and inclination a mystic and increasingly attracted by alchemy, as the long list of his works shows.

As soon as the *Fama* had appeared, he plumped for Rosicrucianism and made himself the great English protagonist of the sect. Yet again there is no indication whatsoever that he was even a member of the association: another pointer to the probability that it never really existed. Already in 1616, two years after the *Fama* was published in Germany, he brought out his own *Apologia Compendiaria Fraternitatem de Rosea Cruce Afluens* in London. It made a considerable impression on English scholars and other erudite people, establishing the Rosicrucian movement on the basis of Fludd's own interpretation, that of a convinced alchemist. The 'true' Rosicrucians, as he called them, were continually travelling from country to country, unknown to all but the members of their fraternity, dedicated to the study of God and Nature's laws; to Fludd, the Rosicrucian voices that warned against indulging in alchemical practices were not those of 'true' brethren.

Fludd's propaganda for the movement, with himself as its leading interpreter, was extremely successful. He also seems to have spread the story, for which little evidence has been found, that the great Francis Bacon himself was the secret 'Imperator' of the fraternity and that the *Fama* had been written under his direction.

Judging by some of the names that have been connected with the founding of a Rosicrucian Society in London, this event must have taken place after Bacon's death (1626) but possibly during the lifetime of Fludd, who died in 1637. There was the Welshman Thomas Vaughan, twin brother of Henry Vaughan the poet, a cleric and alchemist who, under his pen name of Eugenius Philaletes, published an English-language version of the two fundamental Rosicrucian works under the title *The Fame and Confession*. Another founder member was William Lilly, an astrologer from Leicestershire. Born in 1602, he had started his career as a book-keeper, married a rich widow and in later life managed to be employed as star-gazing adviser by both parties in the civil war (Charles I consulted him when planning his attempt to escape from Carisbrooke Castle). A later member was Elias Ashmole, whose books and manuscripts became the core of the Oxford museum that still bears his name; born at Lichfield in 1617, he studied law but also dabbled in alchemy and astrology before making his name as an antiquary and natural scientist.

Another latecomer to the Society was the lawyer Heydon, born in 1629, a fervent propagandist of the Rosicrucians, claiming that they were the guardians of the world's most sublime secrets, on a par with Moses and the Prophet Elias. He was, however, an obvious crank, who believed that eating was mankind's original sin and that for the initiated there was sufficient nutriment in the air. He recommended to the hungry to place on their stomachs a plate of cooked meat and just inhale its aroma, which would satisfy their appetite. Eccentricities of this kind, the mysterious air of the Rosicrucians, and their absurd claims to ancient magic powers provoked a good deal of ridicule. Samuel Butler wrote in his *Hudibras*:

> As for the Rosycross philosophers,
> Whom you will have to be but sorcerers,
> What they pretend to is no more
> Than Trismegistus did before,
> Pythagoras, old Zoroaster,
> And Apollonius their master.

The success of the Rosicrucians in England reverberated over the whole Continent, and they were now identified everywhere with alchemy. There were still a few educated men who professed to be Rosicrucians but condemned the alchemists' search for the Philosophers' Stone, such as the French Abbé de Villars in his curious work, *The Count of Gabalis,* published in 1670. He declared that Rosicrucians did not believe in sorcery, witchcraft and the transmutation of metals, but his own notions were no less mystical. Mankind, he explained, was surrounded by the elemental spirits whom the Rosicrucians could tame for their service to humanity by 'imprisoning' them in a mirror or a ring, forcing them to appear at will (another version of the *jinn* fable from Arabian cabbalistic literature). The Abbé's kind of *jinn* could conquer space and time; it was made of pure elements from the matter which it inhabited, and could live for a thousand years.

In seventeenth-century Germany, torn by the long war between the Catholic and the Protestant forces, denominational Rosicrucianism was the rule. One widespread 'Order' of the Rosicrucians, practising alchemy, had statutes with specific instructions to keep Roman Catholics out. It also had its 'Imperator'. For reasons of secrecy, members had to change their places of residence every ten years. They recognized each other by this exchange of greetings:

A   Ave, frater
B   Roseae et aureae
A   Crucia
Both   Benedictus Deus qui dedit nobis signum

Whereupon each took out his copy of the seal of the brotherhood, which all brethren had to carry with them.

Some 'orders' were no more than a spoof for attracting the gullible and relieving them of membership fees for a virtually non-existent organization. But others, in France as well as in Germany, moulded themselves upon the patterns of the Masonic lodges which were the great intellectual fashion of the time, the late seventeenth century and the eighteenth. Around 1754, for instance, a new Masonic degree became very popular in France, calling itself the Rose Croix Degree. In Germany, these quasi-Masonic Rosicrucian lodges developed into a rite of nine grades indicating the stages of initiation into the secrets of the sect.

One such order, widespread in Central Europe, was the Asiàtic Brethren, a Rosicrucian society based on many traditions of the mysterious East, probably inspired by the notions of the Abbé de Villars. It was said to have been founded in 1780; its lowest grade was that of the Seeker who, after a period of probation, moved up into the grade of Sufferer by way of an elaborate initiation ceremony held in a room completely hung and carpeted with black cloth, lit by candles in five-branched golden candlesticks. The Master, or Magus, conducted the rites from a dais with a black canopy; behind him was the Holiest of Holies with the image of the sun in a triangle, a sword and the Book of the Law, by which the candidate had to swear obedience and secrecy. The ceremony was more or less similar to that practised by the Freemasons with symbolic actions and prescribed questions and answers.

The relationship between Rosicrucians and Freemasons in the eighteenth century was by no means unilateral; the attraction of Rosicrucianism was also exploited by the Freemasons. There was, for instance, a certain Fraxinus, Grand Master of the four United Masonic Lodges in Hamburg, who was running a Rosicrucian Order behind the backs of his Masonic brethren in the early 1780s; the admission fees to the sect were rather stiff and Fraxinus made much money out of them. One Rosicrucian felt that he had been overcharged and attacked the Grand Master in print. The affair caused a great scandal, with Freemasons as well as Rosicrucians exposed to public ridicule because of their gullibility.

Alchemy had its final great fling in those days while men like Lavoisier, Cavendish and Dalton were busy taking the last traces of mystique out of chemistry. A German bestseller published as late as 1788 in Leipzig, entitled *The Secret of All Secrets of the Rosicrucians*, contained dozens of recipes for producing the alkahest, the universal solvent of the Alchemists, 'a treasure that neither an emperor nor a king can afford'. It could be made from sweat, spittle, worms and so on, but the best raw material, the book claimed, was blood: 'One must keep in mind that the spirit of an animal as well as of a human being resides in the blood. . . A secret alkahest can be obtained only from a healthy animal or executed culprit . . . which is better than the blood of a young lion. . . .' The purification of the blood for the purpose would take up to six months, said the recipe. Perhaps the alchemists trying it out lost patience, for none of them seems to have come up with the miracle fluid.

There were persistent stories in Germany that the great Goethe was also a Rosicrucian, at any rate in his twenties when he wrote the first draft of his version of the Dr Faustus story, the *Urfaust*. Like his hero, he had been studying ancient and contemporary natural-philosophical books, but discarded them as unsatisfactory. He was looking for a system of 'beautiful combination' of the natural phenomena, 'though perhaps in a phantastical manner', as he wrote in his autobiography. His train of thought had been started by a Roscrucian book published at Frankfurt in 1723, the *Aurea Catena Homeri*, Homer's 'Golden Chain', which attempted to explain Nature from the alchemist's point of view. In Goethe's definitive *Faust*, however, completed in old age, the rationalist devil Mephistopheles demolishes and ridicules Faust's mysticism, and as it is the devil to whom Goethe gave all the best lines in his drama, one may come to the conclusion that the author himself was making fun of his own youthful speculations on alchemical lines.

In our century Rosicrucianism, with Goethe as one of the principal witnesses, was reawakened by a serious thinker, the Swiss Rudolf Steiner, who established the esoteric philosophical system of Anthroposophy.* In the 1920s, he said in a series of lectures on 'Rosicrucianism and Modern Initiation':

It is difficult to distinguish the true from the false ... and this is what has led many to regard the whole of Rosicrucianism as charlatan. One can understand it, for the true Rosicrucians are extraordinarily hard to find among the charlatans ...

But Steiner believed he knew how the 'true Rosicrucian' could be recognized:

You might find him in some village, gathering herbs for an apothecary, or engaged in some other simple calling. If you are one who takes an interest in special forms and manifestations of the being of man as they show themselves in this or that individuality, then you may meet with such a person. At first you will find him very reserved, he will speak but little, perhaps he will even turn away your attention from what you are trying to find in him by talking in a trivial manner, on purpose to make you think it is not worth while to converse with him. If, however, you know better than to look merely at the content of what a man says, if you know how to listen to the sound of his words, if you can hearken to the way the words come out of him, then you will go on listening, despite all discouragement. And if then out of some karmic connection (the Buddhist concept of *karma* means the sum of a person's actions in one stage of his existence, deciding his fate in the next) he receives the impression that he really should talk to you, he will begin to do so ... carefully and guardedly; and you will make the discovery that he is a kind of wise man. But what he is telling is not earthly wisdom. Neither is there contained in it much of what we now call spiritual science. It is warm words of the heart that he is uttering, far-reaching ethical teachings ...

But even Rudolf Steiner, in his attempt at reviving Rosi-

* It is significant that Steiner chose the name of his system, which has still many followers, from the title of a book, *Anthroposophia Teomagica,* which the Welsh Rosicrucian Thomas Vaughan (*q.v.*) published in 1650.

crucianism, could not explain what these ethical teachings really were, only what he wanted his Anthroposophists to meditate upon. Here is a characteristic passage from his lecture on the 'geometrical figures of the old Rosicrucians', which the aforementioned wise men would show only to people 'who approached them in the right way':

> When they spoke about these figures ... then the conversation would unfold in a strange manner. There were in the old days many who felt interested in the unpretentious wise men before them, but were at the same time overcome with curiosity as to what these strange Rosicrucian pictures really meant, and would ask questions about them. But they received from these wise men, who were as a rule regarded as strange and eccentric, no clear or exact answer. They would receive only the advice: If one studies these figures with the right deepening of soul, then one can see through them as through a window into the spiritual world. The wise men might give as it were a description of what they themselves had been able to *feel* from contemplating the figures; but they were not ready to offer any explanation or interpretation of them ...

In other words, Rudolf Steiner didn't know it either. He went on to analyse Goethe's *Faust* from the same angle of Rosicrucian inquiry, for instance the hero's medieval concepts which the author has put into the scene when Faust conjures up the Earth Spirit, 'although Goethe himself did not understand its true meaning':

> Who is it really that Faust is conjuring up? Goethe himself when he was writing *Faust*, most assuredly did not fully comprehend. But if we go back from Goethe to the mediaeval Faust, in whom Rosicrucian wisdom was living, we find that he too wanted to conjure up a spirit. And who was it he wanted to conjure up? He never spoke of the Earth Spirit, he spoke of *Man*. The longing and striving of mediaeval man was : to be Man. For he felt in the depths of his soul that as Earth Man he is not truly Man ...

And so on, in one vague sentence after the other. Or take Steiner's version of the birth of modern astronomy:

> The Copernican cosmology, for example, was taught in Rosicrucian schools; but in special states of consciousness the ideas contained in it came back in the form I have explained to you. It was the Rosicrucians, above all, who realized that that which man

receives in modern knowledge must first be carried forth, so to speak, must first be *offered to the Gods*, that the Gods may translate it into their language and give it back again to men.

In Britain and the United States, a Rosicrucian revival began in the 1860s. A *Societas Rosicruciana in Anglia* was founded, Rosicrucian Colleges set up. The British Museum still has one tattered little copy of the *Rules and Ordinances of the Rosicrucian Society in England*, published in 1881, printed by the Freemason Printing Works in London. This was surely no coincidence, for the Society was closely tied to the Freemasons despite the statement in the rules that the 'Society of Brethren of the Rosy Cross' was 'totally independent'. In the next paragraph, we read that its members were 'selected from the fraternity of the Masonic Order', which meant, among other restrictions, that women were excluded. There were the traditional nine grades, from Zelator to Supreme Magus, with fees on a sliding scale. The Supreme Magus at the time was a London doctor and one may assume that the activities and interests of the society were charitable deeds and antiquarianism rather than making gold or the cultivation of mystic powers.

In America, however, Rosicrucian mysticism has been attracting followers in the midst of an increasingly materialist society. A Dr P. B. Randolph, who styled himself Professor of Oriental Interior Science, published a *Rosicrucian Dream Book* in Boston in 1871, containing 'solutions of over 3,000 different dreams' in alphabetical order. If you dream of gold coins, for instance, it means 'Thou'rt hated by thy wife'; potatoes mean : 'Someone poisons the mind of those who do thee good'; camels: 'Thy love is better far than he or she looks'; and genitals (Oh for those good old pre-Freudian days!): 'Tame thy passions'.

Today, you may become a Rosicrucian without much ado and at tolerable cost if you join an international organization which has its headquarters in California, an awe-inspiring complex of fake-oriental buildings with two hundred employees and an annual budget of two million dollars. There are an Egyptian Obelisk, a Francis Bacon Auditorium, a museum and astrological planetarium, an art gallery, a Rose-croix University with plaza and fountain, a science collection and physics laboratory (for experiments in vibrations of sound, light, colour 'and other phenomena of Nature'), offices for mailing and correspondence, a research library, and a 'Shrine of Amenhotep IV', for the society traces its history back to 1500 BC; in fact, it was set up in the 1920s by a Dr H. Spencer Lewis, 'First Imperator and founder of the Second Cycle of the Rosicrucian Order for North and South America'.

The Order teaches, by correspondence very much on the lines of Pelmanism, a system of metaphysical and physical philosophy to help the student utilize his natural talents, uniting mysticism, science and the arts in an educational programme 'to free society of the enslaving influence of superstition' and lead the members towards a 'happier and more useful life'. This is to be accomplished 'by a method of personal interaction and guidance'. The organization claims a hundred thousand members, a great number of them in South America. Under its Imperator, a Supreme Secretary and several Grand Masters are at work improving the members' minds and souls. The newcomer, however, is assured that membership does not involve 'strange practices or rites that would bring members into public ridicule'.

A pale shadow, indeed, of the secret Rosicrucian sect of the past in quest of answers to the great mysteries of life, God, Nature and perhaps, *en passant,* of the Philosophers' Stone.

7

Sects
in Politics and War

Soka Gakkai

At the twenty-third Congress of Orientalists at Cambridge in 1954, a Jesuit from Japan, Father W. Schiffer, read a paper on the astonishing diversity of religious resurgence in that country during and immediately after the war. Since 1941, he reported, no fewer than 120 new religions had been granted official recognition, most of them created around 'some inspired divine being' whose word was accepted as absolute law by the faithful. A number of these faiths had a Christian basis, others sprang from Japanese Buddhism, and a few from the other two traditional religions of the country, Shinto and Confucianism. Shintoism itself, however, the spiritual 'cement' of loyalty to state and emperor, appeared to be largely discredited after 1945 because it was identified with the regime that had brought defeat and disaster to the nation; furthermore, its mythology was in obvious contradiction to the modern scientific and technological concepts which appealed so much to the Japanese. There was, therefore, a religious-political gap which those innumerable new beliefs were trying to fill.

Apart from the 120 officially recognized religions, several hundreds of sects were competing for followers among the masses, with faith-healing or sex as their most popular features, one of them cleverly combining the two, offering faith cures through sexual intercourse. Another was based on the concept of what has been termed 'unisex' in the west, worshipping 'The Great God of the Heavenly Womb, uniting the male and female principles'. In striking contrast, the Electricity Culture Religion had elevated Thomas Alva Edison to the status of a god. One sect believed in 'an absolute being who is at the same time a non-absolute being';

another was paying homage to 800 gods. There was also a Perfect Liberty Sect, proclaiming that 'man must practice whatever his first inspiration dictates'.

Father Schiffer admired the lack of interdenominational strife among all these religious groups in Japan, despite their rivalry for the souls and, of course, pockets; there was even a weekly magazine called *The League of New Religions,* serving the interests of all sects. But, as the Jesuit scholar remarked, 'the financial management in quite a number of these new religions seems to have been under the influence of human weakness'.

Perhaps inevitably, the most efficiently organized sect, the one whose psychological appeal covered the broadest sector of the population, was bound to gain ascendency over the rest. It is called 'Soka Gakkai', the 'Value-creating Association', a name sounding, in western ears, like that of a savings or shareholders club, but it seems that the Japanese mind welcomes a combination of material and spiritual values. Although the fabulous success of the Soka Gakkai proves that this combination fulfils a modern need, the roots of the sect go back a very long way.

A thirteenth-century monk called Nichiren Daishonin, a fisherman's son who had for a time been a Samurai (and, to judge by various accounts, a rather cantankerous one), had a revelation that he was the True Buddha. His claim was widely accepted, and *Nichiren Shoshu*, 'True Buddhism', became the first distinctive Japanese Buddhist creed. He was a radical and militant reformer, leaving six disciples to carry on his work. One of them, Nikko, soon broke away, and in later years further sectarianism among the Nichiren followers weakened the movement, while by the turn of our century Nikko's True Buddhism had withered away to a mere shadow of its medieval popularity. It was only in 1930 that a kind of resurrection began, when a former teacher and headmaster from Tokyo called Tsunesaburo Makiguchi, disappointed in his pedagogic work, founded Soka Gakkai on the basis of Nikko's and Nichiren's tenets, ingeniously adapting and complementing them to cater for the particular requirements of Japan's working and lower middle classes. His first important convert was a fellow-teacher, Josei Toda, who had been a Christian; Makiguchi allotted to him the job of organizing the movement after the 'cell' system of the Communist Party.

At first, the growth of the sect was rather slow, but then the first breakthrough came among the impoverished, underpaid coal-miners. Soka Gakkai's religious creed, an intolerant claim to represent the only valid Buddhism, denouncing all its other forms, may have made less impact on the miners than its more practical aims: the pursuit of happiness, higher wages, protection against accidents, healing cures for all kinds of illness, peace and friend-ship, with a strong appeal to Japanese nationalism. Significantly, the movement took its cue from Kant's three values: truth, good and beauty, changing them into gain, good and beauty, in that order.

When Japan entered the war, Makiguchi and Toda got into trouble. By preaching against military service – because Shinto, the state religion that gave the emperor his divine right to wage war, was a heresy in their eyes – they invoked the wrath of the authorities; the two leaders and a number of their disciples were imprisoned. Their misfortunes proved to be of decisive propa-ganda value; Makiguchi died in his cell in 1944 and the move-ment had its great martyr.

After Hiroshima and Nagasaki, Soka Gakkai, with no more than a few thousand believers in 1945, soared to success under Toda, who led it until his death in 1958, when there were some three million of them. He was an extremely tough, efficient and autocratic leader, perhaps thanks to his native roots in Hokkaido, Japan's northernmost island, where life is a permanent struggle for survival. He was a superb propagandist of a practical every-day faith in an age of scepticism. This is how he appealed to the masses for Soka Gakkai, which had been given the nickname of Yen Buddhism by its critics:

I recommend to you this faith because I want you all to enjoy a happy life and no inconvenience in your next life. You should be able to live in a big house, possessing everything from a piano to jewellery; your mother should be a beauty, and you should be born anew with intelligence, a fortune, and excellent health.

The publicity booklet which Toda compiled made these claims:

We often hear of a man whose business is failing, but after becoming a convert to Soka Gakkai he has brilliant ideas, he is prospering again and shares in the divine benefit of the magnificent power of Gohonzon [Nichiren's sacred scroll worshipped by the believers]. It makes baseball players win, inventors succeed, salaries rise, and men get promoted to higher rank.

The booklet also promised miraculous cures for cancer, polio and tuberculosis; even stammering would cease. But he who does not believe in Soka Gakkia may be stricken down with disease. Christianity was called unscientific; Jesus died on the Cross 'because he had no power'.

Under Toda, the movement laid claim to the whole family of a believer: when the father joined the movement, they were all expected to follow suit. Only then would Soka Gakkai confer on them the fullest possible benefit according to the teachings of its martyr Makiguchi:

> The ultimate purpose in life lies in creating the supreme value in this existence ... We must evaluate everything by whether we gain or lose from it. We teach the individual how to redevelop his character and enjoy a happy life, showing all mankind how eternal peace can be established through supreme Buddhism, the religion of mercy and pacifism, by which a person can escape from poverty and live a prosperous life ... Domestic discord vanishes, the home grows serene and happy, a man suffering from disease will recover, a mother worried about her delinquent son will see him recover through the power of the Gohonzon, a husband plagued with a neurotic wife can have her return to normalcy, the timid and irritable gradually become strong and calm. Everyone who believes in Daishonin can solve any problem. The true intention of Daishonin is to save the whole world through the attainment of each individual's happiness in life.

It was Soka Gakkai's third president, Daisaku Ikeda, taking over after Toda's death, who turned the movement into a political force. At that time, in 1958, Ikeda, yet another former teacher, the son of a humble seaweed gatherer from Tokyo Bay, who had joined Soka Gakkai as a student, was only thirty years old; but he had already made a name for himself as 'Japan's Billy Graham', a powerful speaker with a wide rhetoric range, from soulful persuasion to aggressive dogmatism. Critics have said that his speaking technique reminded them of the popular Japanese actress Kobayashi.

And so, under the ambitious Ikeda, the most successful sect which the country had ever had entered the political arena: *obutsu myogo* he called it, 'a fusion of politics and religion', and the party he founded was given the name of *Komeito*, 'clean government'. The party declared itself right from the start against big business, high taxes and inflation, though Ikeda never explained precisely what economic policy Komeito would adopt if voted into power. But he was explicit about nuclear warfare, from which the country had suffered so cruelly: 'We shall use force, if necessary, in our fight against the atom bomb. Leaders of nations which use nuclear weapons would be executed as war criminals.'

When Soka Gakkai began its political activities, there was still much confusion in the minds of the workers, including the white-collar ones, about which political group would act most effectively in their interest. Komeito, with its stress on the necessity of cleaning up political and administrative life and putting an end to corruption and red tape, appealed enormously to small traders and peasants, underpaid employees and the lower brackets of the industrial proletariat. In those years, France's anti-establishment rebel Poujade with his clean-up slogans was much in the news; Ikeda seems to have taken a leaf or two out of the French book, and with greater success than Poujadism ever had in its own country. The Socialist Party, used to dealing with only one major rival, the conservative Liberal Democrats, got rattled. 'Komeito has exactly the social background and many of the characteristics of Fascism', declared a leading Social Democrat.

Soon those characteristics grew even more obvious. The sect and its political arm set up a paramilitary organization similar to those of the German Nazis; in fact, Ikeda confessed to a British reporter that he admired Hitler. There were demonstrations and mass meetings, rousing speeches and strict discipline, 'not as a threat to the democratic system', Ikeda told the journalist, 'but to establish a real democracy for the common people'. It sounded ominously familiar to the European listener.

The teenagers were the main target of the movement's propagandist and activist branches. By the early 1960s, the Youth Corps of Soka Gakkai had roped in 750,000 followers, and by 1970 three million. But there are some typically Japanese features. The 'family organization' consists of squads of fifteen families each, six squads make up a company, ten companies a local regiment, and thirty regiments a regional 'army'. These armies are controlled directly from the Tokyo HQ of the movement, with chiefs of staff responsible only to the Supreme Commander, President Ikeda. A formidable force indeed, and potentially a civil-war force, estimated at nearly twenty million followers, or seven million families.

However, the tasks allotted to it are, at least for the time being, principally sectarian. Campaigning for converts is the first obligation of the members; called *shakubuku* (meaning breaking down), it is their overriding duty in all walks of life. They must constantly scour their neighbourhoods in search of new recruits for Soka Gakkai among the dissatisfied and unhappy. Singing plays a great part in campaigning, especially the chanting of *daimoku*, the basic Gohonzon prayer and invocation of True Buddhism. The candidates are told of the immediate benefits after conversion, when they will understand the nature of True Buddhism and enjoy prosperity, health and happiness. 'Just try it and you will see! ', they are exhorted.

Every Saturday night, new converts are solemnly initiated into the Soka Gakkai community, when they receive a miniature copy of the Gohonzon, the sacred scroll, which is illustrated with a graph of the universe according to the Buddhist concept. They have to swear blind obedience to the leader, whose commands are the ultimate law of the movement.

Apart from its imposing headquarters building in Tokyo, the sect has since 1969 a new centre of worship, a magnificent temple at the foot of Japan's holy mountain, the Fujiyama, at whose summit stands the old Shinto shrine. The temple, said to have cost 100 million dollars, is probably the largest religious building in the world, and some 15,000 pilgrims come each day to worship the sacred scroll, chanting *daimoku*, at the two-hour service, 'from the hour of the Ox to the hour of the Tiger', and to admire a great relic of the faith, Nichiren's tooth.

No other sect in the world has gained so much political influence as Soka Gakkai. The Komeito party is today Japan's 'third force', manoeuvring pragmatically between left and right according to the issues at hand, always with an eye on the mentality of the mass of its working and lower middle class voters. Komeito's first great success came as early as 1959, when it captured 260 seats on the town councils in the local elections. The nervous major parties, the Socialists and the Liberal Democrats, began to court the new movement, and Ikeda agreed to back one or the other in return for various concessions. In 1966, for instance, he swung half a million voters in Tokyo behind the Liberal-Democratic City Governor and got him re-elected against the Socialist candidate.

In national politics, Komeito entered the arena relatively late and not by way of the Lower House – Japan's House of Commons – but through the Upper House. Here, all its fifteen candidates of 1963 got elected; they numbered twenty-five a few years later. Eventually, Komeito also competed for seats in the Lower House and managed to get fifty, over ten per cent, in 1970.

Its political programme, however, is rather vague. It is strongly anti-war (and of course particularly anti-nuclear war), anti-Communist, but in favour of the United Nations and international friendship. This is an important point, not so much in politics, where it means little more than a traditional commonplace, as for Soka Gakkai's own efforts to establish branches in other countries, to make friends and influence people all over the world. These efforts had already begun in the early 1960s when the sect tried to get hold of the most clearly defined body of strangers in the midst of the Japanese people, the American soldiers stationed in the country. They were not directly approached, but by way of their Japanese servants, the bar and nightclub hostesses; in many cases the Japanese wives of US servicemen were pressed to tell them about Soka Gakkai, make them curious about the movement and take them to special meetings for American sympathizers. Within a few years several thousand GIs became members. American Intelligence men could do little about it but worry and wonder what the effect of Soka Gakkai's pacifist teachings would be on the men's fighting morale. But the sect was more interested in gaining a foothold in the United States itself by way of returning and demobilized soldiers, thus establishing the first of its overseas branches.

In 1970, *Life* reporters visited the New York headquarters of the Soka Gakkai sect. They found a black door with big black letters reading NICHIREN SHOSHU on the fifth floor of a Manhattan office block, where every Wednesday evening some one or two hundred people meet, including a number of strangers who were approached in the streets by members with the question, 'Would you like to come to a Buddhist meeting?' Proselytizing, the believers' main duty, is highly successful in the States; according to *Life's* estimate, about forty thousand people were enrolled in 1969, bringing the total up to two hundred thousand by 1970.

At the New York meetings there is a wide variety of participants: white, black and yellow, soberly-suited citizens and bearded hippies, old and young. They all chant the Gohonzon prayer, *'Nam myoho renge kyo'*, 'Adoration of the Lotus Scripture of the True Law', facing the sacred paper scroll and fingering their prayer beads. Other songs follow, some to popular American tunes but with semi-religious lyrics. Between songs, the worshippers cheer – 'ah, ah, oh' – like their fellow-believers in Japan.

Life reporters made notes of some of the testimonials given by members after the singing session. 'My whole attitude changed after joining,' testified a teenage lad. 'I even cleaned up my room.' A middle-aged grocer said that soon after becoming a Soka Gakkai member he heard that his son, a soldier in Vietnam, was the sole survivor of a mortar round which had struck his unit. Another son of his passed all his subjects at college and, after a bout of chanting, his driver's test at the first attempt. 'Let's face it,' said the grocer, 'the church has lost most of my generation and I would say all of the next generation. In church you fall asleep. You don't do that at our meetings; there is too much going on. My children have started chanting, and it has brought about some minor miracles for them.' And he took up his Nichiren beads again, symbolizing the head, arms and legs of the human body and 'the 108 desires of man'. 'Nichiren Shoshu is nice because you participate,' he added. The beads plus a miniature copy of the Gohonzon, the necessary equipment for chanting at home, cost him $4.81.

The Japanese Soka Gakkai organization is a prosperous business concern. It can count on millions of families as subscribers for its weekly and monthly journals, its bulletins and propaganda books, some of them also published in English. The sect has its own large printing works. It also owns a chain of factories for domestic altars, beads, scroll copies and all kinds of sacred paraphernalia for every size of pocket. The uniforms, banners and other propaganda utensils for Soka Gakkai's youth and mass meetings are, of course, big business and are manufactured by the sect's own enterprises.

What, the western observer may ask, is it all in aid of? Profit and power for the leaders? A genuine desire to bring about the spiritual and social salvation of Japan and the world? Political aims? For each of these definitions there are valid pros and cons. To be sure, the sect has proved to be an efficient safety-valve for the disenchanted and underpaid masses bypassed in Japan's rapid postwar development into a highly industrialized, modern state, with inevitable grave conflicts between deep-rooted tradition and burning ambitions to keep up with the Joneses of the west in this technological age. As the third major political movement, Soka Gakkai/Komeito could achieve a great deal at home. But what? It has never said in precise terms. Any sufficiently ruthless and shrewd leader with more sinister and definite aims than Ikeda might steer the movement into a totalitarian course, which would cause violent tremors in the whole world of the Far East.

Many Japanese critics of Soka Gakkai are well aware of the various dangers which the sect's success has engendered. Educated Buddhists condemn its intolerance towards other creeds: 'These people claim to represent True Buddhism; but prejudice and aggressiveness have nothing to do with Buddhism, which strives for total love and total wisdom, and which teaches man to fight his base instincts, his sexual lust, his gluttony and avarice, his desire for material riches and power.' Other opponents of Soka Gakkai have revealed some of the sect's objectionable tactics not only of mass propaganda but of individual pressure, such as promising financial backing to small businessmen to attract them into the fold, and then keeping them in it by economic intimidation. Even instances of Soka Gakkai hooliganism have come to light: the homes of Buddhists of other persuasions were invaded by members of the Youth Corps, shrines smashed up, believers threatened with violence, all because Soka Gakkai declares that no other faith can be tolerated.

Misgivings about the fascist tendencies and techniques of the movement seem to have been confirmed by its development. 'The trouble is,' declared a western observer in Japan some years ago, 'that this nation either wants to lead, or to be led. Soka Gakkai guarantees the fulfilment of these wishes, for the shepherd and the flock, or for some Hitler and his hordes.'

And what does Soka Gakkai want to achieve outside Japan? If we believe what its English-language magazine *Ushio* says (November 1969), it is we westerners, and the people of the developing countries, who ought to be grateful to Soka Gakkai for its efforts to help us:

Many scholars are predicting the decline of western civilization.

The tide of world history has come to a great turning point ... we are witnessing (1) the rise of non-western countries in Asia and Africa; (2) signs of despair about western civilization itself (scientific technology was believed to help mankind to realize the ideal society, but there is only disenchantment and frustration); (3) the transition from one old civilization to new individual cultures, including in 'underdeveloped' countries which had brilliant cultures when Europeans were still primitive.

There is widespread antipathy to christianity among younger people and the trend to seek new guiding principles in oriental philosophy or religion. The tide of history has begun to move from the West to the East.

So Soka Gakkai recommends us to adopt its creed and practice. It does not, however, envisage for itself a lifespan as long as that of the established religions. 'When its revelation has been accepted by the whole world,' say the leaders of the sect, 'then Soka Gakkai will have rendered itself superfluous.'

The Cherubim and Seraphim

Sunday noon outside a large old Congregational church in London's dingy western outskirts. Few people in the street, little traffic. Then, suddenly, the scene grows lively. A well-polished car arrives, then a second, then another half dozen. African women alight, many in colourful native dress with gay elaborate headgear, their children jump out, their menfolk follow: a few in long white cassocks and with round, embroidered caps, but most of them in dark Sunday suits, with neat white shirts and solemn ties. There is much chatter, laughter, bustle as they all make their way into the vestry to prepare themselves for the service. A station wagon parks at the side door of the church, drums and large white sheets are unloaded. There is the unmistakable air of a major social event.

It takes place every Sunday. The Cherubim and Seraphim sect has rented the Congregational church's building for its members, all Yorubas from Nigeria, who will spend three hours at service, keeping up their spiritual link with the homeland in the alien big city. Throughout the week they have to conform with European life and customs; but on Sunday they allow themselves to 'go native', as they call it jokingly, worshipping after their own style and taste as their fellow-believers do back home.

At the entrance, everybody is handed an immaculately dupli-
cated eight-page programme with the order of service and the
texts of the hymns, over half of them in the Yoruba language,
the rest in English. The dignitaries acting during the proceedings
are named in the programme: the Spiritual Leader of the London
branch of the Cherubim and Seraphim is an 'apostle' of the sect,
the President is an 'evangelist', the Vice-President a 'teacher';
there are a couple of 'prophets' and many 'elders', while the rest
of the congregation are plain 'brothers' and 'sisters'. Inside, they
are busy converting the Congregational church into a 'Prayer
House' for the African sect. A white cloth is spread over the
altar; they have brought their own golden cross, candles and a
bell. Flags are put at the side of the altar, one showing a
Union Jack. The drums are set up and tried out for resonance. All
the attendants wear those flowing white gowns and white caps;
hierarchical rank is indicated by coloured waistbands: yellow,
lilac, blue. In between rushing round, some of the men bow, kneel,
pray.

The organ begins to play, but the hall is not yet half full. There
is some ragged hymn-singing. Then the doors open wide, and a
procession of worshippers marches in, women and children first,
all in African dresses into which many have changed in the vestry,
followed by the white-clad men. Suddenly, the drums take over,
drowning the organ's simple European hymn with their sophisticated, irresistible African beat; and the procession takes it up,
dance-stepping, hopping, swaying, singing and clapping hands
in counter-time. One woman throws a fit – rather prematurely, it
seems – and has to be calmed down by the attendants.

When the members of the procession have taken their seats, the
church is chock-full: a gay, colourful congregation, with the
women's enormous headdresses dominating the scene; children
are playing noisily at the back; incense is sprinkled from the aisles.

On the dais around the altar, a dozen men in white sit and
stand around, chatting like members of an informal committee:
prophets, elders, teachers, with the old 'apostle' in their midst.
They do not participate much in the proceedings on the floor of
the hall, where two or three more hymns are being sung, danced,
drummed and clapped, with a good deal of bouncing, shouting,
and waving of hands – now in Yoruba, celebrating the *Egbe Seraf
ati Kerubu*, the Church of Seraphim and Cherubim (the order

of precedence does not seem to matter), now in homespun English:

> This is the day of the Lord,
> Our feast of joy is come,
> Cherubim call Seraphim
> Oh, come, behold the Lord.
> > Halleluhay sing loud, sing loud and loud,
> > Halleluhay Hossah to our King.
>
> This is a thing of wonder
> Concerning Cherubim,
> Since Christ established his Church
> There has never been such.
> > Halleluhay sing loud . . .

And loud are the drums, getting louder from one hymn to the next; the organ has long given up. The drums only stop for prayer and sermon. One of the prophets, swinging a silver baton, says three 'special prayers for pregnant women, little children, Heads of State and all Churches in all parts of the world and in particular for the Band of Glory', the sect's women and youth organization. They sing their own thanksgiving hymn, in Yoruba, which has the whole congregation heaving and swaying. 'Amin! Amin!' everybody shouts at the end. The next item is 'testimonies': members, nearly all of them women, tell of their own faith-healing experiences; there are spontaneous cries of 'Halleluhay' from the listeners, and arms are thrown up.

The sermon is in English, delivered by a 'teacher' holding a heavy, silver-knobbed stick. 'We are ambassadors of Christ,' he tells the congregation. 'I beseech you to present yourselves as a living sacrifice to God.' The members seem to have heard all this many times before, and they know at what points of the sermon they are expected to shout 'Halleluhay' at the top of their voices; the bell on the altar is rung, the band drums a few bars, everybody claps in time with its rhythm, the children at the back make an unholy row. After the sermon, a silver collection; then yet another hymn in praise of Moses Orimolade Tunolase, the founder of the sect. While the congregation heaves and sways, the teachers and elders and prophets walk, almost dancing, through the aisles in procession. The service ends amidst general laughter and singing and bouncing.

Outside, the cars are revving up; after the ecstasy, a sober return home for tea. The white cassocks have been taken off and carefully folded in the vestry, the drums stacked into the station wagon. The women's gay dresses disappear behind the car doors. Within a quarter of an hour or so, the street is as grey and empty as before.

The Cherubim and Seraphim Church is only one of a number of African sects catering for the spiritual needs of black immigrants in England, though probably the biggest and, as the events of 1969–70 showed, the most influential one in its homeland Nigeria. It is characteristic of these sects that each of them originates in one particular African country and has been brought to Europe by emigrants from it. Dahomey, for instance, has sent its Celestial Church of Christ to Britain, where believers meet and worship in the converted parlours of working-class houses in London and the industrial Midlands with their large groups of African expatriates. The Celestial Church owes its existence to the eclipse of the sun in September 1947, visible from West Africa, when a Dahomeyan carpenter by the name of Oschoffa was visited by Jesus, who 'robed him with a white gown studded with stars' and told him : 'I want to send you to the world. Good many people who profess to be Christians will in time of trouble run to the devil and his agents and are usually there given the mark of the beast (Rev. 13, 16). When such people die, they cannot see the glory of heaven and of Jesus Christ. I will show a lot of wonders through you to show the world that I indeed had sent you.'

We do not know what happened to Oschoffa after this communication, but the faithful say that the Celestial Church he founded 'was later revealed by the Holy Spirit to be an earthly branch of the Church in Heaven', and that the Holy Spirit himself gave it its name 'first in French, then in the Dahomeyan language of Egun, and eventually in English and Yoruba when the Church arrived in Nigeria'. The Holy Spirit also gave the sect all the hymns used in worship, and 'more songs descend daily even now'. The Holy Spirit also took the trouble of 'dictating through the prophets' the exact mode of worship: the faithful are allowed to sit on benches and chairs only on Sundays; on all other days they sit on the floor so they can touch the ground with their foreheads. This, and the command to come barefoot, points to Islamic influences; so does the prohibition of alcohol and pork. All full members must worship in white robes whose design 'has been meticulously described through the Holy Spirit to be in agreement with robes used in Heaven above'.

In their little English parlour-chapels, where the believers meet three times a week, ministers practice faith-healing ('Many miracles including the raising of the dead have been wrought by Christ in this Church'). There they often pray and fast all night if a member is seriously ill; tap water is 'made holy' for treatment and baptism; visions and revelations are described by members of the congregation, which responds with singing, shouting, dancing; 'unholy spirits that roam this sinful world' are driven out, for the Celestial Church 'has been given power to overcome all satanic influences – power over witchcraft and sorcery'.

These African exiles in England, unlike the Cherubim and Seraphim members, are mostly poor unskilled labourers; they emphasize that 'Christ's first appearance on earth was in lowly circumstances', and that 'the Church He Himself founded has been disturbed over the centuries by sin and intellectualism' ever since the days when 'the over-enlightened Jewish Rabbis failed to recognize the Messiah'. This and other African sects brought to England by the immigrants, with their strange mixture of missionary Christianity, voodoo concepts, and Mohammedanism, probably fulfil a real need in an often hostile western industrial society even more than in Africa; they are a spiritual and social retreat for a harassed racial minority. But then, amalgams of religious beliefs are almost a tradition in Africa itself. In his book *Through African Doors*, the German explorer Janheinz Jahn writes:

African religion knows many gods. Each is a force, as Man is himself ... The more people worship a god, the stronger he is, the more he can strengthen the power of his worshippers. To offend none of the gods, you must worship them all in due and fitting manner. Many African Christians, I would think, have remained true to their traditional faiths, and many Christian sects in Africa, in their ritual at least, are not 'Christian' by European standards.

The Italian sociologist Vittorio Lanternari, in his fascinating study of modern Messianic cults (*The Religions of the Oppressed*), sees Africa's 'religious ferment' in our time as a historical phenomenon which preceded the political struggle for freedom from colonial rule, accompanied the birthpangs of independence among the new nations, and is still shaking them as they are trying to find a new way of life after liberation. Native societies, says Lanternari, seek relief from their frustration and sufferings under foreign rule in religious ways, often even before they rebel politically: 'In such a situation all the manifestations of the native culture become permeated by a deeply religious spirit.' And ironically it is the foreign oppressor's religion, Christianity, in which the oppressed seek relief, though interspersing it with all kinds of notions from their old tribal beliefs and from other religions. 'At first we had the land, and you had the Bible,' was the African agitators' cry to the whites; 'now we have the Bible, and you have the land.' Even after the land was returned into African hands, how much political and economic influence the whites managed to retain is another matter, the Bible remained, interpreted in various ways by the innumerable sects that had sprung up.

Nigeria, the largest independent African state on the West Coast, has a particularly big share of sects and cults. A few years after independence, the Nigerian edition of the leading African magazine *Drum* reported:

In every nook and corner of Nigeria, at all hours of day or night, voices can be heard, muttering alarmingly or yelling like spirits-possessed. Ominous and awe-inspiring, they warn Nigerians: 'Flee from the imminent wrath to come!'—a crescendo of ecstatic nihilism ... The noise comes from the leaders of certain new churches; they have distinguishing marks: they can be noticed among thousands in the streets of Nigeria by their flowing robes, red and scarlet bands, or the jazzy tunes accompanying them. Many new religions are trying to knock the life out of the established religions—the Cherubim and Seraphim, the Church of Our Lord, the Christ Apostolic Church. The members have in common their love of jazz, their gloating over the approaching doom of mankind, their love of candles and white flowing robes. They are screaming to alert mankind to the realization of the spiritual filth in which it languishes to its unalterable damnation.

Drum quoted one of the leaders of a new sect: 'The trouble in this country is that many churchgoers have surrendered their power of reason to their church leaders. Many Nigerians, like us, should have realized that the Protestant and Catholic dogmas only lead to a dead end, and that they can find their God only by interpreting the Bible, as we are doing, literally.' There is certainly an element of reaction against the 'white man's Christianity' among those scores of separatist churches and their missionaries. Richard Hall, reporter of the Gemini News Service and formerly editor of the *Times of Zambia*, listed some of the bizarre names of Nigerian sects: the Donkey Church, the Kitchen Boys Church, the King-George-the-Fifth-Win-the-War Church; he estimated the total sect membership in thirty African countries at about eight million.

Apart from their belief in the rapid approach of Doomsday, a common feature of these sects is that their members are asked no more than to attend worship and pay their fees regularly: otherwise, the sect leaders seem little interested in them. This is one point about which the established churches express their particular concern. A Roman Catholic priest told *Drum*: 'If you believe that the end of the world is near, of course you will have no need to hoard money. You will have every reason to pay up your tithes. Is there any wonder that the leaders of some of these strange churches live like lords? Their members pay their tickets to heaven, but the money lands in the purses of the leaders.' Or, as *Drum* put it: 'These leaders are well-to-do men and women, wealthier than senior civil servants or big businessmen. They have no other jobs; many gave up their former trades for lucrative sect leadership. They are taking thousands of Nigerians for a spiritual ride.'

It may seem that politics play merely a negative part in African sectarianism, as a symptom of withdrawal from the complexities of community life, a voluntary forsaking of the citizens' right to participate in public and national affairs in favour of spiritual salvation; the sects, which occupy a man's or woman's mind much more than religion does in western countries, are apparently safety valves for emotions that would otherwise find political outlets. Yet there have been instances in which sects took sides in political struggles, or let themselves be misused for political ends. In the early 1900s, only a decade or so after large-scale conversion to Christianity had begun in Buganda, two sects even fought a violent war with each other. In the Belgian Congo, during the Katanga trouble, some sects turned militant and sided with either Lumumba or Tshombe. In Ruanda-Urundi, before independence, some religious bodies cooperated with the colonial administration in supporting the Bahutu, who favoured the *status quo*, in their struggle against the Watusi, who wanted their own state.

Disastrous in human as well as in political terms was the 'holy war' of the fanatical Alice Movement or Lumpa Church in the copperbelt of what was then Northern Rhodesia (now Zambia) in the 1950s and early 1960s. The sect was founded by Alice Lenshina, a simple country girl of the Bemba tribe, who was born in about 1920; she grew up in the same Nyasaland village and went to the same Scottish mission school as Kenneth Kaunda, her junior by a few years, who later, as Prime Minister, ordered his childhood friend to be captured 'dead or alive'.

Alice married a cousin of Kaunda, Petrus Mulenga, a Roman Catholic; however, she felt that she was called upon to found her own church. The dumpy little woman, with a great gift of the gab and much personal magnetism, had discovered that she could sway any size of audience among her fellow-tribesmen. The foundation of the Lumpa movement was a rather dramatic act: having suffered some sort of stroke in 1953, she declared that she had died and gone up to heaven; there she saw the Almighty, who sent her back to earth to preach to the Bembas and other tribes. This she did with enormous fervour and success; the faith she preached was approximately Christian in character, but mixed with African anti-white extremism. She promised immortality, salvation, and God's exclusive help to her followers; she forbade them to go to other missions or churches, and baptized them *en masse*. The story goes that once she ordered the people of her village to strip naked and stand in pouring rain 'to cleanse them from their sins'; but those who had forfeited redemption would be 'struck dead by lightning', and nature obliged soon afterwards: lightning struck a tree, and two people were in fact killed.

Her fame spread quickly, and from all over the region Africans came to hear her preach and to join the Lumpa sect. At one time it was estimated to have some seventy-five thousand members, and the African National Congress, with Kaunda as its general secretary, tried to size it up as a potential ally; but the movement and its prophetess seemed too weird and unpredictable to be of much help on the African countries' road to independence. One day, Alice Lenshina would work up her faithful into hysterics with her battle-cry to drive all whites from African soil; the next day she would assure the politicians that her main targets were the witch doctors and the sway they were exercising over tribal life. In fact, piles of discarded sorcerers' paraphernalia could be seen round all the grass-roofed chapels which her followers had built.

In 1958, friction between the Lumpa and the African nationalists began with Alice's strict ruling that her followers should have nothing to do with any political parties, and particularly not with Kaunda's African National Congress whose canvassers were trying to enroll her followers as members. There were repeated clashes, especially with Kaunda's militant youth organization. The Lumpa sect reacted by forming its own 'warrior' cadres, which started a violent guerilla war against the Congress and the authorities, black and white. Armed with Lenshina's 'passports to heaven' and spears, lethal at twenty yards' range or less, her warriors grew into a serious threat to the social and economic life of a country which had to show the world that it was mature enough for independence. Still Kaunda hesitated to throw the armed forces at his command into the campaign against the troublesome sect, and Lenshina was able to consolidate her rule over a region of hundreds of square miles in Northern Rhodesia, declaring a holy ˙ ar against the state.

Near Chinsali her followers built an enormous shrine of the Lumpa Church, 150 feet long, fifty feet wide and lavishly furnished. For months, many hundreds of them came daily from the surrounding countryside, laying brick upon brick until the building, modelled on a Roman Catholic church some distance away, was finished. The prophetess dedicated it to her warriors. When it was finished, the faithful erected a luxurious bungalow for her, her husband and her five children. But she did not live there for very long; the inevitable great clash came in 1964.

Encouraged by the prophetess's promise either that the enemy's bullets would turn to water or that death for the Lumpa Church would assure them of eternity in paradise, a group of her warriors, together with other fanatic followers and even their women and children, attacked some policemen who were investigating incidents at Chapaula; a white officer was killed, another wounded. Police reinforcements were called in, five Lenshina followers were killed. Further clashes followed, and a platoon of troops were sent to capture Lenshina's stronghold near Chinsali. Sixty-five Lumpas were shot dead in the violent fighting, but Alice had fled. The troubles spread to other districts; in one encounter, 150 people were reported killed, in another seventy-four. After three weeks of holy war, the death roll was estimated at seven hundred. Kaunda, just elected first president of the new state of Zambia, was faced with the urgent problem of quelling the Lumpa uprising and forced to mobilize one third of the national army. Alice Lenshina was found and surrendered to the government troops. She was sent to a remote camp some 160 miles north of the capital, Lusaka, where she was held in restriction while many of her followers were forcibly resettled, with government officials supervising their rehabilitation. About twenty thousand others were said to have fled to the neighbouring Congo.

After a few years, Alice was released, but when she began again to rally groups of believers she was put back in detention as a 'security risk' in 1970.

The African sect which interfered most actively in a full-scale war, thus giving the wheel of history a determined push, were the Cherubim and Seraphim. Watching the happy crowd of their London branch enjoying themselves at their Sunday service, one finds it difficult to think of the sect as a deadly disruptive force during the last stage of the tragic Biafran war in 1969-70. It was a historical episode that could have happened only in Africa.

The cult had been founded by Moses Orimolade Tunolase, a Yoruba from Ikarre in the province of Ondo. He was an Anglican born around 1900 and baptized as a child; he was paralysed in both legs, but his family's fervent prayers – or so they believed – helped him to regain the full use of his limbs by the time he was a young man. He began to evangelise the natives who were still worshipping their tribal gods, and later moved on to Lagos. His prayer meetings were not too well attended, but in 1925 an extraordinary event put him on the road to success. During the Corpus Christi procession in that year, a Yoruba girl, Abiodun Akinsowon, suddenly 'saw a celestial being of wondrous beauty' walking at her side. The divine creature stayed with her for three months, during which the girl fell ill with an obscure disease that nearly killed her.

One day, when Abiodun was delirious with fever or perhaps in a state of trance, she asked to see Moses Orimolade as the only man who could make her well again. He came, prayed for her, and her health was restored. The story spread quickly through Lagos and his following increased at once. He went into a trance, fasted for three days, and then declared that he had been called upon to found a religious society to be call 'Seraphim' after the angels of the highest hierarchical order in heaven, gifted with the power of love and associated with purity, light and ardour. A few days later, some angels appeared to a group of women worshippers, pleading that the name of the sect should be changed to 'Seraphim and Cherubim', thus including the second highest order of celestial beings, gifted with knowledge. Orimolade obeyed, and the number of his followers multiplied again. They were mainly recruited from the masses of villagers pouring into Lagos at a time when the colonial administration tried to impose a new economic and social order on the tribal districts, with disastrous effects of uprooting and unemployment. These people coming to the city from the provinces sought spiritual refuge within the framework of Orimolade's new sect, converts from paganism, Islam and missionary Christianity which did not cater enough for their needs.

Until his death in 1932, Orimolade, revered as 'Baba Aladura', 'Father of the Prayerful', expanded the sect most efficiently, helped by his dedicated disciples who preached in his name up and down Nigeria, particularly the Yoruba regions, and in Dahomey. Abiodun followed him as leader of the Cherubim and Seraphim. Today, the number of followers is estimated at over half a million.

They are most spectacularly in evidence in Lagos. 'Looking out of my window in a suburb,' wrote the British photographer Peter Larsen in his book *Young Africa* (1964), 'I saw a congregation of the Cherubim and Seraphim sect, dancing in a circle, and chanting about the Holy Ghost in the Yoruba language.' Richard Hall, the *Gemini* correspondent in West Africa at the time of the Biafran war, reported that the sect was holding 'hectic meetings at night on the seashore', with flowing white robes, drums, convulsions, orgiastic ecstasy, and bells to drive out evil spirits. 'Political leaders would come from all over the Federation to have their fortunes told . . . The sect also thrives in Ghana and has links with America. Some of its leaders have been to the United States, imitating the religious "spirit-raising" groups which are in business there.' Perhaps the most impressive and frightening picture of a meeting of the sect in its homeland has been given by a *Drum* correspondent, himself an African, in 1968:

It will need a very hard-headed man to stay through a church service of the Cherubim and Seraphim without going ga-ga. The set-up is never laid out to convince reason but to astound it, to bully it and render it useless. For instance, the church songs are never like orthodox church hymns. They have the marching headiness of martial songs or the whimpering of despair for the ultimate agony of mankind—throbbing, hopeless, harsh, jazzy, supplicating, with an undertone that suggests that what is being supplicated for will not be granted. They are songs of people who have renounced the world.

The worship itself also has an alarming setting. All the members pray at the same time in a manner that suggests that they are not requesting but commanding God, in many different tongues and languages. After this will come a moment of silence. All the worshippers will gaze into space, seeing or hearing nobody and nothing, but with their minds presumably fixed on the seventh heaven. Then, suddenly, one of the worshippers will start to yell gibberish—he is possessed by the Holy Spirit. Not even the most worldly and cynical of men will attend one of these services without the impression that the worshippers are often face to face with God—or in warm embrace with the devil himself.

When the Ibos of Eastern Nigeria began their rebellion against the Federation in 1967, there was little evidence that religious factors played a relevant part in what soon developed into a major civil war, with the secession of the whole region as a new state called Biafra. The Ibos, often described as the best educated and most sophisticated people in West Africa, had valid economic and political reasons for their deep dissatisfaction with the Federation which, after all, was a more or less artificial structure that had already been upset by the splitting-off of Camaroun and shaken by *coups d'état* and political assassinations in its short life. There was much friction between the industrious and prosperous Ibos, numbering some six million, and the mainly agricultural five million Yorubas.

At first a local tribal struggle, the Biafran war grew into a battlefield of European and world powers, not unlike the Spanish Civil War in the 1930s. Only here, the ideological frontiers were confused by economic and political interests, with none of the capitalist or Communist countries involved even pretending, as usual, to be on the side of justice and humanity. It was a most unholy alliance that lined up behind the Federation. Russian, American and British planes and Czechoslovak guns went into action against the rebels, who accepted help from whoever was prepared to sell them weapons, such as France, or to fight for money, such as former *Luftwaffe* pilots and Swedish mercenaries, in a savage struggle which devastated one of Africa's best developed regions and reduced a proud people to abject poverty and starvation. An entire generation of Ibo children was decimated, a flourishing economy crushed. 'All told, the war killed roughly two million people,' reported *Life* magazine in January 1970, when it was all over and Biafra had ceased to exist:

Most died of hunger, but countless others were killed in pogrom-like massacres, in modern military engagements fought with the latest European weaponry, in air raids and in hand-to-hand combat. For now at least, conquering Nigeria could claim to have preserved itself as a nation; but its unity is grotesquely diminished by tribal hatreds ... The big powers had given generously of relief supplies and sympathy; but neither they, the United Nations nor other African nations were able to prevent or minimize the suffering. They proved all over again the ineffectiveness of that elusive dream, the 'conscience of the world'.

Yet the sudden collapse of Biafran resistance in the last days of 1969 took the world by surprise, particularly the collapse of the superbly trained and equipped crack division, the Twelfth Division, which had been putting up a magnificent defence on the vital Owerri front. Just before Christmas, the division crumbled; there was a disastrous, chaotic retreat, Owerri was lost, and within a short time Biafra was no more. Immediately after the fiasco of the Twelfth Division, the Biafran leader, General Ojukwu, ordered its disbandment and demoted its commander to head of the fire brigade. This was no 'ordinary' military defeat; some other decisive factor must have been involved, some unknown, even uncanny element. How, for instance, could one explain the ghastly scene of senior Biafran officers, armed only with sticks, walking nonchalantly into the firing line, to be mowed down by a hail of Federal bullets? It happened dozens of times. They did it because they were firmly convinced that they were invisible, or immune to bullets, or both, according to what they had paid for these 'miracles', which again depended on their rank: up to £400 for 'bullet-proofing' and up to £800 for 'invisibility'. Other available spells were supposed to make officers and soldiers immune against rockets, gas, witchcraft, VD or genocide; there was also an 'anti-conscription oil' for civilians. Among the known buyers were one lieutenant-general, several frontline commanders, some tribal chiefs, a leading barrister and the ex-mayor of Port Harcourt; the number of junior officers and other ranks who, by paying spiritual protection money, relied on magic instead of resistance must have run into thousands.

The sellers were leaders of the Cherubim and Seraphim Church. Whether they had come to Biafra merely to start a membership drive and found that spell-mongering in the war-torn, terrified country was good business, or whether it was some kind of Federal plot to undermine Biafran resistance in this way, perhaps we shall never know for sure; but John Porter, war correspondent of the *Scottish Catholic Observer,* managed to bring out documents which seem to point to the latter possibility: that there had been a planned campaign to sabotage, corrupt and disrupt the Biafran army. A senior military administrator handed him the documents in a locked case. 'I thought it was the records of the Marist Brothers [a Roman-Catholic missionary order],' he said. He took it with him when he flew out of beaten Biafra from Uli airport. When he broke it open he found hundreds of documents compiled by Lieutenant-Colonel B. N. Gbulie, the Sandhurst-trained administrator, all relating to the activities of the Cherubim and Seraphim and particularly to their Biafran 'prophet', a man called 'D.D.' by his followers. He was arrested in the last month of the war, and his bank account showed that he had amassed nearly £43,000. His real name was Okenni.

'D.D.' had been responsible for setting up churches and local branches of the sect, which had never made much progress among the well-educated Ibos in peacetime, throughout the breakaway region. Services were always packed; but the great attraction were the spells which his assistants sold with absolute assurance that they were infallible. Joining the sect cost a mere £2 per head, but the spells and 'instant-cure' magic medicines brought in the real money.

This business flourished particularly near the front, where meetings were held every Tuesday night. A favourite performance of the sect was to bring two 'powerful spirits', called Miss Power and Doctor White, 'down through the ceiling'; these spirits were often invoked and asked for their help and advice. Officers and men of the Biafran army, reported Richard Hall in his dispatches for *Gemini,* flocked to the meetings, bringing gifts of money and precious food. Even some senior members of the secessionist government went along during Biafra's last months, seeking advice and comfort. 'To Biafra's outgunned and out-numbered soldiers,' wrote Richard Hall, 'any possible shield against death was worth a try.' One of the sect's top attractions was an anonymous 'prophetess' who specialized in telling high-ranking officers their future for considerable sums.

Lieutenant-Colonel Gbulie wrote to the Biafran leader, General Ojukwu, warning him of the military dangers in the Okenni cult; when action was eventually taken, the churches raided and Okenni arrested, it was too late. Thousands of letters were found; one, quoted by John Porter, came from an officer of the Eighth Infantry, then still at Enugu: 'Our people have gone through the darkest period of agony and sorrow. Thousands have died and many more thousands will die. That is why many of us are begging increasingly that you [the Cherubim and Seraphim] will help us to lessen this agony of pain and death.'

That 'help', in the form of quackery with spells and charms or downright advice to desert, was the final blow against the de-fenders of Biafra. Yet even the palpable failure of the sect's 'magic' did rarely shake the faith of the believers; if a soldier was killed just after paying protection money, the Cherubim and Seraphim explained the mishap away: he had been 'fighting on the wrong day'. Protection money was collected as far away as in London, where the Biafra Office distributed leaflets by the Cherubim and Seraphim, calling on Biafrans in Britain to send donations so that prayers could be said for their relatives at the front or in the war zone. Many of the expatriates paid; would they have done so had they suspected that the sect was Federal Nigeria's secret weapon?

The commander of the Twelfth Division whom Ojukwu sent down to the fire brigade was himself found to be a keen member of the Cherubim and Seraphim, reported Richard Hall. 'The Ibos will be looking for a lot of advice now as they learn to live again with the Nigeria they tried to leave,' he added. 'For better or worse, Miss Power and Doctor White are sure to be waiting.'

8

Twisted
Russian Souls

The Castrators

Some time in the seventeenth century, a deserter from the Russian army called Danilo Filippov felt the urge to become a hermit and made his home in a cave on the banks of the Volga. Equipped with the Bible and other religious books, he devoted himself to preaching to the peasants who came to see the holy man; but after a while he saw that these works could not help him to solve their problems and allay their anxieties. So he packed his books into a sack and threw it into the river. He had come to the conclusion that the 'living book', the Holy Spirit within every man's soul, and not the Bible was the true word of God. Christ, he believed, had been born an ordinary human being, but on the Cross he rose in the spirit as he died in the flesh; and this spirit was resurrected in every generation.

He himself was such a resurrection, he claimed, a new living Christ. He found at least one believer and successor, Ivan Suslov, who carried on and extended Filippov's missionary work. Suslov 'appointed' twelve apostles and established his sect in a ruined church in a Volga village. When Suslov died in 1716, the sect had already split up into various groups, all of them with unusual creeds and rites. Among the new sects which eventually emerged were the Khlysty, from *khlyst* a horsewhip, who expressed their faith by lashing each other in ritual dances; the Dukhobors, from *dukha* spirit and *borets* fighter, and the Skoptsy, the 'castrators'. These sects all acknowledged Danilo Filippov as their spiritual ancestor and leader in dissent from the Russian Orthodox Church, and they all believed more or less in his doctrine of the divine spirit residing in man and in the incessant resurrection of Christ.

Flagellantism as an atonement for one's own sins, whether committed or imaginary, and for the sins of mankind in general, has been known in Christian countries since the thirteenth century, and developed into organized sects after the Black Death in western and central Europe; so the Khlysty were nothing new. Rasputin, the mystic monk at the last Tsar's court, was one of them. But the Skoptsy took the idea to the very end of its tether, and we can only guess what dreadful twist of the Russian soul, what perverted sexual impulse made them adopt castration as the condition of membership and rite of initiation.

Sects of flagellants were still widespread in Russia in the eighteenth century when the movement had all but died out in western Europe, and one such sect gave birth to the Skoptsy in the late 1750s. Only about fifteen years later did the authorities hear about them when a peasant from the district of Orel by the name of Andrei Ivanov was arrested and charged with having incited a dozen of his fellow peasants to mutilate themselves, or one another, by cutting off their genitals amidst orgies of chanting and dancing. The case was heard at a court in St Petersburg, and people in the capital could hardly believe the evidence, confirmed by medical witnesses. Ivanov's examination seemed to point to some strange urge to suppress a man's sexual powers for the greater glory of God, in an ecstasy of cleansing their souls from all 'base' instincts of the flesh.

Ivanov was sentenced to be flogged and exiled to Siberia, where he died, but his principal associate, young Kondratji Selivanov, had escaped. It turned out later that he had gone to the neighbouring district of Tambov, south of Moscow, and started a new branch of the sect there. He preached to the peasants that spiritual fulfilment and salvation could only be attained by the supreme sacrifice of castration, preferably in self-mutilation. Around 1775, Selivanov – a fat and hairless eunuch – moved to Moscow, gathering disciples and holding mutilation meetings at which the Skoptsy worked themselves up into a wild and bloody frenzy. He was caught at last and also flogged and exiled, but he managed to flee from Siberia. Again he turned up in Moscow, again he was caught, in 1797, and brought before Tsar Paul I, who had expressed curiosity about the lunatic sect. Paul had him confined to a madhouse. In 1801, however, the mystical young

Emperor Alexander I acceded to the throne after Paul's assassination, and heard about Selivanov through his woman friend, the Baroness Krüdner, who believed in magic and the occult. She had him released from the asylum, and introduced him to her aristocratic friends, whom she convinced that he was a saint.

Incredibly, Selivanov was able to convert quite a number of the Baroness' friends to his cult, collecting membership fees and donations which paid for a magnificent mansion where he presided over meetings. His disciples believed that he was a reincarnation of Christ himself, by way of some nebulous noble ancestry involving Tsar Peter III and the Tsarina Elizabeth Petrovna, who was said to have lived incognito in the house of a Skoptsy prophet in the Orel district and acquired magic powers – inherited, of course, by Selivanov.

No doubt, this peasant and self-styled saint now enjoyed the protection of the most influential people in Russia, particularly that of State Councillor Jelanski who was said to be a secret member of the sect, himself castrated and a castrator of new aristocratic members; other high officials, however, regarded the sect as a dangerous nuisance and so did the police.

Eventually, the authorities succeeded in getting Selivanov confined to a monastery. Immediately, he declared that he would never die; but he did die, though at a very ripe old age, in 1832. His followers never accepted that their Redeemer, as they called him, had really passed away, and the cult continued to flourish in secrecy. One of Selivanov's most ardent disciples, a former army captain by the name of Sosonovitch, was also sent to a monastery; the monks there brought him back into the fold of the Orthodox Church and the abbot made him reveal a great deal of information about the sect, particularly its cult centres and contacts.

From Sosonovitch's information it appeared that, in European Russia at least, it had spread to most districts and towns; this meant that its appeal must have been equally strong among widely different people, from the Baltic to the Black Sea, and from the borders of Poland to the Urals. Large communities of the People of God, as the Skoptsy liked to call themselves, existed on the shores of the White Sea, in St Petersburg itself, where, curiously, most of the gold and silversmiths were members, and the whole of the Crimea. In other parts of the country it was the builders, carpenters, or hackney-carriage drivers who belonged to the sect in great numbers. A post-Selivanov development (we do not know when it started) was the easing of the dreadful initiation rites: members were allowed to sire two children, in some branches of the sect only one, before having to submit to castration, thus becoming full members.

Tsar Nicholas i, who had suppressed the Dekabrist and the Polish rebellions with cruel determination, ordered the Skoptsy movement to be stamped out ruthlessly. Hundreds were rounded up and sent to Siberia, but thousands remained unknown to the police, spreading the cult like an epidemic; not only in Russia but also in other Slav countries such as Serbia and Bulgaria, where it took the form of political resistance against the Turkish occupants. From there, Turkey itself seems to have become infected, and Skoptsy communities were found as far south as the Lebanon. For all we know, they still exist there.

Students of the sect have come to the conclusion that redemption by castration alone could not have accounted for its enormous attraction; after all, a man's supreme sacrifice would not be undertaken unless he believed that there were important comp-ensations also in this world. Lapsed Skoptsy hinted that there was a secret which was revealed to members only after castration – the secret of power over other people, an almost godlike power, including that of working miracles. No doubt the castrati believed in some such potency, supposed to be vastly superior to the lost sexual one.

Other prophets rose from the ranks of the Skoptsy. In 1865, the authorities in a district bordering on the Sea of Azov were informed that the sect was acquiring greater numbers of new recruits; they were attracted by a peasant woman called Babanina who was said to be able to cure all diseases, speak with the voices of the dead and procure favours from influential people anywhere in Russia by what we might call telepathic hypnotism. The prophetess and many of her followers were banished to Siberia.

In European Russia, the Skoptsy came mainly from the ignorant peasantry on the one hand and from the upper society of idle neurotics on the other, with certain groups of small traders and craftsmen in the middle. But by the end of last century, groups of exiled Skoptsy had settled in Siberia as communities, particularly in the Yakutsk region. They were hard workers and, having deprived themselves of the joys of marital life, seem to have regarded money and possessions as part of their compensation. As there were few young people among them, due to the one- or two-children limitation, they needed workers and found them among another group of exiles, the Dukhobors, spiritually related through their common veneration for Danilo Filippov, the Volga prophet. The Dukhobors, however, found the Skoptsy severe taskmasters: greedy and mean, these 'pious castrati', as the Dukhobors called them, made their labourers work for sixteen hours a day in summer as in winter, with only short intervals for meals. Many Dukhobors got ill and died of cold and exhaustion, having to work in the fields and woods with frost lying on the ground most of the year. The only bright aspect for the Dukhobors was that they were regarded as equals by their employers, in contrast to the rest of Russia where the *kulak*, the land-owning farmer, ruled like a little tsar over his labourers.

Strangely enough, the Dukhobors in Siberia never complained about attempts to convert them by the Skoptsy, although conversion was one of their principal aims in European Russia, for their belief was that one day the whole of the Tsar's realm would be ruled by them; they did not seem to worry about the rapidly falling birthrate if this dream came true. Instant conversions on a mass scale did indeed occur in various places, such as in Morchansk in the Tambov district. On New Year's Eve, 1869, the police chief of the town was trying to forget his worries about the Skoptsy with their orgies and pseudo-religious hallucinations, their influence over the minds of the people and growing power. Suddenly, a messenger appeared with a letter from an important local merchant, asking for the release of three Skoptsy women prisoners just for the night; they would be brought back in the morning. Ten thousand-rouble notes were enclosed as a bribe.

The police chief handed the matter over to the criminal investigation branch, the merchant was arrested, charged with attempted bribery and his house searched, or rather his complex of houses, which turned out to be undercellared with large vaults full of treasure chests containing gold and banknotes. But the police also found files with correspondence with many wealthy people in various parts of Russia, including a well-known banker in St Petersburg, said to be a millionaire. The letters revealed that they were all members of the Skoptsy sect and that their activities were clearly aimed at increasing their influence through bribery, with the ultimate aim of taking over the Russian establishment.

Why did the Morchansk Skoptsy want the three imprisoned women released for one night? Why were women involved at all in a cult that was based on the ritual removal of male genitals? Cross-questioned, the merchant and other Skoptsy brought before the police investigators admitted that the women were needed to whip up the sexual frenzy of the sect's rites. However, for the Skoptsy of Morchansk the time of rites was over. The merchant, twelve other men, and nineteen women, all Skoptsy, were tried and summarily dispatched to Siberia. But the case did not end there. The merchant's correspondence files were sent to the central police authorities in the capital, and orders went out from there to arrest and try on conspiracy charges all those whose membership in the sect was revealed in the letters. A string of trials in various towns, taking up the best part of two years, followed the Morchansk incident; further names of members came to light, some very well-known ones among them, and it was hoped that the sect had now been essentially rooted out. The revelations during questioning were such that the authorities censored the publication of any names and details to prevent unrest among the population.

Neither was the press allowed to hint at the kind of rites in which the Skoptsy indulged, and the true extent of the horrors became known only after the Russian revolution when the secret police files of Tsarist times were found. What the accused revealed, probably under police torture, combined with medical examination, was the most dreadful sexual and sado-masochistic aberration. The castration rite, called 'seal of god' or 'baptism of fire', was believed to be the only way to eternal salvation and, as we know, to magical power over other men. The highest form of sacrifice, called the 'great seal', was the cutting off not only of the scrotum but the penis as well, while the 'lesser seal' meant only 'ordinary' castration, the removal of the testicles. Normal sexual relations, whether marital or extra-marital, were not only the original sin – they were the deadliest sin of all; so the candidate for membership had to write his parents' names on a piece of paper and stamp on it to document his contempt for the sinners who had brought him into the world.

Saturday night was cult night for the Skoptsy. These weekly meetings were routine ones, as distinct from the irregular initiation ceremonies. The meeting room had to be chosen with care to prevent discovery and intrusion; if possible on a farm, far away from other houses; secret doors were often built to make escape into the fields possible in an emergency, and the leading members of the group would sometimes flee through a bee-house to discourage pursuers.

Special dresses were worn on cult night: long, white smocks, closed at the neck and with waist-girdles, by the men; blue nankeen or chintz gowns with white cloths as a headgear, by the women. Both sexes had white handkerchiefs in their hands and wore either white stockings or were barefooted.

Cult meetings were often conducted by a woman, the prophetess, and began with the singing of rhythmical hymns with words that did not make much sense and were not supposed to. What mattered was the rhythm, accentuated by a small drum, compelling one after the other of the worshippers to move and contort their bodies, and accelerating until some of them fell into a trance, speaking with tongues or rapping out commands and prophecies. Eventually, everybody joined in a frenzied dance, arms extended, with jerking steps and twitching faces.

Initiation ceremonies were, of course, a rather different matter. When a Skoptsy had found a likely candidate for conversion, he subjected him to a series of private sermons aimed at making the victim conscious of his sins, instilling the fear of hellfire in him and rousing in him the desire to seek redemption the Skoptsy way. Once he had reached that stage, the tutor remained almost constantly at the candidate's elbow, talking to him about the joys of being a member of such an exclusive, influential group with magic powers that would one day enable them to take over the whole of Russia.

With other candidates, he was introduced to the group at one of their secret meetings and the date of the initiation ceremony was fixed. The candidate had to take this oath: 'I swear that I will come to the Redeemer of my own free will; that I shall keep everything about this holy matter secret from the Tsar, from princes, from my parents, relatives and friends; and that I shall rather endure persecution, torture and death than reveal any part of our mysteries to strangers or enemies.'

What puzzles the student of the history of the Skoptsy is the comparatively high proportion of educated people, aristocrats, officers, civil servants, priests and members of the well-to-do middle classes among them. The documents that have survived offer no explanation for this fact; one report says rather drily that the breakdown of known Skoptsy members according to their social class showed 'the same proportion of peasants to people of rank as among the general population'. In the course of the Morchansk affair, a statistical survey was compiled, according to which the Skoptsy group charged with plotting against the state consisted of 2,736 peasants, 443 soldiers (including some of their wives and daughters), 148 merchants, 119 landowners, ten army and five naval officers, four gentlemen and four ladies of the nobility, 14 civil servants, 19 priests and 220 middle-class citizens, also including many women.

Police records also reveal details about the horrible initiation ceremonies. Investigated cases showed that among more than 600 locations where the operations took place, nearly 100 were carried out in farms and suburban houses, 223 in fields and deserted roads, 136 in woods, 32 in barns, 42 in baths, 6 in cellars and 19 in prisons. No less detailed are the figures of the methods by which castrations were performed. Although the Skoptsy term was baptism of fire, because the sect believed that the operation was originally done with red-hot irons, all kinds of instruments were used. Among about 350 cases, 164 castrations were done with knives, 108 with razors, 30 with small hatchets, 23 with scythes and 17 with pieces of iron, tin, glass and so on. Perhaps the most gruesome fact which came to light was that a great many women were among the 'operators', about 40 among every 100 castrators as an average. The highest proportion of women was found in peasant groups. There are no figures about the rate of self-mutilation compared to castration by other members, nor about the death-rate following operations, which must have been high.

The hope that the sect was finished after the trials in the wake of the Morchansk case was not fulfilled; in fact, the remaining Skoptsy themselves spread the word that victimization only served to increase their power. A number of the convicted members of the sect were put in monasteries, with the effect that they converted some monks to their creed. True to the Skoptsy technique of undermining the establishment by bribes and gifts, the more wealthy among them endowed churches and paid substantial sums to clerics, which made them their supporters and protectors, and as a result many rural and small-town communities looked upon the Skoptsy as their benefactors. This was still the case in the early years of the present century.

It was only with the beginning of the Soviet régime that the sect began to die out slowly. But isolated groups still exist in Russia, as we know from recent Soviet publications, and larger communities appear to have survived in Rumania. However, the fearsome creed itself has seen to it that there are few descendants.

The Dukhobors

The Dukhobors, or spirit-fighters, often translated as 'ghost-wrestlers', would have remained a non-violent, quiet, pacifist sect among the Russian peasantry, had the Tsarist authorities left them in peace. They flourished particularly in the southern Ukraine, where the first of their acknowledged leaders appeared around the middle of the eighteenth century. He was an itinerant preacher by the name of Sylvan Kolesnikov; he claimed to be a guardian of Filippov's teachings and gave his flock as sacraments bread, salt and water, the symbols of life. 'Let us bow to the God in each other,' he preached, 'for we are the image of God on earth.' Until this day, the Dukhobors express this devotion to God in Man by greeting each other with a deep bow, and they kneel and touch the ground with their brows before their leaders.

Kolesnikov was wise enough to make his followers refrain from any obvious heretic rituals: 'So long as you keep goodness within yourselves,' he taught, 'it does not matter to what ceremonials you conform.' So there was little reason for the Church or State authorities to interfere with that harmless sect; besides, the later reign of the Empress Elizabeth and the first years of Catherine the Great were marked by religious tolerance.

After Kolesnikov's death in 1775, the Dukhobors were less lucky in the choice of their leaders. The next one was a dynamic wool merchant, Pobirokhin, who proclaimed himself Christ, chose twelve apostles and as many angels of death to punish those who had incurred his wrath; he completely rejected the Greek Orthodox ceremonials, most of all the worship of images. As Pobirokhin grew older he became more and more tyrannical, trying to establish a theocratic despotism which unfortunately seems to have met with some response among his followers, thus sowing the seeds of their later beliefs. The result of his rule was that the authorities began to investigate the sect, but no action was taken. Pobirokhin, however, removed himself with his apostles to Tambov, proclaimed that he had come to sit in judgment over mankind, and was promptly exiled to Siberia from where he never returned.

But he had brought the Dukhobors into suspicion with the Church and State, and under his successor Kapustin, said to have been Pobirokhin's illegitimate son, persecutions of the sect started in earnest. They got into trouble with Kapustin's doctrine that learning to read and write, commerce and military service were contrary to God's law. He was arrested in 1816 for perverting his followers to heresy and was imprisoned for a while. Then he pretended to die (he was seventy-three), but was discovered hiding in an underground cave from which he controlled his flock.

Worst of all, with Kapustin the rule of the hereditary Christ as the Dukhobors' leader was firmly established. His son and grandson were revered in this rôle without, however, showing Christ's tolerance, for they murdered a number of dissenters, perhaps as many as 400, but were merely exiled to the Caucasus for their crimes; an astonishingly lenient punishment, probably because the authorities welcomed internal strife among the ranks of this irritating sect. As things turned out, it was no punishment at all, for the new leaders, Kapustin's grandson, Peter Kalmikov, and his energetic wife, Lukeriya, built up a well-to-do Dukhobors community of some twelve thousand people in the Caucasus, whom they ruled in the traditional Russian autocratic manner, with the upper crust indulging in philandering, drinking and hunting, and the 'people' doing what they were told. Relations with the authorities were tolerable.

After a long life during which she seems to have been involved in a number of love affairs, Lukeriya died in 1886 and the Dukhobors split into a majority and a minority sect. At that point in their history, they set out on a road which was to lead them right into the limelight of world attention, where they have remained until recent days.

The majority sect went with Peter Vasilivich Verigin, probably Lukeriya's illegitimate son, who now called himself 'Peter the Lordly' and subjected his followers to demands of strict austerity: no meat, alcohol, or tobacco, and later, no sex. The minority preferred to go along with Lukeriya's younger brother, Michael, who was a moderate leader and managed to keep his community out of harm's way, last not least by swearing allegiance to the Tsar. The gesture paid off handsomely, for Michael won for his flock a court case for the possession of the Dukhobor's substantial funds, called 'Zion Treasury'. So Verigin was left to his own devices for making his sect prosperous.

It was Leo Tolstoy through whom the Dukhobors became known all over Russia and in the western world. Prince Khilkov, a fervent disciple of the great writer, country squire, Christian anarchist and humanitarian, had served as an army officer in the Russo-Turkish war of 1877-8, and came to know the Dukhobors' ways and beliefs when he was quartered in their villages. He became a pacifist, resigned from the army and divided his land among the peasants, trying to share their humble existence. When he also publicly rejected the Orthodox Church, he was exiled to the Caucasus where he took a Dukhobor girl as his mistress. Prince Khilkov was in constant touch with Tolstoy, to whom he wrote frequently, and through him the great man heard, probably for the first time, about the sect whose notions were not so different from his own. From now on he took much interest in its fate, which came to a dramatic climax in 1895.

On Easter day of that year, Peter the Lordly ordered his followers who had been conscripted to the army to refuse military duties. They laid down their arms and tore the epaulettes from their uniforms. Eleven of them were arrested, while three Dukhobors communities on Peter's orders burnt all pieces of military equipment they could get hold of, singing hymns. The recruits declared that their only Tsar was the Tsar in Heaven, and that they would rather face the firing squad than kill another human being in war or peace. They were sentenced to three years in penal battalions, where the treatment of offenders was barbaric. More Dukhobors soldiers in Caucasian garrisons followed their example until all conscripts of the sect, some sixty, had laid down their arms and were sent to penal units. Dukhobors who were subsequently called to arms burnt their call-up papers.

Tolstoy, now in direct touch with the sect, was given detailed accounts of the rebels' suffering in the penal battalions. They were flogged with thorny rods; the thorns remained in their flesh. They were confined to cold and dark cells for days on end, then ordered to do military service and again flogged when they refused. This went on for a long time; they were given nothing to eat except a little bread. Many fell sick, and the doctors refused to admit them to hospital as they declared they would eat no meat in accordance with their creed. The chaplains wanted them to attend church and when they refused to go and conform to Orthodox rites they were driven to the house of God with fists and rifle butts. Some did not survive the treatment.

Meanwhile, the rebellious village communities also had to be punished for the burning of government property. Three companies of infantry and three hundred mounted Cossacks were sent there by the governor of Tiflis. Units were billeted in the villages whose inhabitants reacted by lighting more symbolic fires, often on hilltops. The police were called in as reinforcements to stop the riots. The mood of Verigin's followers was growing increasingly militant and desperate; lighting fires, marching around them and singing hymns, the Dukhobors defied the power of the Tsarist State. The local Moslems and Armenians flocked to the rebellious villages. The Cossacks attacked with their knouts but had to retreat before the flames nurtured by kerosene which the Dukhobors kept pouring on. This happened in most of their communities; in the end, arrests were made, but in many cases the Dukhobors were merely escorted to their homes, though some hostages from their ranks were taken away. There were inquiries, trials, sentences of exile; flogging, rape and plunder were the Cossacks' order of the day as soon as the fires were out.

Tolstoy, who had sent one of his disciples to the area, was outraged by reports of the oppression and victimization of a sect trying to live according to his own principles of Christian anarchy. He wrote an article for the London *Times,* entitled 'The Persecution of Christians in Russia', which appeared in October, 1895, following it up with a contribution on the Dukhobors to the *Contemporary Review.* These articles, which carried the enormous international prestige of his name, elaborated upon and confirmed what the *Daily Chronicle* in London had already published by one of its correspondents in Russia on the oppression of the Dukhobors.

The immediate effect of Tolstoy's writings was a Quaker meeting in England at which aid for the victims was discussed. The plan of mass emigration was born, funds were raised and the Dukhobors' opinion sounded. An *Appeal for Help*, with a preface by Tolstoy, was circulated as a pamphlet late in 1896. It told of further cruelties committed against the sect:

> More than four hundred people are suffering and dying from hunger, disease, exhaustion, blows, tortures and other persecutions on the hands of the Russian authorities ... In one place of exile in the Signak district (Georgia), 106 deaths occurred among 100 families, about 1,000 people, settled there. In the Gory district, 147 deaths occurred among 190 families. In the Tionet district, 83 deaths occurred among 100 families ...

In his preface, Tolstoy exaggerated the importance of the sect, but it was all in a good cause, as he saw it; they were not just victims of persecution in an authoritarian state, but witnesses for 'the awakening of the Christian spirit, which is now appearing in all corners of the earth. ... Christ's disciples were just such insignificant, unrefined, unknown people, and other than such the followers of Christ cannot be'. He saw in the Dukhobors 'the true resurrection of Christ', and in their ferocious persecution by the Tsarist authorities the same manifestation of barbarity as that suffered by the early Christians in pagan times. However, he was not at first in favour of emigration plans; he would have liked the Dukhobors to stay in Russia, overcome persecution and develop into a Tolstoyan community in which men filled with inner peace would establish a true Kingdom of God on earth.

At St Petersburg, of course, the English pamphlet created much anger in official and Church circles and when some Tolstoyans tried to submit to the Tsar a memorandum against the Dukhobors' persecution, they were arrested and exiled. One of them, Tchertkov, sought refuge in England where he founded a Tolstoyan community at Purleigh in Essex. He was very active in mobilizing British public opinion for the Dukhobors when the emigration project took a more tangible form.

Peter the Lordly had been exiled, first to Archangelsk in the Arctic, then to northern Siberia; but his hold on the sect, now that he ranked as a martyr, was stronger than ever, and he still ruled them, communicating with his suffering brethren by occasional messengers. Verigin may have been vain, autocratic, and self-indulgent but he was certainly neither a traitor to his cause nor a coward. He risked being sent to the salt mines by addressing, in 1896, an appeal to the Tsarina Alexandra, written almost like a letter from one ruler to another, pleading for a place of safety for his twenty thousand 'subjects' where they could live, work and worship in peace. But he did not have emigration in mind at that stage, any more than Tolstoy did.

The letter had no visible effect, but it must have influenced the Tsarina, and through her the Tsar; for the idea of letting the Dukhobors go and establish their communities elsewhere met with increasing interest in high places. One wanted to get rid of them altogether, for they would have continued to be a nuisance anywhere in Russia. Much sooner than anybody had expected, and without further appeals, the authorities declared that they would grant permission to emigrate to those Dukhobors who desired to leave. The decision was greeted with great joy by the sect.

Now the question was where? What the Dukhobors wanted was some land where they could settle as a group, under a régime that would not object to their religious beliefs. Tolstoy accepted the inevitable and sounded his friends as to the most suitable places on the globe. Writing to the Dukhobors, he suggested Chinese Turkestan (now Sinkiang), Manchuria, Texas or Cyprus. Other suggestions made by sympathizers inside and outside Russia were Hawaii (recently annexed by the USA), Argentina, Brazil and England. Cyprus was strongly supported by the English Quakers, who hoped to be able to get permission from Whitehall; the island was now under British administration. A small advance party of Dukhobors were allowed to leave for Cyprus via England with one-way passports and the stern warning that emigrants would not be allowed back to Russia; the Quakers earmarked £12,000 for the project of settlement. Joseph Chamberlain, then Colonial Secretary, told them that this sum was rather insufficient and that only a handful of refugees could be permitted to settle with such meagre funds.

Still, some land was bought, and although the advance party complained about the climate and the poor quality of the soil, some 1,100 Dukhobors arrived on board an ancient French freighter. They did their best, building houses and tilling the soil with great energy but they soon started quarrelling; discontent was spreading and there was no leader who could have inspired them with the will to hold out. Besides, the Russian peasants' farming methods proved inadequate in Mediterranean conditions. Cyprus was a failure and when the news reached them that Canada had offered the Dukhobors a home, they decided to leave and join their brethren from Russia who were already preparing to emigrate to the New World. In April 1899, the Cyprus settlers departed to what they fervently hoped would be a new life, freedom and prosperity at last, or at least survival.

Altogether, about 7,500 Dukhobors, who now called themselves the Christian Community of Universal Brotherhood, settled in 1899 in three areas allotted to them by the Canadian government: two of them south and north of Yorkton in the Assiniboia Territory and a large reserve near Prince Albert, in Saskatchewan, altogether three-quarters of a million acres, including, however, extensive swamps and rocky ground. Canada needed settlers; strangely enough, none of the Dukhobors' sympathizers had thought of it while scanning the maps for some place for emigration, until a member of the London Quaker committee had by chance read an article on Mennonite colonies in Canada by Prince Kropotkin, the Russian anarchist, in the British magazine *The Nineteenth Century* early in 1898. Canada was seriously underpopulated; on its vast territory of three and a half million square miles, there lived at the turn of the century little more than five million people, compared to over twenty million today.

Immigrants, therefore, were granted all kinds of concessions, apart from complete religious freedom, which had always been part of the Canadian way of life. Like the Mennonites, Quakers and other pacifist groups, the Dukhobors had the benefit of the Militia Act which exempted religious objectors from bearing arms. Education lay in the hands of the provincial governments but was not compulsory in outlying areas; religious education was forced on no one. Marriages, however, had to be registered.

Among the economic advantages enjoyed by immigrants was a 160-acre homestead for each family; until the Dukhobors were settled in their villages, they were given free shelter in 'immigration halls', and a bonus of $5 per head was paid into a special fund for their benefit to provide them with pocket money on arrival. Arrangements for them had been made with the government by Prince Khilkov, who had gone to Canada with some other Tolstoyans before the first immigrants arrived, making the Canadians' mouths water with glowing descriptions of the newcomers from whom the country would benefit enormously. It may have been that idealistic picture of the Dukhobors which made later disappointments particularly grave.

To be sure, minor disappointments were there right from the start. These simple peasants had been uprooted and dumped in an alien country by their own consent, but this did not make their new surroundings any less strange. They spoke only Russian and could not communicate with the Canadians; they were dependent on their western friends who had helped them to come here. Asked to make decisions, they declined and said, 'We cannot decide, we have no power. We must wait until all the brothers can assemble and the matter be discussed.' This was their traditional kind of democracy.

But it was Verigin, Peter the Lordly, who most of all prevented them from becoming ordinary Canadian citizens. From his Siberian exile he issued directions to them which were to ensure their continued existence as a separate sect and community. All who wanted to live with Christ, he wrote to them, must refrain from acquiring private property; land, cattle, mills, granaries, smithies, joiners' shops must be owned communally. Fair enough, one would think; but what Verigin really aimed at was to keep his Dukhobors together by external pressure to prevent assimilation; and as that pressure was not exerted by free Canada's authorities as it had been in Tsarist Russia, he issued instructions to provoke it.

They began by refusing to register individual owners of farms, to have births, marriages and deaths recorded with the registrars, and to comply with Canadian marriage and divorce laws. But Peter the Lordly went even further in his extreme demands:

It is wrong to use metals obtained from the earth, and smelted by the labour of our enslaved brethren; wrong to train horses or cattle to do our work; wrong to use money which bears the image of Caesar: it should be handed back to Caesar. It is wrong to till the soil, for being God's earth it is wrong to spoil it when there are hot countries where men live without working by eating only fruit ...

The effects were most alarming. Many Dukhobors took all their coins with the 'image of Caesar' to the police or immigration authorities, set their horses and cattle free and stopped ploughing and reaping. The Mounted Police, in one operation alone, rounded up 120 horses, nearly 300 cattle and 100 sheep that had survived in the waterless prairie with its coyotes and other beasts of prey. When the animals were auctioned, however, the buyers were other Dukhobors who refused to obey Verigin's outrageous demands. But one of the most harmful results of his exhortations was the general feeling he had instilled into the majority of his brethren: that Canada was merely a half-way house on the road to complete freedom and that it was not worth while putting down roots there, for he would soon come and lead them to some tropical Garden of Eden where they would not have to work.

And he came indeed. In 1902, having completed the fifteen years of exile to which he had been sentenced, he arrived in Canada. With his personal appearance, passive and active resistance against the authorities grew in scope as well as in variety. Peter the Lordly was asked to stop the nuisance, which he promised. He seems to have tried seriously to resettle his flock in a hot country such as Mexico or Paraguay, but considering their record of behaviour in Canada no one was too keen to have them. So the least he could do for them was to buy, in 1908, another 6,500 acres of land for them, fruit land on the Columbia River near Nelson and at Grand Forks for planting orchards, with the funds collected for 'further emigration'. Other purchases followed in subsequent years; by 1912, the Dukhobors were quite prosperous, communally owning many tens of thousands of fruit trees, many saw-mills and flour mills, brick factories, jam factories, dozens of threshing-machines, hospitals and even their own telephone networks. In view of later episodes it is interesting to note that during the hot summer of 1910 they proved of great assistance to the local authorities by fighting the many bush and forest fires that broke out, particularly in British Columbia.

These Dukhobor communities, though keeping strictly apart from the rest of the population, had obviously come to terms with Canada as their permanent homeland. But some never did – at least not until recently. These were the *svobotniki,* or 'sons of freedom', yet another sect within a sect, and one of the most eccentric and aggressive in the world.

The split began only a few months after Verigin's arrival in Canada, when those Dukhobors who had adhered to his instructions to the letter began to be puzzled by his new, apparently moderate attitude. They explained it to themselves with a characteristically Russian twist of logic, developed as a tradition in a long period of persecution, that Verigin wanted his true followers to understand exactly the opposite of what he said in public, which was meant to deceive the authorities and other outsiders. So they developed entirely new ways of serving their cause, which was what the leader expected of them . . . or so they believed.

It was Verigin's own former doctrines which they preached, marching through Dukhobors villages which, to them, had grown tame and conformist: that tilling the soil and using horses and oxen was sinful, and that the 'animal brethren' should be set free. The villagers paid no attention to them and went on with their work. So the *svobotniki* of both sexes took off their clothes in order to make their fellow-Dukhobors take notice of them, and 'to show, in the manner of Adam and Eve, how Man should return to his original home'. About fifty strong, they marched through sixteen villages, until they came upon Verigin himself, who was driving a trap. They set his horse free, but he got another one and rode ahead of them to the seventeenth village on their route. There he mobilized the brethren, who armed themselves with twigs and beat the 'Sons of Freedom' bloody.

In the end, they were arrested and convicted of indecent exposure; they had to work in the prison grounds before being released after a few weeks. The example of that first *svobotniki* demonstration caught on, as was to be expected; the new sect had its martyrs and its rites. Tolstoy, who certainly had no nudist leanings, chided them only mildly: 'One must remember,' he wrote, 'that the material well-being they have now attained thanks to communal life, rests entirely on the religious feeling which showed itself in their movement to free the cattle; and that this feeling is more precious than anything else, and woe not to them in whom it shows itself in a perverted form (I refer to undressing when entering villages), but to him in whom it has dried up.'

The first Sons of Freedom had hardly returned from prison when a kind of shock-brigade formed itself from their ranks, establishing yet another pattern of defiance. Science, they declared, was Satan; it must be extirpated from the life of their Dukhobors brethren by violent means. Their first action was to pull a heavy roller over a field of ripe wheat and set fire to it; then they tried to smash up a threshing machine, but other Dukhobors stopped them. 'Trust not in science but in God,' the Sons of Freedom shouted at their brethren.

If they continued in their belief that this new way of purifying Dukhobor life was what Peter the Lordly really wanted, that belief must have been absolutely blind considering Verigin's counter-action. It was he who asked the police to arrest six of the saboteurs and insisted on their prosecution. They were sent to prison for three years. No doubt, he saw in the *svobotniki* a disruptive element that had to be rooted out for the sake of the whole Dukhobor community in Canada.

He failed. Nude demonstrations and fire-raising continued and increased. During the first years of the sub-sect's activities, these actions were solely aimed at other Dukhobors. But in the early 1920s, the pattern changed. In November 1923, a government school was burnt down. Four more schools followed the same year and five others, a sawmill and Verigin's own house went up in flames the year after. Still, there was an element of doubt in some Dukhobors circles whether Verigin himself was not, after all, behind these attacks; the very fact that his own house was burnt down had raised suspicion. Was he trying to exculpate himself?

However, the outrage that followed on 29 October 1924 ought to have put a stop to any rumours that he was secretly in league with the Sons of Freedom: a bomb exploded underneath a railway carriage in which he was travelling; he and eight other people died. There was no proof that the Sons had planted the time bomb; in fact, Verigin's own son Peter Petrovich, later nicknamed 'the Purger', may have instigated the assassination. He hated his father and at the age of forty five he must have been fed up with waiting for the old man's natural death. He was at the time in Russia, and is supposed to have cooperated with the Soviet authorities in getting the remaining Dukhobors to Canada; but a friend of his, a watchmaker, was among old Verigin's entourage and returned to his native Russia in suspicious haste immediately after the murder.

It was the first time dynamite had been used by the Dukhobors, and this new feature, too, was to become part of the sect's activities, although later they tried, not always successfully, to avoid any loss of human lives. The escalation of the *svobotniki's* struggle for the purification of the sect was mainly due to Peter the Purger, who led them from 1924 to 1939.

He was a most unsavoury character. When still in Russia, he asked his Canadian brethren for money to organize further emigration schemes. The first remittance came and he got so drunk that he beat up some fellow-Dukhobors. After his father's assassination he was permitted to emigrate in order to exert, as he himself put it, a 'sobering influence' on his Canadian followers. Peter the Lordly, to be sure, had been a hypocrite; but Peter the Purger left him far behind. In his first address at a meeting of the Dukhobors, he said:

I stand before you as perfect as a man can be. But right after this meeting I shall be completely different to what you will expect of me: I shall smoke and drink, eat meat and behave like the rest of mankind—in fact, like a hoodlum—for the benefit of our enemies. You alone will know why I do this; so do not judge me by my actions, but pay attention to what I say . . . What is the purpose of all this? If we burn and bomb and fill the jails, the government will grow so anxious to get rid of us that they will send us to another country and provide transport for us and our belongings.

He demanded higher contributions from his followers for the great struggle, and spent the money gambling, whoring and drinking. The emigration scheme never materialized during his rule, but the plans for violent action certainly did. There were over two hundred incidents of arson, bombing and wrecking in those fifteen years, which saw the consolidation of the Sons of Freedom into an implacable, unreformable gang of approximately 2,500 religious zealots. 'Praise be to God,' said Peter the Purger on his deathbed, 'I have completed my task on earth.'

The assembled brethren elected his son Peter Yastrebov, the
Hawk, as their new leader, but he was somewhere in Russia,
perhaps in one of Stalin's prison camps. There was a vacuum in
Canada, an empty space at the top of an extremely gullible sect.
The first adventurer to muscle in was one John Lebedoff, a farmer
from Saskatchewan, who spoke of a mysterious call he had received from God the Father as well as from the Master over the
Water, meaning Peter the Hawk. His short rule was characterized
by the special attraction he had for the Dukhobors women, with
whom he surrounded himself. He was eclipsed by another
Saskatchewan farmer who had turned boarding-house owner in
Vancouver, Michael John Orekoff; he produced documents
saying that the Verigins, to whom he was related, had made him
the trustee of the community funds. The brethren also believed
him when he told them that he had been a visionary since boy-
hood, and he assumed the leadership as Michael the Archangel,
hinting that he was a reincarnation of the celestial general.

He added one or two new features to the protest techniques of
the Sons, such as hunger strikes, and introduced free love as 'an
extension of spiritual communism to break down the barriers
between mine and thine'. He was convicted for seditious conspiracy in 1950 but died before he could be sent to prison.

Another religious adventurer moved in, Stefan S. Sorokin, a
Russian from a displaced persons' camp in Europe, who had
arrived in the New World with a little suitcase and a harp in
1949; he heard that the Dukhobors had just lost their leader,
and decided that this was a job for him. Born in a Russian
Orthodox community, he had made a living in Asia Minor and
Europe as a lay preacher, transferring his allegiance from the
Lutherans and the Plymouth Brethren to the Seventh-Day
Adventists and the Baptists in turn. Why not try the Dukhobors,
for a change? With his long, black beard, his sonorous hymn
voice, and his harp for strumming the accompaniment, he seemed
eminently suited for the rôle of a mysterious new leader.

Sorokin never pretended to be Peter Yastrebov, but it was
tacitly assumed that he was. With his hymn-singing he won over
the Sons of Freedom, who needed a leader; the emigration
schemes of his predecessors had made them increasingly restless;
there were numerous protest marches in the nude, and they
burnt down some of their own houses, dancing around the flames

naked. Four hundred of them were arrested, charged and sent to prison until a mass amnesty freed them. Sorokin took advantage of their dream of emigration, collected $100,000 from the Sons to buy land in South America for them and departed, never to return. He did, in fact, buy land in Uruguay in 1952, but only for himself.

Simma Holt, a Canadian journalist who published a history of the Dukhobors in 1965, visited him in his palatial home near Montevideo, maintained by continuous subscriptions from the Canadian Dukhobors to whom he was still, in his own words, 'the messenger of God, like the Pope', although he had so obviously deserted them. Miss Holt watched him driving around in his luxury limousine, protected by armed bodyguards at day and by a gun under his pillow at night. 'The brotherhood does not complain that I take their money and keep it,' he told her. 'Whatever I tell them they will do. The love of the people for their leader is everlasting. And I alone can solve the problems of the Dukhobors in Canada.'

Few associations, religious or otherwise, would continue in their loyalty to a leader who had absconded with their money, let alone send him further contributions. But the Dukhobors, the main body of the sect as well as the *svobotniki*, found the matter quite in order. They had always accepted that their leaders were entitled to live in style, in contrast to their own frugal way of life; and they had always had a curious weakness for leaders over the water, mysteriously absent from their flock yet giving them orders. And perhaps, by some miracle that only a leader could perform, the gates to the Garden of Eden might one day be flung open to them.

The 'Sons' felt particular admiration for Sorokin because during his two-year direct rule he had done little to restrain them from their terrorist activities, which increased markedly. Within a few weeks in 1950, there were eighteen burnings. In one of them, Lebedoff's house was burnt down by a gang of three dozen zealots; he was still living in it as a retired leader, and just about managed to escape in his pyjamas. When the police came, the arsonists surrendered without resistance, after taking off their clothes. In other incidents, bystanders from the village asked also to be arrested in the nude. When questioned, many were unable to give any reason for their actions; some said they were demonstrating against the third world war. Brought before the magistrate after being forcibly clothed by the police, they would at once strip again, men and women alike.

In 1953, the first year after Sorokin had departed, there were more burnings than ever before and miles of railway lines were blasted with dynamite. Four hundred Sons who had burnt their own homes were living in tents. When school opened in September of that year and parents were told that they would be prosecuted if they prevented their children from attending, they paraded in the nude outside the school buildings as the children came out. About 150 were arrested, and immediately began a hunger strike: 'We will not eat until God tells us to do so,' they declared. Simma Holt spoke to an attractive young woman whose husband had been jailed for taking part in a bomb attack. On the morning after the trial, she rose at three AM, poured coal oil over her furniture, the curtains and the bedding and put a match to the house. Then she took her clothes off and stood outside with her little son, obviously relishing the spectacle. 'I knew I had to do it, just as I have seen my mother do it when I was young,' she told the journalist by way of explanation.

During the 1950s and 1960s, the Sons of Freedom committed an average of a hundred outrages a year; two dozen people died in that period as a result of bombings and burnings, for the zealots had ceased to care whether they endangered human life. Despite their contempt for modern machinery, the Sons had become masters of bombing techniques, from Molotov cocktails to ingenious timing mechanisms operated by wrist watches, or miniature booby traps in the form of cigarette packs. But their most powerful defence weapon against the police was their nudism, which embarrassed even the lion-hearted Mounties. Some police chief thought of using itching powder; the *svobotniki* countered the move by sending their most powerful Amazons forward, who threw a number of policemen to the ground and then sat on their faces, naked. Encouraged by their success, these aggressive Daughters of Freedom staged a coup against their menfolk. One day in the late 1950s, a hundred of them, led by a 240-lb matron, Mrs Florence Storgoff, called 'Big Fanny', burst into the community hall at Krestova, the *svobotniki* centre, where the fifty-two-man council of the sect was holding a secret meeting. 'You men have been playing with this situation long enough,' shouted Florence. 'Now we're going to take over!'

And they did, at least for a while. Four schools for their children were set up to combat forcible education at State schools because 'Canadian education leads to war and killing', as they declared. Besides, they wanted their children to be taught in Russian to emphasize Dukhobor 'apartheid'. The police raided the Krestova school, a cold barn with hard wooden benches, and tried to take some of the children away to New Denver, where the authorities had set up a special dormitory school for Dukhobors youngsters The police managed to pick up two children at Krestova, but when they came back for more, the women turned on them, bombarded them with eggs, rocks and mud, and drove them away.

However, most of the 'assimulated' Dukhobors had already consented to let their children go to State schools, where they were found to be industrious, intelligent and clean, even asking for extra homework. But to the Sons, Canadian schools were concentration camps where their children were tempted to take up smoking and dating and, worst of all, riding in motor-cars. The moderate Dukhobors in one town, many of them car owners, were taken by surprise one day in 1961, when hundreds of *svobotniki* swarmed through the streets, rounded up their automobiles, piled them up high, and set fire to them.

As the plans for further emigration led to one disappointment after another, a new notion began to ripen in the minds of many Dukhobors who were still feeling strangers in Canada, and of the *svobotniki* in particular, that of returning to their homeland, Russia, now that Tsarist oppression had come to an end. As far back as 1922, the Soviets had invited emigré sectarians back. The Dukhobors community sent a cable to the Commissar for Agriculture in Moscow, expressing their interest in the idea, provided they would be given land in a good region where they could grow wheat and fruit, and build a factory for farming machinery; they further asked for tax exemption for twenty years, freedom from military service, from registration and State education for their children. So far as we know the Soviets never replied to these demands and the Dukhobors forgot about the idea of repatriation for the time being. Meanwhile, further Dukhobors were allowed to emigrate to Canada, and it seemed nonsensical to try and reverse the process now. Nor did another scheme for resettlement, in Turkey, come to fruition.

Only as late as 1957 had there seemed to be a chance for the *svobotniki* to return to a homeland which, in fact, the present generation had never seen. A spokesman for the sect had submitted the request to the Soviet Ambassador in Ottawa. 'As we are not getting freedom of religion in Canada,' the spokesman explained, 'we feel that we should go somewhere where that freedom is assured.' The Ambassador promised to send the request with his recommendation to Moscow.

Canada sighed with relief. 'The exodus would bring an abrupt end to the problem that Canada and British Columbia have never solved,' wrote a leading Vancouver paper, 'and which has cost the country millions of dollars in bombing, fires, nude parades, court and prison costs, guards, probes and research.'

A few months went by; then came a Soviet invitation to send a small delegation over and inspect the territory which the government was prepared to allot to them. This was early in 1958; the resettlement region had turned out to be in the Altay province of southern Siberia, practically virgin land. Some faces fell when the Sons of Freedom heard this, but a thousand of them, they now numbered three thousand altogether, voted to 'fly from Canadian persecution'. A further delegation was sent to prepare their reception in Siberia. It was the post-Stalin era, Khrushchev wanted Russia to be a friendly country in the eyes of the world, and there was some propaganda value in accepting back a sect that regarded the Soviet Union as the land of freedom.

Negotiations with the Canadian government started and early in August a formal agreement was reached: those Dukhobors who wanted to emigrate would lose their Canadian citizenship; Canada would assist with transportation and resettlement costs. There was a mass meeting in a clearing near Krestova, and to show their joy the *svobotniki* set fire to the four sides of the surrounding wood. Prayers were said, hymns were sung and there was much dancing in the nude.

By November 1958, 2440 forms renouncing Canadian nationality had been signed and a substantial amount of money collected among the sect to finance the emigration. Only one thing was missing: the green light from Moscow that the exodus could begin.

It never came. Moscow, most likely, had second thoughts about the weird sect with its eccentric variety of Christianity, its record of anarchistic outrages, its violent reaction against anything the State demanded, from military service to education. The mystery is why the Soviets ever seriously considered to let the *svobotniki* come.

As usual, their excitement had expressed itself in the form of fires and dynamiting, and the year of expectation, 1958, was a particularly active one. Bombs were exploded in a widening radius from Krestova (up to 200 miles); apart from railway lines and power poles, the Sons now included hotels, a lake ferry and a bus depot among their objectives, with the result that people were killed or maimed.

The gradual realization that their fellow-Russians did not want them either, and that they were now probably stuck in Canada for better for worse, left them stunned. When the Union of Spiritual Communities, comprising all the Dukhobor factions, accepted the project of reselling community land to private members of the sect, the terrorists sprang to action again. The tomb of father and son Verigin was blown up, two Dukhobors community halls were burnt down and a whole village destroyed by Molotov cocktails. The Mounted Police formed a special D-squad (D for Dukhobors) which cracked down on the Sons in their area in the summer of 1962, searching their homes, setting up road-blocks and arresting 120 of the hard-core terrorists. They were given sentences of up to ten years and sent to the fire-proof prison of Agassiz so that they could not use their traditional method applied in many country jails, that of burning them down and escaping. The prisoners' families, however, reacted in the traditional manner: they set fire to what was left of Krestova, marched off to Agassiz, led by Big Fanny, and laid naked siege to the prison. The police decided to ignore them. They built make-shift huts, where many of the six hundred that had come continued to squat for years; the men found local work as farm labourers.

Big Fanny died of cancer in 1964; she had been the last of the active *svobotniki* leaders, and with her a chapter of their history, perhaps the last, came to an end. Curiously enough, it was Simma Holt's book on the Dukhobors and their violent fringe, *Terror in the Name of God*, that brought about a change of heart among the prisoners at Agassiz and their families. When the advance copies appeared in 1964, the prison authorities had the good sense to let the English-reading convicts see them. They were much impressed by its objectivity: Miss Holt refuted many misconceptions on both sides, the Dukhobors' as well as the authorities', and put the sect in its historical context as just one of a number of fanatical Russian religious groups, though the most troublesome outside their country of origin.

Many of the younger prisoners began to cooperate with the authorities after reading the book, volunteering for work, asking for more reading matter and for teachers, and altogether emerged from that sullenness that had been so characteristic of imprisoned Sons for almost four decades. Within a year, more than a dozen were paroled, and most of the rest had followed them on the road to freedom by 1968. They and their families began to trickle back to the ghost town of Krestova, where wolves had been roaming through streets of charred ruins. Krestova, the 'City of the Cross', came to life again. This is how the authors of a recent history of the Dukhobors, George Woodcock and Ivan Avakumovic, describe the scene :

Krestova, so long a place of violence, has now become one of the most peaceful villages in western Canada . . . The men who live there have found year-long employment on the various construction works in connection with the Columbia River hydro-electric power project, and the traditional Krestova pattern of summer work and winter idleness is a thing of the past. Contrary to all expectations, the 'Sons of Freedom' have recently decided to buy back the land at Krestova, and among the charred, grass-grown ruins on the plateau, new houses are being built, solid structures with none of the air of deliberate impermanence of the old tar-paper shacks. The children at Krestova now have a record of school attendance better than that of the non-Dukhobor children in the neighbourhood. Assimilation started late with the 'Sons of Freedom', but once begun it has been extraordinarily rapid. It is perhaps too early to prophesy that there will be no regressions into violence, but at the time of writing they seem unlikely.

The majority of the Dukhobors, of course, have completed that process of assimilation; all that distinguishes most of them from their fellow-Canadians is their creed and their language. They have kept their Russian mother-tongue, and with it a 'fading vision of the great return', which still haunts them and their children.

9

Murder
as a Sacred Duty

The Assassins

Over nine hundred years ago, three young men at an exclusive religious school at Nishapur in Persia had become great friends and made a pact to help each other whenever they would be able to do so. They had high hopes of making their way in life, for it was well known that students from this school – with the famous Imam Muwafiq as its 'headmaster' – never failed to rise to power or fame.

The story of that students' pact has been told by Edward Fitz-Gerald in the preface to his translation of the *Rubaiyat,* for one of the three friends was Omar Khayyam, later Persia's poet laureate. The second was Nizam-ul-mulk, who was to become Grand Vizier, equivalent to the position of Prime Minister in our time. Almost as a matter of course, he offered his former schoolmates the usual sinecure, a governorship to each. Omar Khayyam, however, refused with thanks; he felt that he was not cut out to be a civil servant. The Grand Vizier granted him a pension instead, which enabled the poet, mathematician, and astronomer to lead a carefree life at Nishapur.

The third friend, too, refused the offer, not because he disliked responsibilities, but because he was aiming higher: a provincial governorship would have tied him down in Persia, whereas he had raised his sights to the centre of Moslem power, to Cairo, to the court of the Caliph. So Nizam, loyal friend that he was, obtained employment for him in the Caliph's service.

The third man's name was Hasan ibn al-Sabbah and he was the son of a pious Shia in north-eastern Persia. The Shiites believed that Ali, the Prophet Mohammed's son-in-law, was his true successor, while the main stream of Moslems followed Abu

Bakr, the first Caliph ('successor of the Prophet'); thus, the Islamic faith suffered its first great crisis soon after the Prophet's death in AD 632. Hasan was raised in the Shiite creed which had many influential men among its adherents. But the sect of the Shia had already given birth to yet another one, the Ismailis, followers of Ismail, the disinherited son of the sixth. Imam ('leader') after Ali; they felt that Ismail – cast out by his father because of his drunkenness – had been treated unjustly and must be revered as the real seventh Imam instead of his younger brother Musa, who was recognized by the majority of Shiites. Persecuted as heretics at first, the Ismailis were a secret and fanatical sect, gathering converts by the thousands from other Islamic groups.

During that first time of persecution, they organized themselves tightly and efficiently while first-rank theological thinkers and writers worked out for them an attractive system of religious and cultural philosophy, with more than a touch of scientific understanding of the world. Of all the numerous Islamic sects of that period, the Ismailis were without doubt the one with the highest intellectual and emotional level, the most progressive group one might say; their power of survival proved to be enormous and today there are still more than ten million Ismailis in Africa and Asia who recognize the Aga Khan as their Imam.

At the time when Hasan went to Cairo, three centuries after the beginning of that movement, the Caliphate, whose reign extended from Spain to the borders of Tibet, was firmly in the hands of the Ismailis. He hastened to become a convert and as such was welcomed at the Caliph's court. Soon he rose to the position of minister.

There are various versions of how Hasan got to Cairo and what actually happened there between him and the young Caliph, Melekshah. Some modern historians, dismissing the schoolmates' pact as a fable, believe that Hasan was an unscrupulous, morbidly ambitious character who plotted against Nizam, an honest and efficient administrator. Hasan got into trouble for harbouring Egyptian secret agents and was on the point of being arrested as an agitator. As a last resort, he asked Nizam to recommend him to the court of the Caliph, and Nizam did so to get Hasan out of Persia. This version appears to be substantiated by a passage in Nizam's autobiographical notes: 'I helped him to

become a minister by my strong and exaggerated recommend-
ations. But like his father he turned out to be a fraud and hypocrite, and altogether a selfish scoundrel. With his pretensions and
lies he managed to capture the trust and sympathies of the
Caliph.'

Hasan remained in Cairo and Alexandria for three years
around 1080. Soon he made himself unpopular with the politicians and the army chiefs by his intrigues; according to one
account he was arrested and deported to North Africa, but the
ship was wrecked. He was saved and brought to Syria. However,
Nizam's account says that Melekshah entrusted him with the
general revisions of Persia's fiscal system, much to Nizam's anger.
Hasan made such a mess of the revision that the Caliph sent him
into exile, and he travelled up and down Persia and Iraq in the
service of the Ismaili organization. But he did not intend to serve
for long – he wanted to lead; his aim was to gather a group of
devoted friends, inspire them with a fanatic belief in him who
would promise them Paradise on earth: in other words, to found
yet another sect, with himself as the leader.

Hasan seems to have been a hypnotic personality who easily
attracted young people, particularly in those eastern regions of
the Caliph's empire where the civilizing influence of Islam had
been merely superficial and the age-old tribal instincts were still
lurking in men's souls. Defiance of authority, frustration because
of hard economic conditions, the traditional warrior spirit – all
this made the outlying districts near the Caspian Sea a fertile
ground for rebellious movements of all kinds. It was here that
Hasan looked for a centre and stronghold for his new movement.
He picked the castle of Alamut, in the heart of the Elburz
Mountains, built by some ancient king of the Daylam people,
dominating a thirty-mile-long valley from the rock on which it
stood. This was to be Hasan's 'Paradise on earth', his hideout
and strategic base.

Marco Polo, to whom Europe owes the first information about
Hasan, passed this way two hundred years later, in 1271:

In a beautiful valley, enclosed between two lofty mountains [he
wrote], there is a luxurious landscape of gardens full of every kind
of delicious fruit and every fragrant shrub on earth. There are
palaces of many sizes and designs, decorated with gold, silk, precious furniture and paintings. By means of small conduits, streams

of wine, milk, honey, and the purest water are made to flow everywhere. The inhabitants of these palaces were elegant and beautiful ladies, accomplished in the arts of singing and playing of musical instruments, dancing, and especially dalliance and amorous allurement. Clothed in expensive dresses, they were continually seen amusing themselves in the gardens and pavilions ... The aim of the man who had created all this [Hasan] had been as follows: Mohammed, the Prophet, had promised to the faithful the enjoyments of Paradise, where any kind of gratification of the senses would be found; but Hasan wanted to prove that he, too, was a prophet and a peer of Mohammed, and that he had the power of admitting to his earthly paradise everyone he chose to favour. In order to prevent others from gaining admission to that delicious valley it is guarded by a strong and unconquerable castle at the opening of the valley, which can be entered only by a secret passage ...

The way in which Hasan acquired the castle of Alamut in the autumn of 1090 is characteristic of his methods. The seizure was planned meticulously. First he sent his 'missionaries' into the valley; they succeeded in converting some of the people of Alamut to Ismailism. Their chief, Mihdi, who held it for the Sultan of the Seljuq dynasty, smelt a rat; he pretended to be won over, but when most of Hasan's men had left again he threw out all the converts, closed the gates, and let Hasan know that the castle belonged to the Sultan and no one else. Hasan and his men hid in the neighbourhood until one of his missionaries inside found an opportunity to bring him secretly and in disguise into the castle. For a while he remained inside without being detected – long enough to smuggle in a number of his armed followers. Suddenly, Mihdi was confronted with the invaders. Hasan offered him three thousand gold dinars if he would move out, and Mihdi accepted. The castle was in Hasan's hands. It is said that during the following thirty-five years, until his death, he never left it.

The next stage was the recruitment of more and more young men from the surrounding villages; most of them were under twenty. He accepted even boys from twelve years onwards, providing they looked strong enough to bear arms and seemed willing to follow his orders blindly. Soon the whole of the valley with its forts and palaces was theirs; now Hasan sent missionaries and agents further afield to survey other castles and strongholds in the vicinity and to discover rocks that might be suitable for building forts. At the same time, converts were made among the gentry, the landowning class, as well as among the villagers who owed them allegiance.

The doctrine of the new sect, as yet nameless, began to take shape. Hasan assumed the title of Sheikh al Jebal, 'Old Man of the Mountain', implying that he was an incarnation of the Prophet and declaring that his sect represented the genuine Ismaili creed. A number of the castles he wanted were freely surrendered to his missionaries on the strength of these claims, pressed on a largely ignorant population with all kinds of propaganda tricks. Where peaceful conversion did not work, the 'missionaries' used force. Murder, pillage, rape, arson were committed without the slightest scruples; in fact, Hasan's doctrine demanded the killing of enemies as a sacred religious duty.

Several contemporary and later writers have claimed that in order to induce in his followers a state of fanatic ecstasy, Hasan made them take hashish – Indian hemp, or 'pot', as it is called nowadays – before sending them out on military expeditions. Marco Polo tells a slightly different story:

The Old Man desired to make his adherents believe that Alamut and the valley beneath it was actually Paradise. At his court he kept a number of youths from the countryside to whom he would tell stories about Paradise, just as Mohammed had done, and they believed in him as the orthodox Moslems believed in the Prophet. He would then take them into his garden, some four to ten at a time, having first made them drink a certain potion which made them fall into a deep sleep; on awaking, they found themselves in a place so wonderful that it seemed to them Paradise in very truth. There, the ladies [like the houris in Mohammed's tales] dallied with them to their hearts' content so that they had what all young men desire, and none of the Ashishin ever wanted to leave the place.

The Old Man kept his court in a grand and noble style, making the simple hill people in the neighbourhood believe firmly that he was a great Imam. When he wanted to send one of his Ashishin on a mission he would cause that potion to be given to him in the garden, and then had him carried back into the castle. So when the young man awoke there, he found himself no longer in Paradise, which displeased him. The Old Man would then ask him in the presence of other newcomers where he had been, and get the answer: in Paradise. This, of course, roused in the other young men, who had not yet been admitted, the greatest desire to see it also. So when the Old Man wanted to have any prince slain, he would tell one of the youths: 'Go and kill so-and-so; when you return, my angels shall carry you to Paradise. And should you die in the course of duty, I shall also send my angels to that place.' . . . Thus there was no command of his that they would not obey, and in this way he got his men to murder anyone he wanted to get rid of; and the great fear he inspired in many princes made them become his vassals so that they might be spared. The Old Man also had certain others under him who adopted the same proceedings in other regions such as Damascus and Kurdistan.

At the time when Marco Polo wrote, the term *Ashishin* or 'Assassins' was already well known in Europe as the name for the Persian Ismailis. In fact the story of the hashish-taking killers had been brought back by the first crusaders who had fought their way into Syria in 1097, where they made the unpleasant acquaintance of Hasan's men and methods. Gradually, the words assassin and assassination, for political killer and murder, became part of the everyday vocabulary first in France and then in England.

By the early twelfth century, Hasan's Ismailis had already grown far beyond their beginnings as a murderous religious sect. Their power, cemented by fanaticism and terror, was now a political factor. Although it first extended to the east and south of Alamut, with more and more princes being forced to join them or pay them handsome tributes, it was in the west, particularly in Syria, that the Assassins fought their way into world history. The Cairo Caliphate, weakened by its internal struggles and external onslaughts by the Turks on the one hand and the crusaders on the other, was now faced with a well-organized, treacherous and completely unscrupulous enemy within its gates. One by one, the Syrian castles and hill forts fell to Hasan's *fedayin*, his devotees, acting in absolute obedience to the Old Man of the Mountain and the regional grand priors he had set up to execute his orders. The secrecy of their rites and aims confused their victims and enemies. Their hierarchy was by now well established: under the 'divinely appointed' Imam Hasan and his three grand priors there were the religious and political emissaries or 'missionaries'; the fellows of the order who were admitted under solemn oaths; the *fedayin* who did the actual fighting and killing; the lay brethren or 'believers'; and the profane, the ordinary people of the territories ruled by the sect. Contemporary sources estimate that the *fedayin*, the militant members of the sect, numbered more than forty thousand at the height of their power.

They achieved their decisive success in Syria in 1113 by murdering the Turkish emir of Damascus; it was the Turks against whom the Assassins waged war in the first place, attacking the crusaders only when under pressure of circumstances. Syria was now their new base of operations. The close proximity of Christians and Assassins has been a favourite subject of historical speculation: did they learn anything from each other? The Templars were later accused by their Christian enemies of having been corrupted by the Assassins. The Assassins may have picked up some useful practical ideas in weaponry and warfare from the Templars, who seem to have accustomed themselves, to a certain extent, to the treacherous methods of the Persian Ismailis. Thus William of Tyre, the historian of the crusades, tells us that the Assassins sent an ambassador to the Christian King of Jerusalem, promising to become Christians themselves if the King stopped paying annual tributes to the Templars. The offer, which was not taken seriously, was rejected; but on his way home the ambassador was waylaid and murdered by a Templar, who was subsequently protected by his Grand Master. This and other unpleasant stories about the Knights Templar – including accusations of heresy and blasphemy – were used to justify their persecution and suppression, in the fourteenth century, by the English and French church authorities. Oriental historians have also claimed that the crusaders borrowed from the Assassins certain conceptions which in later times led to the formation of a number of European secret societies, such as the Jesuits.

There were, of course, many clashes between crusaders and Assassins, usually followed by periods of neighbourly coexistence and even collaboration. One of the major collisions was caused by the assassination of the crusader Count Raymond II of Tripoli – the Assassins' first Frankish victim – in 1130. The enraged Knights invaded and ravaged the Assassins' territory, forcing them to pay an annual tribute of two thousand pieces of gold. The money was handed over for some years until the Assassins again had the upper hand in that region.

What disturbs Christian historians most of all are the stories, too many of them and too well substantiated to be dismissed as fables, which tell of political and military cooperation, secret or open, between the crusaders and the Assassins later in the twelfth century, especially in the time of Sultan Saladin and his great opponent, Richard Coeur-de-Lion. Two Assassins – to mention the most famous of these stories – disguised themselves as Christian monks and gained admission to the court of the Marquis Conrad de Montferrat, King of Jerusalem, in Tyre. As soon as they had a chance, they stabbed him to death, and when caught and interrogated under torture, confessed that they had acted at the instigation of King Richard. The English ruler had, in fact, a certain interest in getting rid of the Marquis; very soon after the murder, his protégé, Count Henri de Champagne, married the latter's widow and succeeded to the throne of Jerusalem.

Had Richard really enlisted the help of the Assassins, and what was the price their leader exacted from him? Did he secretly contribute to the funds? Anything was possible in those confused times when the Assassins were able to run their protection racket all over the Middle East, and their reputation as efficient killers ensured that any ruler, secular or spiritual, paid up on the nail when approached by the emissaries from Alamut or Damascus with direct or indirect hints that his life was 'in danger'. At the height of their power, in the thirteenth century, the Syrian Assassins graciously accepted gifts worth tens of thousands of dinars from no less a sovereign than the German Emperor Frederick II, who personally led a crusade to add the title of King of Jerusalem to his distinctions. In return for the gifts the Assassins caused no trouble to the crusaders.

After Frederick's departure the Knights Hospitallers – later called the Knights of Malta – again demanded tributes from the Assassins. They replied 'Don't you know that your Emperor has given to us – how can you expect us then that we give to you?' The Hospitallers, however, did not take no for an answer, they attacked an Assassin stronghold, conquered it, and carried off a great deal of booty.

The Assassins had a way of impressing visitors with their

power over the *fedayin* and the discipline and obedience among them. Count Henri de Champagne, the King of Jerusalem after Monferrat's assassination, was travelling through Ismaili country when a superior officer of the missionaries invited him to his castle. The Count was received with every mark of honour, as he wrote in his reminiscences, and asked to accompany his host up to the tallest tower – not only, as it turned out, to admire the view. Two *fedayin* stood at the top as sentinels. 'These men,' said the Assassin chief, 'obey me much better than your Christian soldiers obey their lords.' He gave a signal, and the two men flung themselves down, smashing themselves to death. 'In this spirit,' the Assassin told his horrified guest, 'the faithful fight the enemies of our Imam.'

Hasan ibn al-Sabbah, the first Old Man of the Mountain, died in 1124, probably at the age of ninety. During his earthly days he had been responsible for the deaths of thousands of people, among them some fifty outstanding personalities – including his old schoolmate and benefactor, Nizam-ul-mulk, who became the very first victim of the Old Man's *fedayin*. It seems that Hasan was afraid of the ridicule his claims to divinity would provoke from a man who had known him so long and so well. The murderer disguised himself as a *sufi,* a member of a harmless mystical sect, and stabbed the Grand Vizier to death as he was being carried to his harem tent in a litter. Even more horrifying is the fact that Hasan killed both his own sons, one for committing an assassination without his father's specific orders, and the other for getting drunk.

What was the purpose, if any, of all the terrible slaughter the Old Man of the Mountain caused among his fellow Moslems? Had it been nothing but the excesses of a fanatical, hashish-drunk sect for the greater glory of its self-styled prophet, it would surely have died with Hasan himself. But it did not; for almost a century and a half after his death, it flourished and progressed. Under the prevailing, often chaotic conditions, with the Caliphate, the crusaders, the Turks and various factions of Mohammedanism fighting for supremacy in the Middle East, the Assassins had not only the advantage of rigid discipline and centralized leadership but also of a creed that inspired courage and sacrifice in what they believed to be a great religious and political cause.

First of all, it is significant that most of their victims were representatives, great or small, of the Sunnite 'establishment', the imperialist Caliphate that ruled, or fought to maintain its rule, over the whole of the Islamic world from its Egyptian head-quarters. The word *sunna* means custom, that is, the custom of Mohammed; the majority of Moslems, whether they recognized the early caliphs as rightful successors to the Prophet or not, were, therefore, Sunnites, and as such supporters of the establishment. And it was this that the militant Persian Ismailis regarded as their principal enemy, an enemy that had to be weakened by terror and ultimately crushed, so that they themselves could take over the Islamic Empire and render the Islamic creed victorious. Combinations of political and religious aims, to be achieved by unscrupulous slaughter, were of course no purely Oriental feature; after all, Charlemagne had enlarged his empire and 'Christianized' the Saxons three centuries earlier by slaying tens of thousands of them.

Indiscriminate though the Assassins' murders and extortions may have seemed to the Christian Europeans who were not familiar with the subtleties of Moslem sectarianism, they were as a rule committed against selected individuals, Sunnites who stood in the way of the sect's ambitions; native Christians and Jews, as well as other Shiite sects who also opposed the estab-lishment, were left alone. Nor were the Assassins' supporters all recruited from the ranks of the simple hill folk or those who had grudges against the Caliphate; like Hasan himself, many were educated townspeople, teachers and doctors, intellectuals and clerics; in short, they came from a class that had already found Ismailism an attractive alternative to orthodox Mohammed-anism and to whom Hasan's militant 'new preaching' appealed to a certain degree. They discovered an element of social and economic rebellion in it, rebellion against an arbitrary bureau-cracy and a corrupt ruling class; and they welcomed the Ismailis as a powerful resistance movement against the barbarian invaders from the east, the Seljuq Turks, who were trying to impose their new order on an older and superior civilization.

At least equally strong was the mystical appeal of the Assassins. To be sure, they had started out as just another of many Messianic sects with secret rites, magic numbers, such as the seven degrees of initiation, blood-curdling oaths and a creed in which resurrection, reincarnation and revelation were important elements. But the activities of the Assassin sect had a few additional attractions, from Hasan's Paradise on earth to the use of hashish for inducing a visionary state. However, the most powerful attraction, in a turbulent period and part of the world, seems to have been the discipline that the Old Man of the Mountain was able to enforce among his followers, and the system of well-planned organization he had established: an attraction which has worked throughout history in favour of dictatorship, right up to our own century.

For Hasan himself was not just the callous and ambitious maniac as portrayed by his enemies. With all his terrifying ruthlessness, he was a philosopher and theologian as well as a man of planning and action; some of his writings have survived and show him as the principal creator of the 'new preaching', the reformed Ismaili doctrine which claimed that he was the true representative of the 'hidden Imam', a central concept of the Ismaili faith – divinely appointed and inspired, infallible and all-knowing, commanding implicit obedience. Hasan was the *hudja,* the proof and source of the 'hidden Imam', and guided by him as the executive of his will and teaching. Others who also claimed to be representatives of the Imam were frauds and their followers sinners who had to be led on the right way or, if they persisted in their error, destroyed.

The first Old Man of the Mountain himself designated the second as his successor: Kia Buzurg-Umid ('Great Promise'), Hasan's most trusted military commander for twenty years. The pattern of activities continued under him: units of regimental strength attacked forts and castles, funds were collected by blackmail, individual opponents were killed (including two Caliphs), converts gained, territories consolidated. A brief flirtation with the Turks ended in a major setback for the Assassins: Buzurg-Umid concluded a secret treaty with the crusader King Baldwin II of Jerusalem, which involved handing over Tyre to the sect if it succeeded by a treacherous ruse in opening the gates of Turkish-held Damascus to the crusaders. The plan was betrayed: six thousand Assassins within the city, including the Ismaili vizier, were killed by the Turks in revenge, and the Turkish garrison of Damascus attacked and defeated the crusaders. From then on, the Assassins and the Turks were deadly enemies.

Kia Buzurg-Umid was succeeded by his son, who turned out to be a weak leader, soon to be eclipsed by his own son, Hasan II. This magnetic personality was also a megalomaniac who claimed to be no other than the 'hidden Imam' himself, a direct descendant of the Prophet Mohammed. He was assassinated by his brother-in-law. The next Old Man of the Mountain was Mohammed II who fancied himself as a man of letters, but the thirty-five years of his rule as leader of the Assassins were characterized rather by the iron rod which he wielded over his followers, quite justifiably so, from his point of view. It was the time when the Assassins had at last found their match in the shape of Saladin, the great architect of Moslem unity, and, as such, the arch enemy of the Assassins no less than of the crusaders.

Sultan Saladin had overthrown the Ismaili Caliphate in Egypt to re-establish the orthodox Islamic faith, fought a successful war against the crusaders in Palestine and proceeded to purge all Syria of the Assassins. While he was besieging Aleppo, Mohammed II sent his *fedayin* into the Sultan's camp to do away with him, but the attempt failed; so did a second a year and a half later, in 1176, when a group of Assassins who had infiltrated into the ranks of Saladin's soldiers attacked him with knives. However, his armour protected him and he received only flesh wounds.

Now it looked as though a fight to the end was inevitable. The Sultan invaded the Assassins' territory and laid it waste. Then, suddenly, the onslaught stopped. There are several versions of why Saladin did not pursue his avowed aim to wipe out the sect. The Assassins say that he sued for peace, overawed by their mysterious powers; but it is much more likely that the Assassins were the ones who asked for mercy, offering the Sultan a solemn promise never to attack him again, and that he accepted readily as he wanted to have his hands free against the crusaders. At any rate, there were no more attempts against his life and no more clashes of arms between Assassins and Saladin's troops. Even when the Sultan was defeated by Richard Coeur-de-Lion (with whom, as we know, the Assassins seem to have arranged a certain degree of collaboration) they did not attack Saladin from behind to finish him off, as they might have done.

A few years before the turn of the thirteenth century, Mohammed II died and was succeeded as Old Man of the Mountain by a Persian. With him began a period of comparative quiet and even cooperation with other Islamic groups, which lasted for half a century. Orders from Alamut went out to the Syrian Assassins to build mosques, observe rites, obey the holy laws – and to spare the lives of fellow Moslems. A few Christians of rank did, however, die at the hands of the *fedayin* in that period, but on the whole the mere threat of assassination succeeded with Moslems and Christians alike, thus securing the sect a comfortable income. The proselytizing ardour of the old days seemed to have fizzled out. They had also adopted the practice of keeping at Alamut some distinguished and useful personalities as captives – perhaps not entirely unwilling ones, considering the attractions of Paradise valley: artists, physicians, astrologers, philosophers, military historians, linguists. To the foreign visitor, such as Emperor Frederick II in 1227, the sect may have appeared almost harmless and probably much-maligned; his gifts were accepted with the grace of cultured and educated people.

Had the good life made them soft, inclined to ignore the writing on the wall? Did they underrate the danger from the Mongols approaching from the east, steadily destroying the Islamic civilization in their path? Genghis Khan had died in 1227, but his sons and grandsons continued the advance to the west. By the middle of the thirteenth century Genghis's grandson Hulaku was leading his hordes into Persia. The Caliphate of Baghdad was crushed. Too late the Assassins woke up to the peril; they put an army in the field, but it was utterly defeated in 1256 and twelve thousand Assassins were slain.

As the Mongols were sweeping westward into Syria the survivors of the sect were ordered to 'go underground', conceal their faith and join other Moslem forces in resisting the invaders. Baybars, the Mameluke Sultan of Egypt, succeeded in repelling the Mongols; as a gesture of gratitude for the Assassins' help he restored Alamut to them, but forced them to pay him the tribute they had formerly sent to the Frankish crusaders. They soon found that they had now got a new master rather than an ally. Baybars assigned the Assassins' lands in fief to one of his military commanders, who squeezed them dry with his tax demands. The end came when Baybars used a real or alleged plot to assassinate him to justify the systematic suppression of the sect, though he went on to employ the traditional skill of individual Assassins for his own purposes; some of the murders and murderous attempts against opponents, such as Prince Edward of England in 1272, appear to have been the work of Assassins in the Sultan's service. A few castles of the Assassins held out until 1273, when the last one fell under Mameluke rule.

Yet some pockets of the sect survived, almost unnoticed, for over half a millennium; it was only in 1811 that the French consul in Aleppo discovered during a journey to Persia that there were people who acknowledged allegiance to an Ismaili Imam called Shah Khalilullah, living in Kehk, an out-of-the-way village between Teheran and Isfahan; he was alleged to have miraculous powers and claimed to be a descendant of the fourth Old Man of the Mountain. The consul did some research on the subject and found that there were Ismailis 'as far away as India' who went on pilgrimages to the Imam 'to receive his blessing in return for the pious and magnificent offerings they bring him'.

Little more was heard of the sect until, in 1850, a British court in Bombay had to deal with a case in which nineteen men were accused of having murdered four men in broad daylight – both killers and victims being members of a local Moslem sect of traders called Khojas, which numbered tens of thousands. It turned out that some Khojas had refused to pay their annual dues to the head of the sect – in fact, the son of Shah Kalilullah who had been murdered in 1817. The Shah of Persia had appointed the son governor of the district and given him the title of 'Aga Khan' (Turkish for 'lord' and 'ruler') in 1818. From his seat at Kehk he had sent his requests for the customary contributions to his followers in India, but since 1827 a group of Bombay Khojas had refused to pay up. The matter developed into a split within the community, feelings grew strong on both sides and the murders of 1850 were the result. Meanwhile, the Aga Khan had led an unsuccessful rebellion against the Shah and fled to India, where he took an active part as head of the Khojas.

The case was tried by Sir Joseph Arnould, the Chief Justice; four of the murderers were convicted and hanged, but the dispute over the Aga Khan's claim to be the legitimate leader of the sect dragged on for over fifteen years. It ended, after a host of witnesses and experts had been heard, with Sir Joseph's findings: their creed was that of the Ismailis and they were 'a sect of people whose ancestors ... were converted to, and had throughout abided in the faith of the Shia Imamee Ismailis, which has always been and still is bound by ties of spiritual allegiance to the hereditary Imams of the Ismailis', the latest of whom was the Aga Khan, a direct descendant of the Old Man of the Mountain at Alamut, through whom he claimed descent from the Caliphs of Egypt and ultimately from the Prophet Mohammed. In other words: the modern Ismailis are the successors of the Assassins, and the Aga Khan – the title was confirmed by Queen Victoria to the present Aga Khan's grandfather in recognition of his co-operation with the British Government – is their spiritual head.

Not only India and Pakistan, but also Syria, the Lebanon, Persia, Central Asia and Tanzania still have many communities of the Ismaili sect. They are law-abiding, peaceful citizens of their respective countries; the old ambitions of overthrowing the Islamic establishment are forgotten, and so are their ancient ways of treachery, blackmail and assassination.

The Thugs

It may be pure coincidence that the earliest record of the activities of an Indian sect called *thag* – Hindi for 'deceiver' – dates from the thirteenth century, the time when the Mongol invasion made the Persian Assassins go underground. However, it is certainly possible that a number of them sought refuge and anonymity in the teeming masses of the Indian population, to wait for an opportunity to start some kind of a branch movement. Such an opportunity (assuming that the theory is correct) seems to have come soon enough, for that record appears in the writings of the Sultan of Delhi, who speaks of no less than one thousand *Thags* – or 'Thugs', the spelling later adopted by the English – who had been brought before him. They were members of a secret society or brotherhood who believed that they were supernaturally inspired and commanded by the Deity to strangle and rob people. The Sultan, unwilling to offend such strong religious feelings, merely exiled the Thugs from his territory, sending them to Bengal, where they promptly developed an even more efficient and ruthless form of 'Thuggee'.

But perhaps the ancestry of the Indian Thugs goes farther back even than the beginnings of the Assassins. Among the great number of extremist Shiite sects that flourished in southern Iraq in the early eighth century, there was one that practised strangling with cords as a sacred duty: and this is precisely what the Thugs did. Only their divine command to kill did not issue from any self-styled prophet but, according to their ardent belief, directly from the Hindu goddess Kali (meaning 'the Black One'), wife of Siva and the acme of bloodthirstiness, whose idols are black, with red eyes; she has at least four arms, often eight or even ten, bloodstained palms, matted hair, huge fang-like teeth and a protruding tongue that drips with blood. As a rule she wears a necklace of skulls, earrings in the shape of small corpses, and is girdled with snakes. She is the goddess of death and destruction in Hindu mythology, and demands bloody sacrifices, of humans (customary until the end of the eighteenth century) as well as of animals.

The Kali mythology of popular Hinduism explains the Thug cult. The principal Hindu gods are Vishnu the Creator and Siva the Destroyer, but more widely worshipped than these are Siva's female companions, Devi (or Durga), the goddess of fertility and Kali (or Bhowani), the goddess of destruction. She was born of Siva, but she is also his consort and may be regarded as another 'aspect' of Devi-Durga, for the elaborate temple rituals in her honour include prostitution (with priests and worshippers as the prostitutes' partners) and other sexual and fertility elements. Kali's devotees submit to dreadful torments: they are beaten by the priests, hooks are passed through their muscles with ropes attached which lead over a tall pole and whose other ends are embedded in the ground; the poles are swung around, and the devotees, streaming with blood, are whirled above the heads of the ecstatic worshippers, who shout, 'Victory to Mother Kali!'

The traditional Thuggee legend says that Kali built an image of herself and breathed life into it. She then gathered a number of her votaries, whom she gave the name of Thugs, instructing them in the art of killing by strangling the living image she had made. She endowed the Thugs with superior intelligence and cunning, sent them forth to worship her by deceit and destruction, permitting them to keep the plunder from their victims as reward. She also promised to give them certain omens whereby they could foretell the success or otherwise of their plans; the observation of these omens formed an important part of the Thuggee rites.

We have some reliable accounts of the inititation ceremonies of the sect. The novice was bathed and dressed in a clean loin-cloth that had never been bleached. His guru, or spiritual leader, then took him to a room where the elders of the Thug band were seated on a white sheet. The guru asked them whether they were willing to receive the novice as a brother. After they had assented he was led out in the open air, where the guru raised his hands and eyes to heaven and exclaimed, 'O Bhowani, Mother of the World, whose devotees we are, receive this thy servant; vouch-safe him thy protection; grant to us an omen that may assure us of thy consent!' Now they waited in silence until some omen occurred, perhaps the cry or movement of a bird or animal. Then the novice was taken back into the presence of the elders, and a pick-axe was placed in his right hand. He had to raise it and repeat after the elders the sacred oath of the sect, binding himself to be faithful, brave and secretive, and to attempt the destruction of every human being whose death the goddess would demand. Women, being the source of life, were to be spared, but only in theory; so were priests, fakirs, men with cows, beggars, dancers, musicians, sweepers, blacksmiths, carpenters, cripples and lepers. In practice, however, most witnesses of the Thugs' murders were also killed, whatever their sex or caste.

Some branches of the sect, especially after their exploits had made them affluent, gave the novice a huge feast where he was handed jasmine flowers (whose colour is pleasing to Kali) and sprayed with rosewater; some naked girls danced before him but he was not supposed to yield to temptation.

One of the most interesting features of Thuggee is that Hindus and Moslems alike – notwithstanding the ban on killing laid down in the Koran – joined the Thugs, and here one might detect another link with the Assassins. The traditional Thug greeting was, 'Ali bhai salaam', meaning 'Salutation to Ali my brother', which seems to be a reference to the successor of the Prophet revered by the Ismailis. The fact is that the murderous sect of the Thugs united, as no other Indian organization did, the two traditionally opposed religious groups, and that very few

incidences of friction or violence between them within the
fraternity have been known. One common bond was the secret
Thug jargon spoken and understood by all members from whatever region they came.

At any rate, the bloodthirsty black goddess became also the
Moslem novice's ruler as soon as he joined the Thugs. It has been
said that the Moslems' contribution to the sect was their military
tradition – the Thug bands were organized according to the
Persian system of units and ranks – while the Hindus looked after
the spiritual and ritualistic side. Though it did not surprise the
British administration in India that certain groups of Hindus
regarded murder as a sacred duty, the participation of Mohammedans seemed rather puzzling. As late as 1838, Colonel
Meadows Taylor, in his *Confessions of a Thug*, wrote:

> Strange that Hindu and Moslem of every sect and denomination
> should join with one accord in the superstition from which this
> horrible trade has arisen. In the Hindu, perhaps, it is not to be
> wondered at, as the goddess who protects him is one whom all castes
> regard with reverence and hold in the utmost dread : but as for the
> Moslem, unless his conduct springs from that terrible doctrine of
> Fatalism, with which every true believer is thoroughly imbued from
> the first dawn of his reason, it is difficult to assign a reason for the
> horrible pursuit he has engaged in.

The Colonel wrote this at a time when a great deal was already
known about the sect, whose Hindi name was then just beginning
to edge into everyday English at home as a new term for ruffian
or cut-throat. In India, the British also called them 'Stranglers';
in the south of the sub-continent, the sect itself preferred the
name of *Phansigars*, from the Hindi word *phansi* for noose.

We know next to nothing about the development and activities of the Thugs from the thirteenth century, when the Sultan
of Delhi had to deal with them, until the early nineteenth, when
British rule extended over two-thirds of the Indian peninsula.
The younger Pitt's India Bill of 1784 had shifted the political
and military control of the country from the hands of the East
India Company into those of the British Government, and with
it the full responsibility for enforcing law and order. Thus the
administrators found themselves faced with the formidable task
of stamping out apparently well-organized bands of murderers

and robbers who made tens of thousands of people disappear mysteriously every year on their cross-country travels. India's vast interior was still beyond the reach of the British military and police forces; in 1812, for instance, about forty thousand people were estimated to have been killed and robbed, with only a handful of suspects being caught. There were several gangs: the mounted Pindaris, numbering some thirty thousand, who roamed the countryside in units of regimental strength, torturing, murdering, pillaging, raping and maiming their victims, often with women participating in their activities; the Dacoits, whose numbers in northern India and Burma were at least five thousand; and above all the Thugs, who operated all over the peninsula in countless groups. Trade between cities and districts was paralyzed, so that India's craftsmen, particularly the handloom weavers, had become impoverished. The East India Company found it easy to turn these into a cheap labour force for the mass production of low-quality cloth for Britain's new industrial proletariat.

In 1809, at the age of twenty-one, William Sleeman, the son of a sea captain from Cornwall, joined the Bengal Army. He was a conscientious, hard-working and devoted cadet, a non-smoker and non-drinker who spent his leisure time in India reading philosophical works and studying Oriental religions and the Hindi language. In 1815, as a young officer, he happened to read an article which was to change his whole life. It was written by Dr Robert C. Sherwood of the Madras Medical Service, and dealt with the sect of the *Phansigars,* probably the first detailed account ever to be published on the subject. The doctor had studied them thoroughly and the tale he had to tell was frightening.

The Phansigars [he wrote] are indistinguishable from their neighbours so long as they live peacefully in their villages, which they do for most of the year. Then, suddenly, they vanish from their homes and go on their annual expeditions, strangling travellers, rifling and maiming their bodies, then killing all witnesses except young boys, who are adopted by them and initiated into the 'horrible mysteries' of the sect on reaching puberty. The Phansigars operate in gangs of from ten to fifty people, disguised as ordinary travellers, waiting for a chance to single out a genuine traveller, who is then attacked by groups of three Phansigars and strangled. The gashed and cut-up body is buried by the wayside.

On the religious basis of the cult, Dr Sherwood wrote:

Kali is regarded as their tutelary deity. Before an expedition is determined on, an entertainment is given, when the ceremony of sacrificing a sheep is performed. The head of the sheep being cut off, it is placed with a burning lamp upon it and the right forefoot in the mouth before the image of Kali, and the goddess is entreated to reveal to them whether she approves of the expedition ... White and yellow being considered the favourite colours of Kali, the cloths for strangling are of one or other of these.

Dr Sherwood noted that he had heard of no instance of a European having been murdered by the sect, probably because they were too well armed and guarded on their journeys and because scrupulous enquiries were made if one disappeared 'in the dominions of the East India Company', while the disappearance of natives in such large numbers 'excites little interest with the authorities'. There was, however, one exception: Lieutenant Maunsell of the Bengal Infantry became a victim of the sect in the Northwest Territories in 1812. A favourite trick of the stranglers, said Dr Sherwood, was to send out an attractive woman on the road, with dishevelled hair and apparently in distress; she would tell the travellers some sob story, and as a rule one of them would ask her to mount his horse behind him, whereupon she would strangle him as her companions came out of ambush.

The doctor's account impressed Sleeman deeply, and he decided to do something about it. As a junior officer, however, he had not enough authority and opportunity for the job; so he asked to be transferred to the Civil Service, and was in 1819 appointed Junior Magistrate in the Saugor and Narbada Territories in Central India, where the British held a comparatively narrow strip of land. He began to enquire systematically into Thug activities from village to village. Bodies were dug up or lifted from disused wells, usually with grisly injuries. The villagers, however, were too frightened to say what they knew, or perhaps they really knew nothing. At that stage, all he could find out was the basis and background of the Thug cult, the

Kali legend, their 'holy writ that inspired them to kill without fear', as he put it in his report.

The authorities, anxious not to interfere with anything that looked like religious customs, refused to take any action; it was only in 1828, when General Lord William Bentinck, Duke of Portland, the Whig administrator, was appointed first Governor-General of India, that Sleeman, at his own request, was charged with reporting on Thug and anti-Thug operations over an extensive area of Central India to the Governor-General. His reports are still kept at the library of the India Office, now the Commonwealth Relations office, in London, and reveal one of the most dramatic stories from the period of the British Raj.

At first, Sleeman made only slow progress. Judges were reluctant to convict Thugs on circumstantial evidence, and witnesses would not talk. One major stumbling block was that the Thugs knew the art of camouflage to perfection. They were not only model citizens in their communities, discharging their civil and religious duties most scrupulously; they also paid very high land rents to their landlords, thus making them beneficiaries of their robberies. Sleeman's attempts at inducing people to talk usually ran up against a brick wall of silence, while the authorities were unwilling to antagonize the rich and influential major landlords by putting them under pressure to reveal what they knew. The Thugs' families would not or could not disclose anything either, except that their men were devoted husbands and fathers, which was the truth. Sleeman was a little luckier with the Moslems; one of them, arrested as a member of a Thug gang, told him during interrogation why those loving husbands and fathers would not hesitate to kill women and children to eliminate witnesses: 'When omens are favourable, we consider them as victims thrown into our hands by the deity; we are mere instruments in her hands to destroy them; if we do not kill them she will never again be propitious to us, and we and our families will have to endure misery and want.'

Lord Bentinck had the courage to grip firmly a good many hot irons in India. Among his major reforms was, for instance, the ban on *sati*, the burning or interment of widows. Yet he still hesitated to authorize a full-scale campaign against the Thugs as demanded by Sleeman in his reports. Exasperated at having been given a job but not the tools to finish it, Sleeman sought help, as a last resort, from public opinion. He wrote an unsigned letter, nearly six thousand words long, to the editor of the Calcutta Literary Gazette. The letter, which was printed early in October 1830, was the first public disclosure of Thug beliefs, activities, and rites; most of this was information which Sleeman himself had gathered. A particularly interesting passage revealed what went on at a certain Thug temple, one of the major centres of the sect:

Kali's temple at Bindachul, a few miles west of Mirzapore on the Ganges, is constantly filled with murderers from every quarter of India between the rivers Narbada, Ganges and Indus, who go there to offer up in person a share of the booty they have acquired from their victims strangled in their annual excursions ... The priests of this temple know perfectly well the source from which they derive their offerings and the motives from which they are made, and they possibly console themselves with the conclusion that if they do not condescend to take them, the priests of other temples will ... They suggest expeditions and promise the murderers in the name of their mistress immunity and wealth, provided a due share be offered up to their shrine, and none of the rites and ceremonies be neglected. If they (the Thugs) die by the sword in the execution of these murderous duties by Kali assigned or sanctioned, she promises them paradise in its most exquisite delights, but if they are taken and executed, it must arise from her displeasure, incurred by some neglect of the duties they owe to her, and they must as disturbed spirits inhabit mid-air until her wrath be appeased ...

Writing anonymously, Sleeman could not, of course, suggest in detail any steps that would have come under his responsibility. However, he was able to discuss the likely reaction to the publication of his letter:

To pull down the temple at Bindachul and hang the priests would no doubt be the wish of every honest Christian, but it would answer no useful purpose. Others would soon be found to answer the same purposes, and probably the attention drawn to this temple by this communication will be sufficient of itself to deprive the priests of the offerings which they have been accustomed to receive from the Thugs ...

At the end, Sleeman came to these impressive conclusions:

> Under the sanction of religious rites and promises the pest is
> spreading . . . It is an organized system of religious and civil polity
> prepared to receive converts from all religions and sects and urge
> them the murder of their fellow creatures under the assurance of
> high rewards in this world and the next. Sad experience teaches us
> how prone mankind has been in all ages and nations to prey upon
> the lives and property of each other under such assurances or under
> any sanction of law, human or divine, which they deem sufficient . . .
> If these people are led by priests to expect great rewards in this
> world and the next, we must oppose to it a greater dread of immedi-
> ate punishment, and if our present establishments are not suitable
> for the purpose we should employ others that are, till the evil be re-
> moved, for it is the imperious duty of the Supreme Government of
> this country to put an end in some way or other to this dreadful
> system of murder, by which thousands of human beings are now
> annually sacrificed upon every great road throughout India . . .
> These men (the Thugs) may be found often most securely estab-
> lished in the very seats of our principal judiciary establishments;
> and of late years they are known to have formed some settlements
> to the east of the Ganges in parts that they used merely to visit in
> the course of their annual excursions . . .

Few 'letters to the editor' have ever caused such a sensation as
this one, anonymous though it was. Public opinion in India,
meaning the British Establishment, was deeply shocked. Here
was a man, whoever he was, who not only revealed in the most
dreadful details a widespread and powerful murder organization,
but was also accusing the Government of doing little to suppress
it. This was a challenge which the British Raj could not ignore.

Lord Bentinck wrote at once to Curwen Smith, his Agent
in the Saugor and Narbada Territories, who had been in constant touch with Sleeman about the latter's plans to stop Thuggee.
It was now time, wrote the Governor-General, to seize the Thug
leaders who were 'still at large'; in fact, none of them had been
caught as yet.

With this in view [Bentinck continued], you will be pleased to
endeavour to ascertain the writer of the letter, who appears to
possess extensive knowledge of the character and habits of the
Thugs . . . You will request him to communicate to you such further
particulars as may promote the object in view of apprehending the

Thugs ... whether by offer of rewards, the employment of spies near the temple at which they are said to make their offerings, or such other mode as may appear to seem the most advisable, and report your sentiments for the consideration of the Government.

Curwen Smith must have known quite well, and Bentinck may have guessed, that Sleeman was the writer; at any rate, Sleeman now had no reason to remain anonymous. He had achieved what he wanted. He went to work with Smith.

They both drew up a reply to the Governor-General, submitting to him what they called a 'Plan for the Eventual Destruction of the Associations of Thugs'. A body of fifty mounted irregular troops for the arrest of suspected Thugs was to be recruited, acting under a superintendent with full authority for the job in a wide area of central and northern India, including the states of the independent princes in that region. The arrested suspects were to be committed for trial by the agent, Curwen Smith, at Saugor or Jubbulpore. Rewards of up to a thousand rupees – then about £100 – were to be offered for information leading to the arrest of prominent Thugs. Apart from the mounted irregulars, called *nujeebs*, the superintendent should be given detachments of sepoys, Indian soldiers from the British Army, and help by the police wherever required. Heavy penalties should be inflicted on the chiefs in whose villages Thugs had been harboured and, a measure which must have appeared detestable to many Englishmen, authority should be given to detain the wives and children of Thugs against whom information had been laid until he was arrested. But Sleeman and Curwen Smith explained that 'Thugs are generally hereditary; there could be no injustice therefore in chaining the lion's whelps until the lion himself is disposed of'. All British Residents, the government agents residing at the princes' courts, should be directed to have all known or suspected Thugs arrested; the princes would then have to be asked to permit the suspects to be tried, which was the required procedure. Curwen Smith signed the document and added a rider: 'Captain Sleeman is undoubtedly in my opinion the most proper person for the situation of Superintendent.' Lord Bentinck took the advice, and Sleeman was appointed.

At least, there would now be no more anonymous letters.

The task which Sleeman accepted at the end of 1830 was daunting, or would have been for anyone without the new super-intendent's zeal and courage. The mere size of the territory, twice as large as England, Scotland and Wales, was frighten-ing; most of it was desert, but there was also plenty of bush to offer cover for attackers or fugitives. The main roads carried what today is often called 'bunched' traffic; caravans and wagon trains with dozens or even hundreds of travellers, and then long gaps with no more than a few stragglers, for there was safety only in numbers. When Sleeman took over, all the armed protection which the travellers had was what they themselves could afford in the way of hired guards, which more often than not was very little. And at the end of the road there was always some densely populated town affording shelter to murderers and robbers on the run.

An estimated five thousand Thugs were active in the area over which Sleeman organized his campaign. But they were not just gangs looking for victims where they could find them. They, too, were strictly organized, a hierarchy with certain classes, each of which had to carry out special duties. A *sotha*, for instance, was to act as a decoy, joining groups of travellers, getting friendly with some of them, and attempting to separate them from the main caravan; a *shumshea* had the task of distracting the attention of the victim at the vital moment when his comrades emerged from the bush, and the *bhuttote* approached the victim from behind with the noose in his hand. The *lugha* had to prepare the grave; the usual procedure was that he went in advance of the gang to find a suitable spot for the grave and start digging so that the body, or bodies, could be disposed of with the minimum delay.

The rites of the sect demanded that the most important man of each gang, the *bhuttote,* should pass through special ceremonies before being accepted for the task of strangling the victims. He had to fast for four days, taking only milk; during that period every chance omen was carefully watched. On the fifth day, he was annointed and a vermilion mark put on his forehead. He was given the murder weapon, a silken handkerchief with a silver coin knotted into it. After acquiring some experience he was expected to be able to break a man's neck with this weapon within a second or two. When the *bhuttote* had completed his first murder there was a ceremony at which he was invited to sit on the white sheet with the elders. He would then untie the knot in his handkerchief and give the silver coin, together with some additional money from the booty, to his guru, whose feet he would touch in reverence. This was the last part of a young Thug's initiation; he was now a fully-fledged *bhuttote*.

A general ceremony for all who had returned safely from a gang's annual expedition was also customary, a 'thanksgiving' to Kali. The party would bring some *goor,* unrefined sugar, to the priest. The leader of the expedition would take his seat on the white sheet facing west; before him, the *goor*, the sacred pick-axe and pieces of silver were spread out. A small hole was made in the ground, some *goor* poured into it, and Kali was invoked by the priest while he was sprinkling holy water on the hole and the pick-axe. Each member of the party then ate a little of the *goor* and drank some holy water in silence.

Often enough, of course, things went wrong on an expedition. Sleeman reported a case in which a gang of Thugs had murdered a whole party of religious mendicants on their way home after a successful begging trip; killing beggars was one of Kali's taboos, but the rich booty had tempted the stranglers. They were just about to bury their victims when a party of horsemen approached on the road.

In great alarm they concealed themselves behind a mound of earth at some distance, leaving the bodies on the ground [wrote Sleeman]. The horsemen passed by without stopping, but when the Thugs returned to the grave they found that the dead bodies had disappeared! The approvers [informers], who have been questioned on the subject of the disappearance of the bodies, are unable, or pretended to be so, to account for the circumstance. They admit that the goddess Bhowani ... had probably removed the bodies, adding: though this interference on the part of the deity would argue a dereliction of duties on their [the Thugs'] parts, in having put such holy persons to death, yet as they had unlimited authority from Bhowani herself to commit murder, and the mendicants had through their means obtained a speedy passage to Paradise, no sin can possibly attach to them from the commission of the act.

Sleeman did not reveal whether he had an explanation of his own for the mystery of the vanished bodies.

Sleeman had recruited a whole army of spies, called 'approvers' in official euphemistic language; they told the police or soldiers where bodies of victims were to be found, and these exhumations were, as a rule, a rather shocking experience for the villagers in the neighbourhood. Now they began to come forward to report on vanished relatives at the police stations, even mentioning names of suspected Thugs. The first arrests were made, and the local magistrates were at last willing to co-operate and commit suspects for trial. Sleeman collected all the information he could get in files, a system which must have seemed ultra-modern in the 1830s; thus he was able to build up detailed dossiers on the various gangs operating in the area, and on their favourite routes. Sepoy units were sent on patrol along these routes, guided by 'approvers' with information about dates of annual Thug excursions, and in an increasing number of cases the murderers were caught red-handed.

Superstitious fear because more and more excursions ended in disaster – believed to indicate Kali's anger – began to work in Sleeman's favour. Thugs who had been arrested offered their services as informers, and revealed the names of other members of the sect to save their own skins. The Thug's oath of secrecy was losing its power of protection. The process of demoralization among the gangs had set in: no member could be sure any longer that his fellow-Thug would not send him to the gallows.

There was one name that kept appearing in the interrogations, that of a supreme leader called Feringeea. Sleeman's file on him grew. The man was in his mid-twenties, an intelligent, educated and good-looking Brahmin. He was well-guarded and elusive. If he could be caught, perhaps the Thug movement would fizzle out. A concerted action to get hold of him began, at first without any information about his home village or hideout. In fact, he lived with his family in the independent State of Gwalior in north-west India.

Feringeea was so sure of himself that he organized his annual expedition as usual in 1831, with a gang of forty men. But everything seemed to go wrong. For a whole week, no victims were found. One day a spy came to Sleeman's headquarters: Feringeea's gang had been seen only thirty miles away. At once a mounted detachment was sent off to intercept them. The spy was also able to reveal the leader's home village, and a second unit was dispatched to wait for him there in case he got away.

The gang was discovered resting by the roadside after its first success; they had murdered a man and three women. The *nujeebs* charged with their spears; a dozen Thugs managed to escape, but twenty-eight were caught. Feringeea was not among them. He was galloping towards his home, 175 miles away, to take his wife and children to some safe place. When he arrived three days later his servants told him that *nujeebs* had been seen in the area and he rode on without bothering about his family. Shortly afterwards the Irregulars burst into his house. Feringeea's wife and children were sent to headquarters under escort. He remained in the district, sleeping in one of five different villages every night. Sleeman had each of them watched as soon as it became known that Feringeea had been seen there and an extra reward of five hundred rupees was offered for information leading to his arrest. Several times the soldiers arrived too late, to find that the bird had flown.

There was a last chance to catch him in a village that had not yet been searched. Two sepoys knocked on the door of a known friend of Feringeea's. To their surprise, he came out himself without trying to escape; he must have thought a large unit had been sent to arrest him because of his importance. He was bound and brought to the Thug prison at Saugor, where his family was already. His interrogation, conducted by Sleeman himself, was more like a conversation between two educated people who had just finished playing a game of chess. The loser told the winner his story with surprising frankness. Feringeea's ancestors had been Thugs for eleven generations; he himself had been active as a member and eventually leader for many years, but his family had had no idea until they were arrested. 'I allowed myself to be captured,' he said, 'because I was afraid they might suffer.'

To Sleeman's disappointment, Feringeea proved to be no different from other captured Thugs; he pleaded for his life and offered information on other members of the sect in return, particularly on a meeting of several large gangs in Jypore that was to take place soon. Curwen Smith agreed to spare Feringeea's life if these gangs were caught, so that the leader's betrayal would become known throughout the fraternity. During the talks between Feringeea and Sleeman, which the latter recorded, the Thug leader explained what in his opinion was the reason for his bad luck: 'We had murdered women, although Kali forbids it. It was all due to our misfortune . . . and it was their fate to die by our hands. We all feel pity sometimes, but the sacrifices to Kali changes our nature. Let any man taste it, and he will be a Thug for life.'

Sleeman: 'So you believe that the killing of women has been the chief cause of your misfortune?'

Feringeea: 'Yes. It was fate, theirs and ours.'

The captured leader's treachery did in fact result in the arrest of all the Thugs assembled at Jypore. Saugor prison was crowded with them, most of them eager to inform against their brothers. In one house which served as a hiding place for booty, the sepoys found two thousand pearls, eight-five diamonds, a large chest full of gold coins, hundreds of gold trinkets accumulated over generations. The soldiers got extra rewards.

Thuggee had all but ceased in Central India by the autumn of 1831; only in the north-west were the gangs still operating. A large one, numbering 125 men, killed 108 people during the three-months' excursion 'season' of that year. But in 1832 Sleeman broke the Thugs' power in that area as well. 'We have incurred Kali's wrath,' said the arrested men. 'That is why we are doomed.'

Mass trials were conducted by Curwen Smith. 'In all my judicial experience,' he reported to Bentinck, 'I have never heard of such atrocities or presided over such trials, such cold-blooded murder, such heart-rending scenes of distress and misery, such base ingratitude, such total abandonment of every principle which binds man to man. . . . Mercy to such wretches would be the extreme of cruelty to mankind, and they must be paid in their own wages by rigid adherence to the law of *lex talionis* [an eye for an eye].' But passing death sentences on 110 of 'my fellow creatures', as Curwen Smith put it, was an 'ordeal' to him, and he used every chance to exert mercy, for instance in cases of only circumstantial evidence, or when Thugs had turned King's evidence against their fellows.

Completing the mopping-up process, however, took Sleeman another sixteen years. By the end of 1841 almost four thousand Thugs had been captured and tried. Although the sect as a whole was wiped out to all intents and purposes, a few pockets of

Thuggery still remained; these were cleaned up by 1848, with another five hundred arrests. One of the brighter chapters of the British Raj had ended, and back home they had a new word of contempt and condemnation.

Sleeman's devoted work had cost him his health. He accepted the easier position of Resident at Lucknow, with promotion to the rank of major-general and a knighthood to follow. In 1856, a severely sick man, he decided to return to England with his family; but he died of a heart attack aboard the ship that should have taken him home.

10

Drugs, Devil Worship, Dogs, and Snakes

Religion and Ecstasy

In 1970, the distinguished British scholar John Allegro, whose work in connection with the deciphering of the Dead Sea Scrolls had won international acclaim, startled the Christian world with his book, *The Sacred Mushroom and The Cross*, in which he suggested that the entire New Testament was a hoax in coded language, made up deliberately as a cover for instructions to members of a sect that was addicted to a hallucinatory drug. Jesus and the Apostles never existed, the Crucifixion story was a ruse to guard the cult of the 'Sacred Mushroom' – the toadstool, poisonous as well as an obvious phallic symbol – at a time when the practitioners of the cult were scattered all over the Mediterranean world after the fall of Jerusalem in AD 70. But the code was never understood, the symbolic tales were taken at their face value, and the drug cult vanished. Says Allegro: 'What began as a hoax became a trap even to those who believed themselves to be the spiritual heirs of the mystery religion, and took to themselves the name: "Christians".' That new cult needed no drug as a key to heaven; its religious and ecstatic experience stemmed from another source: the 'cover' story of the crucified rabbi called Jesus.

Allegro backs his claims etymologically: 'The main factor that has made this new discovery possible,' he says, 'has been the recovery of the oldest written language known to us: Sumerian cuneiform texts, dating back to about 3,500 BC.' However, scholarly as his explications may be, he has found rather little support for his sensational theories on the origins of the Christian faith.

To be sure, the taking of hallucinatory drugs as the central rite of a sect does not seem unusual or far-fetched in the twentieth century, and why should it not be an ancient practice? Our modern addicts often appear to hover on the borderline between hypersensitivity and religious fantasies, as we know from their own descriptions. Aldous Huxley (in his *Doors of Perception*) reports on his 'mystical' experiences after taking mescaline, a derivative of the peyote cactus which grows in the Rio Grande Valley, and which is the basis of the creed of the Native American Church, a sect with more than fifty thousand members among forty-six Indian tribes in the west and south-west of the USA and in Canada, particularly among the Navahos.

They cut off and dry the cactus tops, or buttons, and eat them in night-long ceremonies, achieving what they believe to be an immediate communication with God, the Great Spirit – an experience far more exciting than the anaemic liturgies of the paleface missionaries who have tried to Christianize them for centuries. The cult seems to have been popular long before the Spanish conquest; the old Aztec word for the cactus, still in use, is *peyote*. Some tribes pick the flowering tops, from which they brew a kind of tea; the vivid hallucinations produced by peyote are said to be the effect of a reduction of the glucose supply to the brain. The drug is considered to be the special gift from God to the American Indians. In the lore of the sect, its origin is described like this, in the words of one worshipper: 'In the first creation, God himself used to talk to all the people and tell them what to do. Then Christ came among the white people and told them what to do. Now white people have everything, the Indians have nothing. But then God gave us peyote, and that's how we found God.'

The Native American Church, founded towards the end of the First World War, has attempted to incorporate Christian elements into the peyote cult: the sect believes in the Holy Trinity and the divinity of Christ, but the drug makes their faith an immediate reality *en lieu* of conventional prayers. The Church holds conventions, meetings extending over several days; here the delegates sit cross-legged around a 'sacred fire', helping themselves to peyote buttons or cups of peyote tea which are passed around. They begin to chant to the soft rhythmic beat of the calabash. When the effects of the drug have worn off, the delegates elect their new president and committee like any other church gathering.

Nevertheless, the Federal Bureau of Indian Affairs, prompted by the conventional Christian churches, have repeatedly tried to stamp out the cult, but with little success. Peyote has been banned several times under the narcotic laws, only to be legalized again as a prop for 'religious purposes', as in 1959 by the New Mexico House of Representatives; in 1964, the Supreme Court of California ruled: 'To forbid the use of peyote is to remove the theological heart of peyotism', and quashed the conviction of three Navahos caught drinking peyote tea.

Mail Order Religion

It seems to be just as easy to set oneself up as a sect leader at the eastern shore of the American Continent, particularly in Greenwich Village. An Indian newspaperman tried it as a journalistic experiment, and reported on his experience in the London *Guardian* in 1969. All the capital he needed were a few dollars for an advertisment in the *Village Voice*: 'Guru Chakravarti assists achieve Brahman thought by Hatha Yoga'. In fact, his knowledge of the subject was, as he admitted, minimal. Within a day or two he found himself the centre of a new cult. 'Of course there had been others before me,' he wrote. 'There was the Maharishi Mahesh Yogi who had bagged Mia Farrow and the Beatles . . . But there was an idol much nearer home: an Indian who had gone up to Princeton to read chemistry, and having mystically ploughed all his exams, had decided to adopt the selfless goal of disseminating the "message" – for a consideration, of course.'

Deliberately using the claptrap terminology coined before him by other sages from the mysterious East, the reporter made such rapid progress in assembling disciples round him that he got a little frightened. When one sari-clad New Yorker told him that she knew all along that he was a *swami*, and that she knew she had 'touched God', he felt in all honesty that it was high time to shut up shop.

It may strike us as ridiculous, absurd or pathetic that a mere advertisement can trigger off such strong human impulses towards spiritual quests. No one knows them, and utilizes them, better than the people who run what has been called 'mail-order religion'. Like, for instance, the 'Archbishop of Psychiana' whose standard ads in hundreds of English-language newspapers and periodicals

claim, 'I TALKED WITH GOD, SO CAN YOU – IT'S EASY!' At the
advertisers' headquarters in Moscow, Idaho, up to two thousand
letters arrive every day from people who want to know how it's
done. They can learn it by mail in twenty primary and thirty
advanced lessons for a few dozen dollars, but they are also exhorted
to buy the Archbishop's books, which sets them back by another
one hundred dollars or more.

A former minister of the Methodist Episcopal Church, Professor Charles S. Braden, reported in his book on minority religious
groups in America, *These Also Believe* (published in 1949),
how Psychiana developed. It was founded in 1929 by forty-year-
old Frank B. Robinson, the son of an English Baptist minister
who had taken to drink and engaged in amorous intrigues with
the female members of his congregation. This put the son off
orthodox religion; still, after emigrating from England to Canada,
he accepted a scholarship in Toronto's Baptist training school but
broke off his studies and took to the road. He drifted from job
to job, joined the Salvation Army for a while, and worked as a
pharmacist all over the US; but he kept having bouts of heavy
drinking like his father before him, and sought in vain inner peace
in the churches of various denominations. At last it dawned on
him that what these clergymen told the people was not what the
people wanted. They wanted to return to their childhood dream
of God and he decided to help them do so.

He had $500, all his savings, with which he wanted to start an
advertisement campaign. The agent he asked to organize it for
him just laughed: the sum was so ridiculous. So he placed the first
few ads himself. The result was astonishing; money came rolling
in fast from people who wanted to 'talk with God', and Robinson
was soon able to extend his campaign to the whole of the States.
Within twenty years, he enrolled over a million students for his
Psychiana courses. Did he give them value for their money? If it
is worth a few dollars to be told what you would like to hear, then
the answer is definitely yes. There is no need to wait for the great
Beyond to find happiness, the 'lessons' say; everything is here and
available *now*, but 'the unseen, spiritual realm is the real, permanent one from which all material things must come'. Mental
exercises, prayers, meditation will teach the student to 'use the
mighty God-power that is there for the asking, the immense pos-
sibilities lying in your hands'. And God himself, true to that

childhood dream, is shown as the helpful father figure, while Jesus is every believer's 'pal from old Galilee', lovable and always approachable : your all-American friendly neighbourhood deity, one might call 'Archbishop' Robinson's concept. The members of the Psychiana sect never met, but were made to feel like one big, worldwide congregation. Most of them, after taking the course, did not go to church again.

'Whether Psychiana lives or dies,' wrote Professor Braden, 'it will stand out prominently as a remarkable movement, born just at the end of a period of great prosperity, and drawing to itself, during the greatest depression and the Second World War, multitudes of those who felt deeply the need for a ministry which for some reason or other they failed to find within the established churches. It stands as symptomatic of that period of confusion, uncertainty, insecurity and fear.'

The Snake Cult

There can be no greater contrast than that between the comforting and comfortable teachings of Psychiana and the cult based on Christ's words as reported in the Gospel of St Mark: 'In my name shall they cast out devils; they shall speak with new tongues; they shall take up serpents, and if they drink any deadly thing, it shall in no wise hurt them; they shall lay hands on the sick, and they shall recover.' It is the creed of a weird sect with groups in West Virginia, Tennessee, Kentucky and North Carolina, popularly called the Snake Cult, and it seems to be a relic of ancient serpent-worship cults in Asia, Africa and Mexico.

In 1968, a Virginia Circuit Court of Appeals convicted a member of the Big Stone Gap congregation, Roscoe Mullins, of violating a state law against handling snakes in a dangerous manner. In the witness box, Mullins took the Bible in his left hand; he had no right one: it was amputated in 1953 after he had been bitten by a rattlesnake. Yet his faith remained unshaken.

A year before the court hearing, during a Sunday service at the Holiness Church of God in Jesus's Name at Big Stone Gap, another member of the sect had been standing before the congregation, holding a pair of writhing rattlesnakes above his head and ecstatically crying, 'I believe, Jesus, O Jesus, I believe, thank you, Jesus!' One of the snakes bit him in the left temple. He was taken home, refused all medical attention and died a few hours later. 'It was God's will,' commented Mullins. 'He died one hundred per cent in his faith.'

It is an extreme fundamentalist movement which started at the turn of the century, spreading to a number of remote rural areas. Every Sunday, in their bare little wooden chapels, the faithful indulge in masochistic ecstasies of an intensity as only the darkest Middle Ages knew it. The snake-handling is the central ceremony of the service. 'Women, with eyes shut and hands waving in jerky spasms, circle the floor to a monotonous, almost toneless chant,' a British newspaperman described the scene he witnessed. 'Men plunge bare arms and hands into fire and take up living serpents, coiling them about their heads and bodies.' The preacher, microphone in hand to achieve maximum amplification, moves through the congregation, shouting: 'Our daughters are running around with their skirts over their heads. Our children are criticizing their parents. They want free sex. I tell you, God will punish them.' And the congregation breaks into cries of 'Jesus, yes, Jesus, yes, praise the Lord.' At the height of the ecstasy, tears are running down the men's cheeks, women collapse, others are lost in a trance or 'speak with strange tongues'.

Every year, an estimated seventy-five or eighty people are bitten by snakes during these services, but at the time of writing no Federal law had yet been passed against the cult; only in some States such as Virignia are there legal prohibitions but they are difficult to enforce.

World Healer

At another extreme end of the American sectarian scene we find the extrovert cranks who insist on healing all the world's ills. One who went to great lengths of practising what he preached was Mr Homer A. Tomlinson from Queen's Village, New York, Bishop of the Church of God, a sect founded by his father in a mountain log-cabin back in 1903. In the late 1950s, then sixty-five years old, Bishop Homer started on a grand tour of the world, equipped with a collapsible throne, a sceptre, an inflatable globe, and a lightweight crown, all the insignia and props necessary for the purpose of crowning himself King of the World. The journey was financed by his 1,500 followers in the US and was, as the procedure of coronation did not require the consent of his 'subjects', a complete success.

A squat, amiable, chubby, bespectacled Yankee, he enacted the ceremony of crowning himself King of England and the Rest of the World at Speaker's Corner in London's Hyde Park, watched by five, rain-drenched English devotees. Clad in a Chinese silk robe and waving his red, white, and blue banner, he delivered a half-hour speech about his world capital, Ecclesia, a strip of desert land south of the Sea of Galilee, which he intended to sow with winter wheat seed (he produced some from a plastic bag labelled 'Californian carrots'). This, he proclaimed, will be mankind's new Garden of Eden and a place of refuge for all nations. Then he went on to Trafalgar Square, where he again put on his tin crown, blew up his plastic globe, and proclaimed himself 'King of All Asia' to a congregation of unattentive pigeons and one damp policeman.

In Glasgow's George Square he solemnly announced, 'I am King of Scotia'. Again it was raining. 'It always rains at coronations,' he confessed cheerfully to the assembled two reporters. In Switzerland, in Zürich, in the mistaken belief that it is the country's capital, he made the old republic a monarchy again, promising to 'send the Devil back to Hell for the next 1,000 years'. In West Berlin he pledged that 'tomorrow, by faith, I shall remove the Berlin Wall' from his portable throne, set up in front of the Brandenburg Gate.

He had guts, for that is surely what it takes to proclaim oneself 'King of the Soviet Union' in the middle of the Red Square, next to Lenin's tomb. Watched by scores of grinning Muscovites who could not understand a word he said, he conducted his coronation with his usual expert facility, and declared: 'I believe there is more real Christianity in the Soviet Union today than ever before.' Fortunately, the militiamen on duty did not understand his speech either, but moved him gently on as he was causing a traffic obstruction.

Back home, he was able to tell his flock that he was now king of over a hundred nations who would all recognize his rule and pay ten per cent of their income to his 'government'. Following his final coronation as 'King of the World', the United Nations would move to Jerusalem to be next door to Ecclesia, from where the actual ruling would be done. That, however, was the last the world heard from its sovereign.

Black Masses and Devil Worship

It must seem to leaders of expansive American sects that the British Isles are fair game for their missionary zeal, if for reasons of language alone. However, many who banked on this were disappointed when their US-made creeds flopped on the other side of the Atlantic because of different mentality and attitudes, and they had to learn the truth of G. B. Shaw's shrewd observation that England and America are two nations divided by a common language.

There are, of course, exceptions. Using commercially available broadcasting stations on the European Continent and inserting large ads in British papers, the Californian-based Radio Church of God, run by two Armstrongs, father and son, seemed to have scored some progress among British listeners in the 1960s, making several thousand converts. Some English church leaders grew worried, and warned the public in general to keep away from the Radio Church. The warning, which was broadcast by the BBC in the autumn of 1970, explained the dangers to family life inherent in the American sect: it was asking for strict discipline and obedience in the home; wives had to call their husbands 'sir', children were forbidden to attend parties. It exerted its hold on members by means of fear and suspicion: predicting the end of the world and hell on earth within a few years, it exhorted them to 'pay their debt to God' (i.e. to the Radio Church) even *before* paying their rent or putting money aside for their children. The sect, by the way, also claimed to represent the famous lost tribes of Israel, and one of its predictions was that the Pope would soon move his headquarters from the Vatican to Jerusalem.

But the British do not need the Americans to teach them the Doomsday game. They can play it even better by themselves, or so it appears from the emergence of a bizarre cult called 'The Process, Church of the Final Judgment', also in the late 1960s. It was launched, at considerable expense, from a fashionable Mayfair address and with masses of propaganda literature, including a psychedelic picture magazine, by a small group of young people around a long-haired, bearded man they called alternatively 'God', 'Satan', 'The Oracle', or 'Christ of Carnaby Street'. He called himself Robert Moor Sylvester de Grimston, but he was born plain Robert Moor at Shanghai in 1935. After a short spell in the British Army and as a student of architecture, he joined the Scientologists and took a course, during which he met the daughter of a Scots mill girl, Mary Ann, whom he married. They decided to start their own 'mind cult', and Robert's father, who lived in retirement in Kensington, gave them the necessary sum of money.

They took the term 'Process' over from the Scientologists, but added their own arguments for joining the new sect: 'The world is dying – you can live!' they promised. Their basic premise was that mankind is doomed because it is intent on destroying itself. Only a few people will survive general destruction by pollution, noise, drugs, the effects of science, anxiety, sickness, violence, disease and insanity. To achieve survival, their minds must be 'processed' in the Church of the Final Judgment which provides 'a short-circuit of the machine of thought, a bolt of energy that sparks across the gap of unsuppressed feelings with knowledge and emotion, music, chants, singing, rhythm, readings, ritual. Must be seen and felt to be believed!'

For half a pound to a pound admission fee per evening the faithful were able to savour that miracle. There were telepathy circles, midnight meditation, 'I Ching' interpretations, awareness and process games (for instance one called 'Rape'), guidance in tarot and cabbala. Many of the activities took place in a coffee bar called Satan's Cavern in the basement of the Mayfair home of the sect, much to the displeasure of the noise-sensitive neighbours. But what do you expect of people who claim to be in direct contact not only with Christ but also Satan?

One issue of the magazine *Process* (which folded up after a few issues) was almost completely devoted to sex. But not what those genteel neighbours would have understood by the term. A contributor describing himself as 'Satan's Advocate' exhorted the reader:

Take your choice, indulge, explore the very limits. Leave nothing out and use every means of sharpening the senses: alcohol to set the blood coursing in your veins, narcotics to heighten your feelings to a peak of sensitivity so that the very lowest depths of physical sensation can be plumbed and wallowed in. The farthest reaches of the body's strange delights must be passed over ... Let no so-called sin, perversion or depravity escape your searching senses ...

As regards practical advice towards this end, the writer suggested, among other things, to make love in an alleyway while watching people walk past, necrophilia, flagellation, sex in a cemetery and, to top it all, a Black Mass which must finish in 'divine degradation'.

By the grace of England's eccentric laws, the Church of the Final Judgment was accepted as a charity by the Commissioners in 1969, exempting it from the tax-payer's burden which other business enterprises have to carry. However, Mr Robert Moor Sylvester de Grimston, his good lady and their disciples were not to enjoy their privilege for very long, at least not in Mayfair. A High Court judgment, passed on the Church of the Final Judgment, ruled that they had to get out of their house by the end of December 1970, as the goings-on had been a breach of the lease and an annoyance to the neighbours, what with chanting, gong-banging and the like, to say nothing of the incessant revving-up of the motor-bicycles outside Satan's Cavern. At the time of writing, the Process was still looking for a new abode.

Cult groups which worship the devil, indulge in black magic and hold Black Masses have appeared in growing numbers in western countries. If they are serious about their revival of these age-old mystic traditions, then we must assume that they are, in fact, religious people: for you cannot believe in Satan if you don't believe in God. However, a great number of these groups cannot be taken seriously, except by the police, if their activities, ranging from cemetery vandalism to ritual murder, violate the law. Nor do we have to concern ourselves, in the context of this book, with a parallel phenomenon, the fashionable revival of witchcraft in modern society. Whole libraries of volumes have been written about the subject; but it may be argued that a group of ordinary citizens of both sexes, prancing around stark naked in the woods on a chilly night, do not make up a sect.

The only sect of any importance which appeared in England practising Satanism and black magic was that of Aleister Crowley, alias 'The Beast 666'. He was a weird and colourful personality, difficult to characterize and impossible to analyse.

Born Edward Alexander Crowley in Leamington, Warwickshire, in 1875, he was brought up by parents who both belonged to the strict fundamentalist sect of the Plymouth Brethren. As a Cambridge undergraduate he wrote poetry in Swinburne's sensualist manner; then, at least according to his own accounts, he travelled through the whole of Tibet and proved to be a good mountaineer. At any rate he established himself in London as a practitioner of the mystical arts before the First World War; his midnight rites were attended by wealthy, well-known people, including the wife of a famous statesman, who contributed generously to his upkeep. He was by now calling himself Aleister, which is the Gaelic form of Alexander, and assumed the title of 'Master Therion', the Greek word for 'beast'. For he believed that he was the Great Beast foreshadowed in St John's Gospel and the Book of Revelations, with the mystical number 666 according to the Cabbalists' interpretation.

Crowley's creed, which he liked to impart to anybody who would listen, was 'Do what thou wilt', which sounds very much like the modern 'Do your own thing', and 'Love is the law'. He summoned his followers to practise that creed at the Abbey of Thelema, a temple at Cefalù in Sicily, which he took over as a ritual centre in the early 1920s. It was here that he became involved in a resounding scandal which made his name known all over England. An Oxford undergraduate, Raoul Loveday, and his wife Betty May, an artist's model from London, had been persuaded by Crowley to join him at the Abbey of Thelema. The somewhat unbalanced twenty-three-year-old Loveday, morbidly attracted to Master Therion's mysticism and strange rites, submitted faithfully to the outrageous discipline of the sect. Drugs had to be taken; a cat was sacrificially killed and its blood was drunk; every time a disciple happened to use the word 'I', he had to observe the penance of gashing his arms with a razor. Loveday fell desperately ill and died. There was a public outcry in England, and the authorities expelled the sect from Italy. Crowley first went to Tunis and then to Paris, where his extravagant love-life shocked even the local Bohemians; thrown out of France as an undesirable alien and suspected spy, he moved to Leipzig and Berlin before returning to England in the late 1920s. Wherever he went, he found disciples and got involved in scandals. His books on his own brand of magic were eagerly read, but his expensive tastes prevented him from holding on to the money he earned by his book sales, or which his wealthy followers gave him. He would invite a friend to a luxurious lunch at the Café Royal, and then 'touch' him for a few pounds. Newspaper exposures made great play of the sexual-orgiastic aspects of Crowley's cult; he sued some of them for libel but rejoiced in his reputation of utter wickedness. It was even said that he had killed two of his own children during a nocturnal rite and that their bodies had been found in the Thames near his house, with their hearts cut out; however, the police never got enough evidence for charging him with murder.

He spent his last years in Brighton, 'an old, deflated, querulous man with a pouchy, sallow face and staring eyes', as someone who knew him intimately described him. There was little left of 'The Beast', and the circle of his disciples had shrunk to a few faithful cranks. His last 'success', if one may call it that, was when William Joyce, 'Lord Haw-Haw', the English Fascist who broadcast from Hitler Germany during the Second World War, suggested sarcastically that as Britain's Intercession services did not seem to be doing her much good, Aleister Crowley should be asked to celebrate a Black Mass in Westminster Abbey. He would have loved to oblige. He died from chronic bronchitis, seventy-two years old, at Brighton in 1947. Many of his former followers gathered for the cremation, and a 'Gnostic Requiem' was recited for the wickedest man in the world, as he hoped to be known to posterity.

The people of London have not tolerated the insane activities of the Rev Piggot, who presented himself to his flock as the returned Messiah, for very long, [wrote a continental illustrated magazine in 1902]. 'After the exposure of his religious swindle they interrupted his sermon by booing and hooting, reviled him on his way from a church in Clapton to his house, and would have made short shrift of him had not the police protected the "new Messiah" from the fury of the mob. Piggot escaped to Spaxton, the headquarters of the Agapemonite sect, whose leader he is and where he wanted to preach again; but there, too, an angry crowd gathered to sack the church, smash the windows, and make an unholy row. From that scene, too, Piggot has now disappeared. His image is no longer that of an exalted man but that of a smart deceiver. Let us hope,' the magazine concluded its report, 'that after the fall of their leader the Agape-monites will come to their senses.'

If the journalist meant with that remark that the sect should dissolve itself, he must have been disappointed. In fact, it existed for sixty more years. Nor was Mr John Hugh Smyth Piggott its first leader, though the most dramatic personality they had in their history. Agapemone, meaning 'Abode of Love', was the name given to a community of divinity students at Spaxton Village near Bridgwater, Somerset, by its founder, Henry James Prince, a renegade Church of England curate from the nearby parish of Charlinch, in 1846. Convinced that the Second Coming was at hand and that he himself was a second St John the Baptist, he built the Agapemone with a handsome legacy from his wife. The students took a number of girls and women with them to live in a single building, the Abode, sharing their possessions under the leadership of the Lord, as they called Prince. One rich London businessman brought with him his whole fortune and served Prince as a liveried butler.

Soon, the women outnumbered the men, and there were stories that Prince permitted free love. Several lawsuits were started by the girls' relatives, and he had to return some of the money they had brought along. At any rate, 'breaches of decorum and man-ners' were evidenced by the proceedings in the Chancery Court in 1860. But the Agapemonites were for many years a flourishing community and saw nothing wrong in the grand style in which Prince lived; he travelled extensively abroad in a magnificent coach-and-six, accompanied by outriders – also liveried – and a pack of hounds. 'The time of prayer is past,' he told his followers, 'and the time of grace has come.'

In 1896, as an old man of eighty-five, he decided to open a branch of the sect in London. At Clapton, a northern suburb, he built a magnificent church with a mansion, standing in its own grounds. Over the porch of the church were carved the words 'Love in Judgment and Judgment unto Victory', and the name which Prince gave the edifice was Ark of the Covenant. He attracted a great number of new members. But three years after the consecration, the Agapemonites were deeply shocked; 'the Lord', who had boasted immortality, died. It was then that the Reverend John Hugh Smyth Pigott, Prince's favourite follower, took over. He was fifty, had been an Anglican curate like Prince, and later a major in the Salvation Army: a lean, tall man with fiery dark eyes and a resounding voice.

For the next three years, the Agapemonites consolidated their position in London's religious life. Then, one Sunday evening in 1902, came the bombshell. Pigott mounted the pulpit in the Ark of Covenant and declared in his most sonorous tone that he was none other than Jesus Christ, the Messiah returned to earth at God's command, as foretold by Henry James Prince. The congregation of several hundred Agapemonites fell on their knees, cried in blissful astonishment, and shed tears of excitement.

The news spread like wildfire through north London. The following Sunday, some six thousand people waited from the crack of dawn in the hope of seeing and hearing Pigott in the evening, and mounted police had to control the increasingly hysterical crowd – not all of them, though, hysterical with joy at the 'Second Coming', but many with fury about the impertinent blasphemer. This latter section won the upper hand at the fracas that broke out when Pigott arrived. Hundreds swarmed over the iron railings and thronged the church to shout him down, and he had to dodge a shower of stones and bricks when he emerged again after the service. 'This self-styled Messiah,' wrote a London paper, 'would probably have been thrown into the pond at Clapton Common but for the protection of the mounted police.'

So he collected his wife Kathie and a young woman, Ruth Preece, whom he called his spiritual bride, and retired to the sect's original Abode of Love in Somerset. Contrary to the continental magazine's report, the local people left the community and its leader in peace, and Pigott seems to have refrained from repeating his outrageous claim; in fact, he was soon preoccupied with worldlier matters. His spiritual bride gave birth to two children, boys called Glory and Power, with the result that the Bishop of Bath and Wells had him arraigned before a Consistory Court on charges of immorality; strangely enough, he was still regarded (and regarded himself) as a member of the Anglican clergy, and even more strangely, the Church authorities never put him on the carpet for claiming to be Jesus Christ. It was merely for his dissolute private life that he was unfrocked in Wells Cathedral in 1909.

It made no difference to the Agapemonites. The community,

by that time consisting of about a hundred women and only a handful of men, worshipped him as before. Sister Ruth bore him a third child; his legal wife was ignored. As time went on, the community shrank with Pigott's waning charisma. He died in 1927 at the Agapemone; Sister Ruth carried on until her own death, in her eighties, in 1956, mourned by the remaining fifteen members of the sect. A few years later, the Abode of Love was sold and converted into council flats while another sect, the Ancient Catholics, took over the Ark of the Covenant in Clapton, once the scene of the 'Second Coming'.

Ancient Catholics, and Essenes

The Ancient Catholics must not be confused with the Old English Catholic Church, whose Archbishop was sentenced to a year in jail for fraud in 1960; he had been collecting funds for a non-existent parish magazine. But ten years later the sect was still flourishing, with headquarters at Richmond, Surrey, tended by a whole bevy of bishops of whom four had also served prison sentences, two of them for indecency offences, yet they were running a youth club. Another dignitary of the sect killed himself in 1969 by taking a combination of drink and drugs because he was worried about being prosecuted for a car tax offence. The church secretary, on the other hand, was convicted for receiving goods by false pretences, in company with a 'bishop' of the sect. The stories of these 'Old English Catholics' were published in the newspapers; yet the sect continued to exist in London and some provincial towns. 'Bishops' in colourful velvet robes, with large crosses dangling on their chests, held services, chanting prayers in Latin; as a rule, however, the priests outnumbered their flock at these ceremonies.

What made the worshippers come? None of the reporters who attended the services was able to come up with an answer. It is easier to find one in the case, say, of the Close Brethren who were much talked about in Scotland in 1970 when their seventy-one-year-old American 'Archangel' was allegedly found in bed with a married follower. At their rites in Aberdeen, the 'sisters' of the sect had to wear long, loose dresses with nothing underneath, not even brassieres. Then there was the Naturian Kindred sect, which attracted many followers to its 'church', an ordinary middle-class house in Ealing, London, in the 1950s; it put nudism on a religious basis : members of both sexes and all ages were scampering about naked at the sect's weekly meetings under a self-appointed 'Reverend Father'. As these gymnastics were taking place indoors, behind drawn curtains, their nude bodies could not expect any benefit from the sun; perhaps their souls did, though.

Two black chauffeur-driven Rolls-Royces pulled up outside the main entrance of the British Museum in January 1966, and a party of middle-aged men and women stepped out, carrying shepherd's crooks and wearing ornate brass crosses on their chests. One, addressed by the others as 'Leader', was dressed in maroon robes; a black-haired lady, with a golden crown on her head, was called 'The Centre'. They represented the Brotherhood of the Essenes and demanded to see the Dead Sea Scrolls which were being exhibited by the Museum. But they were not allowed to jump the long queue of ordinary citizens who also wanted to see the newly discovered scrolls, and were told to come back on another day despite their claim to a particularly close connection with the ancient relics from the Holy Land.

One of the smallest yet strangest sects in England – it has only about three hundred members, very carefully chosen – the Essenes take their name from the puritanical and mystical Jewish community which originated about the second century BC. They probably wrote the Dead Sea Scrolls and hid them in caves from their enemies. They held doctrines which are said to have influenced Jesus, and they abhorred animal slaughter. Apart from vegetarianism, their modern successors, or rather the 'reincarnated' twentieth-century Essenes, have somewhat different notions, and indeed weird ones considering that many of them are professional or otherwise educated people. They say that their brotherhood began when they were reborn to assist humanity after the First World War, but it seems more likely that the sect was founded after the Second by a London doctor, who was succeeded as sect leader by another doctor from Wolverhampton.

Stripped of its messianic, astrological and other mystical elements, the cult of the Essenes is, to put it crudely, dog worship. Not that they dote on toy poodles or panting pekes. They believe that there was a King Dog at the time of Christ, and that it died on the day of the Crucifixion. Dogs meet the departed souls and accompany them on the road to Heaven; but a soul may only enter on giving certain responses to the dogs, which the soul knows only if it belonged to a good man on earth. At the end of Christ's coming thousand-year reign over mankind, another King Dog will appear, and with him the Kingdom of Heaven.

But wait! There was also a King Dog in our own time. It appears to have died a sacrificial death at the hands of the Essenes in December 1969, at Glastonbury Tor in Somerset, which according to the sect's belief is the magnetic centre of the world, where they can feel heavenly vibrations.

A team of London journalists investigated the rumours that the ritual killing of a dog had taken place at Glastonbury, where the Essenes meet once a year. Witnesses were not difficult to find; a crowd of a few hundred people, many of them children and adolescents, had been attracted to the Tor by a band of robed men and women assembling there one evening around the signs of the zodiac, laid out with sticks and ropes in the grass. A dog, whose description varied, could be seen moving about by the flickering light of torches. Suddenly, all torches were extinguished simultaneously, a gong was banged three times, and prayers chanted. A three-minute silence followed; then the torches were lit again, one by one, and threw their light on a ghastly scene: the dog was lying dead in a pool of blood: its throat had been cut ... at least according to the eyewitnesses' accounts.

Later that evening the Essene brethren and sisters, about twenty of them, sat down in their robes in the town hall for a vegetarian dinner. Behind the crowned lady called 'The Centre', who presided at the meal, there were two large photographs of a beautiful Samoyed dog (or were they two Samoyeds?), flanking a picture of royal insignia; above them, a nine-armed candlestick, making the arrangement look like a kind of altar.

Was the dog that had been sacrificed a Samoyed, 'King Dog II' if you count the dog that died on Crucifixion Day as number one? No use asking the Essenes, who are very secretive about their rites; but some years before, a newspaperman who visited their 'temple' in Potters Bar, Middlesex, met not only The Centre there but also her two Samoyeds which, she told him, 'played an important part in their rituals'.

At any rate, a *Daily Express* reporter witnessed the solemn burial of a Samoyed dog, about ten years old, a day or two after the Glastonbury scene. The burial, attended by many members of the sect, took place in the Cornish village of Mithian near a house belonging to a couple who described themselves as founder-members of the Brotherhood. The dog, King Dog, as they called it, had belonged to 'a middle-aged woman called Anna-Maria' who lived in Potters Bar and revealed to the sect members the 'edicts from Heaven' that governed their lives.

The dog's body was buried in an ornate mahogany coffin after a ceremony during which some of the Essenes, dressed in flowing robes, formed intricate patterns with their long shepherd's crooks. The dog that died had been 'the sentinel of the animal kingdom', the reporter was told.

Spiritualism amid Primitives

Compared to the great number of weird and eccentric sects in the western industrialized and educationally advanced world, the backward, underprivileged, and traditionally superstitious peoples have surprisingly little to show in this field of human activities. Furthermore, they seem to need a few Christian or other occidental notions to fertilize their native imagination and produce a new sect.

The Caodaists are a case in point. Their creed is a strange blend of isms, eastern and western ones: Roman Catholicism, Buddhism, Taoism, Spiritualism and Confucianism. It is difficult to say how they survived the war in Vietnam, where they have their religious and administrative centre; but in the early 1950s it was estimated that two million South Vietnamese out of a population of six million believed in Caodai. At that time, the sect had also enrolled hundreds of thousands of members in Cambodia.

Its founder and first Pope was a bad egg. Called Le Van Trung, he was a Vietnamese from Cholon near Saigon. After the First World War, as a young man, he led a riotous life; he came from a wealthy family, and indulged in opium-smoking. But in 1925, a friend took him to a spiritualist séance during which *cao dai*, the Supreme Being, revealed himself to Le Van Trung, who forthwith became a changed man.

He went, at divine command, to Tayninh, fifty miles north of

Saigon, where he founded the Holy See of his new cult, devoting all his money to making it as splendid as possible. He built an enormous pagoda, or rather cathedral, combining a dozen different architectural styles: the twin towers are French Catholic, the main doors Chinese, the pillars Gothic with twisted dragons; the papal throne is formed by four snakes. The huge interior, with an Indian-style tiled floor, looks at a first glance like early Disney. There are great roaring, pawing lions made of stone, and perched on the roof is a more than life-size, bearded guardian on horseback, with a snake coiling from his arm to his head. A large picture in the entrance hall shows the first three saints of the sect: Sun Yat Sen, China's liberator; Nguyen Binh Khiem, a famous sixteenth-century Vietnamese poet; and Victor Hugo, in a cocked hat, depicted in the process of writing *Dieu et Humanité, Amour et Justice* on the wall.

But the most fantastic sight in this extraordinary temple is the altar. Beyond huge yellow and blue curtains a hundred feet or more long, the statues of Buddha, Confucius, Christ and Lao-Tse are ascending steps towards an immense blue globe, dimly lit and apparently floating in the air; and from the centre of this star-spangled sphere, a huge human eye, complete with lids and eyebrow, stares at the congregation. It symbolizes the essence of Caodaism, or the Universal Conscience in the Universal Cosmos.

There is nothing unusual in the discipline which the sect's Pope, cardinals, archbishops, bishops, priests and deacons have to take upon themselves: poverty, chastity, fidelity and vegetarianism. But all the more curious is the way in which this Catholic-style hierarchy receives its instructions: by spiritualist messages. The reason why the three great men depicted in the entrance hall have been made saints is that they are the best communicators from the Beyond; and since the painting was done, more saints have joined them for the same reason: Chateaubriand, Churchill, Descartes and Joan of Arc. Many messages have also been received from George Washington, Franklin D. Roosevelt, Gandhi, and Queen Elizabeth i, with whom discussions have been going on about the possible canonization of Shakespeare, who is a magnificent message-giver. Victor Hugo, however, tops them all; the library at Tayninh boasts no fewer than eleven novels of his, all written after his death.

Such fertile communication cannot be done without special facilities. The sect trains as mediums those members of its clergy who show a particular talent for falling into trance, and instructs them in the use of an ingenious Caodaist invention, the *corbeille à bec*, or 'basket with a beak'. It is a spiritualist writing-machine which achieves the speed of an accomplished shorthand typist. The messages have a wide range of content; they provide guidance to everyday affairs, comment on the political situation, expound philosophical ideas, forecast the future. Some spirits, who had no time to do it on earth, dictate their memoirs, and Khiem transmits his 'new' poems. Unfortunately, Shakespeare has not come up yet with any new plays.

What we do not know about the sect, which has always been strongly anti-Communist, is the fate of its army. Before the Americans came to South Vietnam, the Caodai Pope commanded a well-equipped force of 20,000 men whose job it was to defend the Tayninh district with its fertile, well-kept fields, its neat red-tiled houses, its flourishing shops. Has all this, too, been devastated in the war like so much of the rest of South Vietnam?

Spiritualism is also the essence of the messianic negro and mulatto sect called Umbanda, which is very strong in southern Brazil. Here, too, great men of the past are 'called back' from the dead to guide the living, and some – like Napoleon and Abraham Lincoln, because of their sympathy with the coloured people – are believed to be continually re-incarnated among them. But the emphasis lies on the evocation of the spirits of the negroes' African forefathers.

Brazil also has the only spiritualist city in the world, Palmelo, about 160 miles from the capital, Brasilia. It has some two thousand inhabitants and a rather curious history. There was a French scientist, Professor Denizard Hippolyte Léon Rivail, born at Lyons in 1804, who was a pupil of the great educationalist, Pestalozzi, in Switzerland, and later taught mathematics and natural science in Paris. At that time, the middle of the nineteenth century, a new American craze was spreading in France – table-rapping. Professor Rivail took part in these spiritualist séances, and during one of them he was told that in a former 'incarnation' he had been the Druid Allan Kardec. This was the pen-name he chose for the books he now began to write, attempting to synthesize spiritualist and scientific concepts.

There has never been a plausible explanation for the fact that the multi-racial society of Brazil has been particularly receptive for spiritualism. The name of Allan Kardec, practically forgotten in France, is still famous in Brazil, so much so that a public celebration was held, and special postage stamps issued, in 1964 on the one-hundredth anniversary of the publication of Kardec's principal work, *O Evangelho* or 'The Gospel according to Spiritualism', in the Portuguese language. His twentieth-century prophet in Brazil was Jeronimo Candido Gomide, who began by curing lunatics in his country shack in 1925; some were so mad that their relatives brought them tied to a monkey. As the number of patients he was asked to heal increased to a flood, he built some houses and a church dedicated to the memory of Kardec. Within a few years, Gomide's sectarian settlement grew into a small town, Palmelo. Its population has a very high percentage of spiritualist mediums. Gomide regards himself as Kardec's 'instrument' and the Evangelho as the bible of the sect.

One of the strangest and most interesting cults among primitive people has developed in the Pacific, in the Melanesian islands. It is called the 'Cargo Cult', and its main object of worship today is the aircraft. It has attracted the attention of dozens of European and American anthropologists, and quite a number of books and scientific papers have been written about it – yet they all tell somewhat different stories, for the cult has taken on various forms and thrives on various beliefs and legends among the islanders in widely separated parts of Melanesia, who have no physical communication with each other. Still, there is one common denominator: the conviction that the intruding white man has deprived them of the wealth and happiness which they feel are due to them.

There is more than a grain of truth in that argument. Throughout the last century and well into the twentieth, the native populations were decimated by 'labour recruiting' – nothing better than slave trade – especially for Fiji and Queensland; called 'blackbirding' by the brutal operators, it has left a legacy of bitterness among the islanders and gave rise to messianic creeds different from those which the white missionaries had to offer, and anchored in pagan tradition.

It is natural for an island tribe to believe that important events are connected with their only link with the outside world, the ship. Dead souls depart in a ship, and they may return in a ship as spirits. When the deliverer appears, he will come the same way. Inevitably, the first explorer to pay friendly visits to the islands, from 1871–83, the Russian Baron Nikolai Miklouho-Maclay, was welcomed as a god, particularly as he travelled on board an impressive Russian frigate. It seems that it was the Baron who started the first phase of the Cargo Cult; cargo, in Melanesian pidgin English, means goods, particularly western goods, which the natives – then hardly more advanced than Stone Age men – had never seen before, and which they believed to originate in the world of gods and spirits. White people who did not give them cargo were regarded as enemies; they were withholding those goods from the islanders by keeping for themselves the religious secrets by which cargo could be obtained.

When the Germans appeared on the scene to take possession of their colonies in Melanesia after 1884, they, too, were largely believed to be deities of the Cargo Cult. Its elements on the various islands underwent a good many changes, particularly after 1914 with the influx of more missionaries, when Christian beliefs began to play a more important part; some renegade native mission workers turned into Cargo Cult prophets. But the most important development started in 1940, with the arrival of the first American military aircraft, especially on the large, fertile island of Tanna in the southern New Hebrides.

Transport planes brought the most fantastic goods, magic cargo such as radios, cans of beer, paraffin lamps, even automobiles. They also brought white and black men, and the natives watched them at their most impressive ceremony: marching up and down, dressed in identical clothes, shouldering fire-spitting sticks that could bring instant death. The Tannese emulated that ritual, rather pathetically, by improvising uniforms and carrying sticks; they also spoke into empty beer cans as they had seen the Americans talk into microphones, for this would bring more cargo-carrying aircraft to the island.

The anthropologists have not been able to agree on the origins of the new Cargo Cult which spread across Tanna and the neighbouring islands as a result of the US occupation, and what has particularly puzzled them is the messianic figure around which the cult centred. Its name was, and still is, John Frum (or Jonfrum), perhaps derived from 'broom' – for sweeping the whites from Tanna. Natives who claimed to have seen John Frum described him as 'a mysterious little man with bleached hair, a high-pitched voice and a coat with shining buttons'; he was said to appear only at night 'in the faint light of a fire' and before a meeting of men under the influence of kava, the local narcotic drink. Meetings from which whites were barred began to be held soon after 1940, to receive 'messages' from John Frum, at first quite peaceful ones: instructions against idleness and for organizing communal gardening and other cooperative activities; he also encouraged dancing and kava-drinking. At that stage, 'John Frum' was not aggressively anti-white, but told his followers to hide him on a mountain from whites and from women; they regarded him as the incarnation of the god residing on Tanna's highest volcanic mountain.

After the Japanese attack on Pearl Harbor, when the whole of the Pacific turned into a theatre of war, more US troops arrived on Tanna, with a higher percentage of negroes. This puzzled the islanders at first, but the phenomenon was soon incorporated in the John Frum Cargo Cult. The black Americans, said the cult leaders, would fight with the islanders to achieve the beginning of the millenium. There would be a cataclysm in Tanna, the volcanic mountains would fall and riverbeds become fertile plains; John Frum would reveal himself to all, the whites would return to their country, old natives would get back their youth and there would be no sickness. The islanders could then kill their cattle and throw the white man's money into the sea – they would need neither as John Frum would provide riches for all. John Frum believers in the New Guinea highlands even prophesied that come the millenium, black skins would be shed for white ones.

The cult reached such an intensity that there were a number of rebellions by its followers; the US occupation forces quelled them, and the Dutch and Australian administrations imposed prison sentences on the leading rebels. The islanders warned their womenfolk to avoid sexual relations with the occupants, who had 'snakes which would enter their vulvae and kill them'.

When the Second World War ended and the troops departed, things quietened down considerably, but the messianic Cargo

Cult is still strong in Melanesia, especially Tanna. A BBC film team, under the documentary producer David Attenborough, found in 1960 a primitive, open-sided chapel made of bamboo with a life-size effigy of John Frum, his face painted white, his dress scarlet, his arms outstretched, and one of his legs bent as though he were running (or flying?). In front of him, there was a scarlet wooden cross; and beside the cross a reasonably good model, also carved from wood, of a four-engined aircraft, complete with propellers. 'Wherever you go on the island,' said Attenborough, 'you will see wooden crosses and gates painted scarlet, John Frum's colour; they have been erected in his name. There is also a scarlet cross at the top of the volcano in the south of the island, because in the inferno at the bottom of the crater live many of Frum's men.'

The Cargo Cult has largely replaced the Presbyterian Church to which the majority of the converted people in Tanna and many other Melanesian islands used to belong. 'It represents the reaction of people living in cultural and material poverty to the sudden appearance among them of new and unimagined riches from across the sea,' writes Lanternari. 'It echoes Christianity with its promise of the hereafter and contains a variety of beliefs and rituals.' John Frum, with his wonderful cargo, will set things to rights when he assumes power, as he promised to do. Then all the remaining white men will go, and the islanders will be kings again in their own islands, only richer and happier than before.

Swiss Cults

Switzerland has never been an underprivileged country since William Tell, or the liberation movement he symbolizes, rid it of its Habsburg overlords and welded it into a nation six and a half centuries ago. But it has always had its little sects, not because it needed messianic creeds as an antidote for material misery, but because individualism and non-conformity have always been features of these self-willed mountain tribes, particularly the Allemanic ones of northern and eastern Switzerland.

What one would not expect, however, is the blatantly sexual character of some of the most successful sects among the pious Swiss. Already around 1800, a former shepherd, Anton Unternährer, founded the Antoni sect which had many followers in the Berne-Lucerne region; in all his writings he interpreted the Bible stories as having sexual-symbolic meanings, explained the Fall of Man as the liberation of humanity ('The eating of the apple is Man's supreme sacrament, his only true communion'), branded the feelings of shame and guilt as Satan's propaganda and declared that the incest was 'just as sacred as other acts of divine service'. Brought to trial, he would declare that God had distinguished him from ordinary men by endowing him with three testicles.

Unternährer may have merely preached incest, but Johannes Binggeli, founder and prophet of the Forest Brotherhood in the Schwarzenburg district, practised it. Binggeli, a dwarfish man with a family history of alcoholism and schizophrenia, was born in 1834 and apprenticed to a tailor. In his mid-thirties he published a book in which he narrated a long series of ghost stories, hallucinations, encounters with devils and angels, visits to Heaven and Hell which he claimed to have experienced; the book was a great success and made him famous throughout German-speaking Switzerland. At the same time, he began to fall into trances, which he could predict, inviting his friends to witness the spectacle. This was the origin of his Forest Brotherhood.

It was an overtly phallic cult. Binggeli called his own genitals the box of Christ and his urine heavenly balm; the sect members used it eagerly as a panacea for all kinds of diseases. He also claimed to be able to exorcize bewitched women by sleeping with them. This he did in 1896 with his own daughter, who became pregnant. He was arrested, but sent to a lunatic asylum instead of prison. Binggeli's followers campaigned energetically for his release, and he was set free after five years, but forbidden to return to his former home and Brotherhood centre. The sect faded away, though his famous book was reprinted for many years.

French-speaking Switzerland, the home of Calvin, has produced comparatively few sects; one, however, which flourished recently, deserves to be mentioned because it aimed at enthroning Queen Elizabeth II as Holy Empress of the World, with the Duke of Edinburgh by her side. It called itself the Rainbow Sect, and was founded at Lausanne in the 1950s by bearded Frédéric Bussy, a former Pentecostal missionary. When America tested her first H-bomb at Bikini and people all over the world grew frightened at the prospect of a third world war that would put an end to organic life on our planet, Father Bussy thought of a solution: an alliance of all religions, which would result in an alliance of all mankind.

His idea attracted some fifty citizens of Lausanne, most of them female. Twice a week they would meet in a large room in a modest apartment house, Bussy's home. They would dress in long white garbs and white caps, take off their shoes, and shake their tambourines which were essential props for the Rainbow service. So were the two kettledrums with which Father Bussy, in a more elaborate, colourfully embroidered priestly outfit, provided the rhythm for the monotonous sing-song prayers that would go on until two o'clock in the morning. Then came a frugal breakfast, and the sect members went home to return to their everyday jobs as housewives, secretaries, salesgirls, civil servants or engineers. Some had also brought along their guitars, mandolins, or flutes to add to the musical treat.

The symbol of the Rainbow Sect, prominently displayed at these sessions, was a Star of David with a cross in the middle, and Father Bussy had on his pulpit three little flags, those of Switzerland, Britain and Israel. The most important pieces of furniture, however, were two comfortable leather armchairs standing in front of the simple wooden chairs of the congregation. One of them had a cushion showing the British royal coat of arms; the other was unembellished . No member of the sect ever sat in them, for they were reserved for Her Majesty Queen Elizabeth and Prince Philip. At least once per evening, the worshippers kneeled behind these armchairs and kissed the floor, praying that they would soon be occupied by the Empress of the World and her consort.

Why Queen Elizabeth? Because, and here the Rainbow sect echoed the creed of the British Israelites, she is a descendant of the kings of Judah. The last of them, they say, had a daughter, Tephi, who escaped to Ireland when Nebuchadnezzar occupied Palestine. She carried with her the ruby which still adorns the British crown, as well as the Stone of Scone on which all British sovereigns sit at their coronation. Princess Tephi must have had quite heavy baggage on her flight. At any rate, Queen Elizabeth, according to the Rainbow sect, is the only legal successor to King David; and she alone can save mankind from the holocaust.

Sects to the End of the World

But why bother about nuclear war? The world is coming to an end anyway, or so innumerable prophets of doom have been predicting for nearly one thousand years. The earliest recorded world's-end panic gripped the Christian countries in AD 999; surely, things could not go on for ever, and the year 1000, a nice round figure, seemed just the right time for God to call a halt to it all. People saw fearful apparitions in the sky, predicting imminent catastrophe; many gave away their money to gain admission to Heaven, others partook of the joys of life as much as they could while there was still time. 1 January 1000 was rather an anti-climax when everybody realized that the world was going on as before.

Not forever, of course. The second millenium has heard countless predictions of The End, sometimes based on supernatural revelations to selected individuals (such as Doomsday Sedgwick, a seventeenth-century crank who burst upon a party of gentlemen playing at bowls in a Cambridgeshire stately home, telling them to leave off and prepare for the approaching dissolution of the world), and sometimes on incomprehensible calculations on the cube root of the Third Pyramid. Doomsday sects have sprung up every few years; since 1930, at least half a dozen of them have come and gone in the western world. What is their special attraction? Perhaps the unlucky in life want to feel some kind of satisfaction, not to say *Schadenfreude,* that those blessed with earthly riches will now go down with themselves; perhaps people who shrink from the competition in modern society welcome a reason for sitting back and waiting for the great termination of human sweat and toil. Other sects derive their success from promising that their members alone, provided they take part in certain rites, will be spared and survive.

This was the fond hope of the Brotherhood of the White Temple, who retreated to the Colorado mountains under the leadership of a Dr Doreal in 1950; the doctor claimed to be receiving survival instructions by telepathy in Sanskrit directly from some high priests in Tibet. At Easter, 1969, a middle-aged fruiterer and spare-time universal saviour in Bavaria climbed a hill, which he claimed was under special protection, accompanied by a small crowd of fellow-believers: here, they were told, they would survive, and the fruiterer would then take over what was left of the world as its supreme ruler. His prediction of the end was based on an old peasants' almanac published in 1800.

In the second week of July 1960, a subscriber to a Swiss magazine wrote to the editor, asking him to publish the next issue a day earlier as the world would cease to exist on the fourteenth at precisely 1.45 pm, Central European time. The reader may have written tongue in cheek, but in fact thousands of people in northern Italy and Switzerland believed what Brother Emman, head of the Community of the White Mountain Before the Coming of God, had predicted. His dead sister had communicated with him from the Beyond, foretelling him that a new American nuclear device, the E Bomb, would be exploded at the North Pole on that day, shifting the earth's axis and setting off world-wide earthquakes, huge tidal waves, and a new Great Flood. But the top of Mont Blanc, like the biblical Ararat, would be one of the few safe places; another was Mount Everest.

It did not sound all that improbable, considering that before the first nuclear test explosion in 1945 even some scientists at Los Alamos had their nagging doubts if the chain reaction might not engulf our whole planet and its atmosphere. And 'Brother Emman' was an educated man, too: he was Dr Giuseppe Bianco, a children's doctor from Milan, who practised faith healing and spiritualism in his leisure time. To the members of his sect he was King of the Reign of God and Priest in Perpetuity according to the Order of Melchizedek.

So a day or two before the fourteenth, seven thousand followers of Dr Bianco's sect set off from Milan, Rome and Turin, leaving their homes and jobs behind, and made for Mont Blanc. 'Every member counts,' the doctor had said, 'for after the catastrophe we shall have to help rebuild a shattered world.' The press, of course, went with them.

Most of the members, however, were incautious enough to stop at the lower slopes of the mountain; only some hundred went to the very top with the doctor. Solemnly the pressmen counted out the minutes. At 1.43 came an imminent warning : a TV cameraman's alarm clock went off. At 1.45 the Last Trump sounded, blown by a statuesque blonde from Milan on a Boy Scout's cornet. But that was all. The world was still there. A quarter of an hour later, Brother Emman announced apologetically, 'Our calculations must have been inaccurate.' A British pressman murmured, rubbing his icy hands, 'That's the understatement of the century.'

The next end of the world failed to take place on 4 February 1962. Nine members of the Aetherius Society climbed up the 2,600-ft Coniston Old Man in the Lake District for a non-stop prayer meeting under the direction of a Yorkshire weaver. Here, they hoped, they would be better heard in Heaven. What they were praying for, kneeling in mist and drizzle on the wet grass, was the at least temporary postponement of the end of the world, which was in obvious danger because of a rare event in the sky : the sun, moon and earth and the planets Mercury, Mars, Jupiter, Venus and Saturn were all in line, which had not happened for eight centuries.

As was to be expected, their prayers were answered, and the London members of the Aetherius Society, pleased with their work, returned to their headquarters over a health-food shop in the Fulham Road. The sect believes that Jesus was a spaceman from another planet; the Star of Bethlehem was, of course, a spacecraft pin-pointing the stable. UFOs, popularly known as flying saucers, are sent to us from outer space, radiating energy for mankind's benefit. The standard prayer of the sect is the Tibetan mystic formula *Om mani padme hum* ('The jewel is in the lotus, amen'). The Aetherians boast the membership of a lady who can manipulate the weather by sending out cosmic power. In 1967, she recalls, she felt that she had to stop a cricket match by bringing on rain when the English side were in danger of losing. A noble sentiment, to be sure; but is it cricket?

End-of-the-world prophecies, scares for the many, hopes for a few, will never cease until it really comes, with a bang or a whimper. Those of us who are satisfied with another 260-odd years' grace can take comfort in the prediction of the oldest existing sect, the Jews. According to rabbinical tradition, the world is to last six thousand years, because Jehova's name has six letters and He created the world in six days. And as this took place in 3760 BC, by Old Testament calculations, the end will not come before the year 2240; so there is no reason as yet to start worrying.

Bibliography

General

ARKON DARAUL, *Secret Societies* (Frederick Muller, 1961).

JOHN HERON LEPPER, *Famous Secret Societies* (Sampson Low, 1932).

VITTORIO LANTERNARI, *The Religions of the Oppressed* (Alfred A. Knopf, New York, 1963).

CHARLES MACKAY, *Extraordinary Popular Delusions and the Madness of Crowds* (1841, 1852; George G. Harrap, 1956).

E. and M. A. RADFORD (ed. Christina Hole), *Encyclopaedia of Superstitions* (Hutchinson, 1961).

BRYAN R. WILSON, *Patterns of Sectarianism* (Heinemann, 1967).

Chapter 1

W. H. BENNETT, *An Introduction to the British-Israel Evangel* (British Israel World Federation, 1968).

REV. CLAUD COFFIN, *Christianity and Israel* (BIWF, 1946).

W. E. FILMER, *A Synopsis of the Migrations of Israel* (BIWF, 1964).

HOWARD B. RAND, *The Bible and Space Travel* (Destiny Publishers, Merrimac, Mass., 1969).

GLADYS TAYLOR, *What Happened to Judah?'* (BIWF, 1969).

JOHN TIMBS, *English Eccentrics and Eccentricities* (Chatto and Windus, 1875).

Chapter 3

SARA HARRIS, *The Incredible Father Divine* (W. H. Allen, 1954).

Chapter 4

RUDOLF OLDEN (ed.), *Das Wunderbare* (Rowohlt, Berlin, 1932).

Chapter 6

The Fame and Confession of the Rosicrucians (1652).

Das Geheimniss aller Geheimnisse (Leipzig, 1788).

K. K. DOBERER, *Goldsucher, Goldmacher* (Prestel Verlag, Munich, 1960).

DR. P. B. RANDOLPH, *The Rosicrucian Dream Book* (Boston, Mass., 1871).

Rules and Ordinances of the Rosicrucian Society in England (London, 1881).

Who and What are the Rosicrucians? (AMORC, San José, California, 1938).

RUDOLF STEINER, *Rosicrucianism and Modern Initiation* (Rudolf Steiner Press, 1950).

Chapter 7

The Nichiren Shoshu Soka Gakkai (Seikyo Press, Tokyo, 1966).

JANHEINZ JAHN, *Through African Doors* (Faber and Faber, 1962).

PETER LARSEN, *Young Africa* (J. M. Dent, 1964).

Chapter 8

SIMMA HOLT, *Terror in the Name of God: The Story of the Freedom Doukhobors* (McClelland and Stewart, Toronto, 1965).

GEORGE WOODCOCK AND IVAN AVAKUMOVIC, *The Doukhobors* (Faber and Faber, 1968).

Chapter 9

GEORGE BRUCE, *The Stranglers: The Cult of Thuggee* (Longmans, 1968).

BERNARD LEWIS, *The Assassins* (Weidenfeld and Nicolson, 1967).

Chapter 10

JOHN ALLEGRO, *The Sacred Mushroom and the Cross* (Hodder and Stoughton, 1970).

CHARLES S. BRADEN, *These Also Believe* (Macmillan, New York, 1949).

PETER LAWRENCE, *Road Belong Cargo* (Manchester University Press, 1964).

PEDRO MCGREGOR, *The Moon and Two Mountains: Brazilian Spiritism* (Souvenir Press, 1966).

SAMUEL MAUNDER, *The Biographical Treasury* (Longmans, Green, 1862).

JOHN SYMONDS, *The Great Beast: The Life of Aleister Crowley* (Rider, 1951).

PETER WORSLEY, *The Trumpet Shall Sound: A Study of 'Cargo' Cults in Melanesia* (MacGibbon & Kee, London, 1957).

Acknowledgments

The author wishes to express his sincere thanks to Mr H. Tasiemka, London, for allowing him the run of his magnificent international newspaper cuttings and reference library; to Mr Derek Ingram, then editor of the *Gemini* News Service, London, and Mr Richard Hall, then its African correspondent, for permission to use dispatch material from the Biafran War; to Mr John Porter, Branstone near Lincoln, then Biafran war correspondent of the *Scottish Catholic Observer*, for permission to use some information broadcast on the BBC radio service; and to Mr John Harold, London editor of *Drum*, for permission to quote from this magazine.

Index